P9-DXM-639

# The Wishing Year

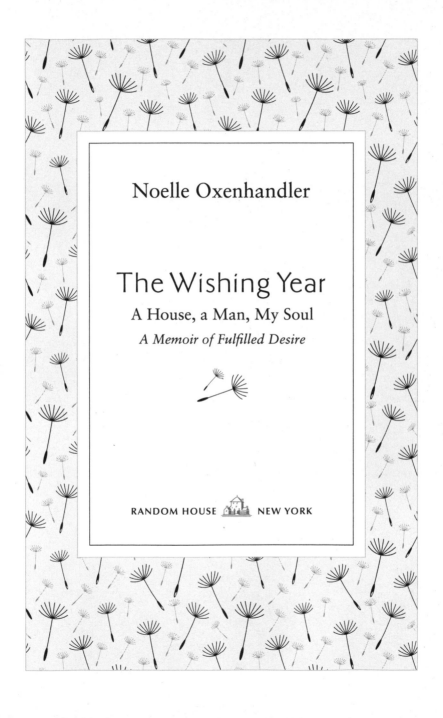

Noelle Oxenhandler

# The Wishing Year

## A House, a Man, My Soul

*A Memoir of Fulfilled Desire*

RANDOM HOUSE    NEW YORK

Published in the United States by Random House, an imprint of The Random House Publishing Group, a division of Random House, Inc., New York.

RANDOM HOUSE and colophon are registered trademarks of Random House, Inc.

Some portions of this work first appeared in
*Tricycle* and *Utne Reader*.

LIBRARY OF CONGRESS CATALOGING-IN-PUBLICATION DATA

Oxenhandler, Noelle.
The wishing year: a house, a man, my soul—a memoir of fulfilled desire /
Noelle Oxenhandler.
p.    cm.
ISBN 978-1-4000-6485-4
1. Desire.    2. Success—Psychological aspects.    I. Title.
BF575.D4O94 2008
818'.603—dc22   2007032252

Printed in the United States of America on acid-free paper

www.atrandom.com

2  4  6  8  9  7  5  3  1

First Edition

*Book design by Laurie Jewell*

We're never truly separate from
what we wish for.

—KYTHE HELLER,
*IMMOLATION*

# Contents

## Author's Note

This is a work of nonfiction. The names and certain identifying characteristics of some of the people who appear in its pages have been changed.

# Introduction

It is, in itself, an ancient wish: the wish that a wish makes something happen. Wish for a palace, and the fisherman's shanty becomes a palace. Wish to be home, and one's glittering red shoes are suddenly planted in Kansas.

Which one of us, throwing a coin into a fountain, is entirely immune from the belief that the act of wishing—from the thought in the mind to the coin making its *plink* in the water—will somehow provoke an actual outcome? We *will* pass the exam. Overcome illness. Conceive a child. Find a house in the country.

Is such belief merely childish, superstitious, unscientific? "Wishful thinking," people say, and the expression conveys disdain for the act of wishing. Disdain, and the belief that wishing is impotent. After all, if wishes were horses, wouldn't beggars ride?

For Sigmund Freud, who considered himself first and foremost a scientist, the wish and the real are fundamentally opposed. According to him, we are each born with the grandiose and deluded notion that the world exists to gratify our every wish. As we grow older, this primal "pleasure principle" must yield inexorably to the "reality principle." At night when we dream, we return to the primal world of the wish—a world that Freud regarded, with great respect, as an inexhaustibly rich reservoir of meaning. If we're truly adults, however, we must open our eyes and let our wishes die back in the harsh morning light.

Some of the most dynamic and successful people I know have insisted to me, with an edge of indignation in their tone: "I don't wish. I make plans." Strong adherents of the reality principle, they see wishing as the very opposite of the clear-eyed, self-reliant, 100 percent pragmatic approach that brings about tangible results. And they seem to have little of Freud's empathy for both wishes and wishers. For them, wishing is not much more than a sign of weakness and a temptation to be avoided. The province of airheads, fools, quacks, and losers.

Yet other people—quite serious and substantial people—insist that there is, indeed, true power in the act of wishing, and an art in tapping it. For them, wishing is not only perfectly compatible with a pragmatic approach to life but a crucial component. They would tell us, "If a beggar genuinely wanted a horse, and effectively harnessed the energy of his wish, then the chances are good that he would find himself riding. Indeed, much better than if he'd never permitted himself to wish in the first place!"

*The Wishing Year* dives into the heart of this controversy, setting out with an—almost—equal mix of hope and skepticism. I say "almost" because by temperament I tilt toward a certain pessimistic melancholy, at least where earthly happiness is concerned. And I am also cursed with a need for rigorous argument, which means that a certain kind of "positive thinking" doesn't seem so much like real thinking to me as a kind of incantation or trance.

Yet despite my penchant for both logic and melancholy, I persisted, and this book reveals the fruit of that persistence. It is the record of my own deliberate attempt to make three very different wishes come true—the wish for a house, the wish for a new love, and the wish for spiritual healing. And it is simultaneously a reflection on the quintessentially human act of wishing, which begins with ancient cave dwellers beseeching the gods for rain, deer, fertility, and extends all the way to New Age prophets preaching affirmations, visualizations, the "law of attraction," and the practice of "Putting It Out There."

In its reflection, the book focuses on these fundamental questions: Does a wish have power? If so, what kind of power is it, and how can this power be tapped? Is there danger in wishing? If so, what sort of danger is it, and how can this danger be avoided? At the root of these questions is one perennial mystery: the connection between mind and matter, psyche and substance, soul and world. Ancient human thought assumed a continuity between these two dimensions ("Being and thought are One," declared Parmenides in the sixth century B.C.), but with the rise of scientific thought, a gap arose. Now, as the latest medical and scientific research begin to dissolve this gap, it becomes more and more urgent for a thinking person to distinguish between fact and superstition, between real power and false promise.

But before going any further: *what is a wish?*

As I see it, a wish begins with a desire—a desire for things to be somehow other than they are. Thus, when I say "I wish," it means first of all that I have a desire to possess something that I don't yet possess, to ward off something that might be a threat, to become or to experience something that at present eludes me, or to hold on to something that might otherwise disappear.

We often use the words *wish* and *desire* as though they were one and the same, but I want to say that a wish is *a desire with something added*. For while a desire can remain quite passive, latent, held within the realm of possibility, a wish, as I intend to use the word, takes aim. It tries to cross the threshold between the possible and the actual. It's a desire with ambition, a desire poised for action. "Hope is the thing with feathers," said Emily Dickinson. And a wish, as I understand it, is a desire with feathers—an arrow's feathers and an arrow's sharp point.

So then, how is a wish distinguished from a hope? To me, it's the sharp point that makes the difference. For while hope implies loft, the aspiration to soar toward what is yet to come, I see it primarily as an inner state, a kind of trusting readiness that does not necessarily propel itself into the air to snag its object. As for a wish: only with both feathers and sharp point can it reach what it aims for, crossing the threshold from idea in the mind to actual occurrence.

Over the course of my year's experiment, I was amazed to discover that, one by one, all three of my wishes really did cross the threshold and come true. Indeed, the intensity of my amazement revealed to me just how skeptical I had been. Even as I gave myself over to my experiment, there was a large grain of salt that never dissolved. And still hasn't, really! How can that be? I don't know. Perhaps that grain of salt is a way of holding the capricious gods at bay, of warding off the jealous neighbor's evil eye, keeping the other shoe from falling, enticing the skeptical reader to turn the next page. What I do know is this: the story that follows is a true story. It's a story that ultimately went beyond my own three wishes, raising new questions, presenting new challenges, and interweaving itself with other people and other places in ways that I could never have foreseen. But it begins in the small northern California town where I live, on the first day of the New Year. . . .

# PART ONE

# Putting It Out There

*In which I openly declare
three desires—to heal my soul,
buy a house, and find a man—
and am initiated into the
art of wishing*

# CHAPTER ONE

# January

## *Shrines: Honoring Desire*

It's New Year's Day: bright and cold, with wind moving through the tops of the eucalyptus trees and silver clouds gathering in the distance. Beside me on the table are the remains of last night's rather quiet celebration: in a glass bowl, four walnut sailboats float on water, their mission accomplished. Bobbing in a small sea of varying good fortunes, each made its way to one particular rolled-up paper message, tied with a gold ribbon. Mine read: "This year you will make a remarkable voyage to a place you've never been."

Hawaii?

Whenever I encounter the word *voyage,* the word *Hawaii* springs up like a flower. For as long as I can remember, it's been my wish place, a place in whose actual existence I've never fully believed. I've looked through travel books, gazed at other people's photographs, and tried to imagine myself actually there among its iridescent green valleys, its waterfalls and lava beds, its banks of plumeria, hibiscus, and bromeliad. Yet Hawaii has always seemed out of reach to me, a place for which I lacked some crucial piece of paper, a ticket or permit saying, "Let her pass."

In any case, I already sense that the fortune I've drawn is about a different kind of voyage—not so much to a place as to a different state of mind.

Fortunes, oracles, signs, and omens: don't they belong to the same family as the wish? They all spring from that great human need to gain some purchase on the future—if not actually to alter its course, then at least to see into its shape, discern its contours, its pattern of light and dark.

When I look up the word *wish* in the dictionary, here's what I find: it comes from the Middle English *wen,* and is related to the Latin *venus* as well as *venom* (originally a kind of love potion) and to *venereal* (referring to love disease), along with *venison* (containing a link to hunting).

Already, in that one small word, so much is gathered: desire, danger, seeking. It seems in itself a kind of omen for the "remarkable voyage" I'm about to embark on. But let me begin by laying my cards on the table, alongside the glass bowl with its four walnut boats.

Like most people I know, I have a long list of wishes for the world around me. However, when it comes to things on the cosmic scale—things as immense and complex as ending war, hunger, poverty, disease, and the destruction of the natural environment—I don't yet have much faith in the power of wishing. Perhaps such faith will emerge as I move forward, but for now I need to focus on a smaller scale. Using my own life as a petri dish, I'm going to start with the two wishes at the top of my personal list.

One is to be spiritually healed. The second is to buy a house.

Is it crazy, a kind of blasphemy even, to set these two cards alongside each other, as though they belong to the same deck?

Not long ago, while I was slumped on the sofa late at night, I happened to catch a popular TV evangelist who was dressed to the nines with big hair, major earrings, and bright makeup. "I'm expecting radical favor!" she beamed, raising her bejeweled hands toward God in His heaven. "I'm expecting favor, blessings, and the best cut of meat in the house!" Her audience beamed back from their stadium seats, as though God, at that very moment, was processing their order for prime rib.

Where does such chutzpah come from? I wondered. When I was young I was taught not to engage in petitionary prayer. Or rather, I was taught that it was all right to petition God for things of the spirit, but not for things of the world. *Ask and ye shall receive*, I was taught. But it was understood that what ye asked for was grace, peace, forgiveness—not jewels on your fingers or Angus beef.

Of course, you might pray for someone who was ill to be healed, for someone who'd lost his job to find employment, for a family whose house had burned to find shelter—but such specific requests for divine intervention in earthly affairs were reserved for dire occasions, for situations of acute suffering and drastic need. Though God was omnipotent and omniscient, the source of time and the end of time, He didn't have time to fritter away. He had to focus on matters of supreme importance—sustaining the universe from moment to moment, forgiving sins, granting life everlasting. You didn't badger Him for lesser favors, and you trusted Him to take care of your deepest needs.

A few nights ago I was invited to join a gathering of women in a beautiful house in Sausalito, which is just south of where I live. They ranged in age from thirty to sixty-something, and among them were therapists, artists, writers, musicians, entrepreneurs. They were an impressive group: highly educated, well traveled, creative, accomplished, and spiritually oriented. Though most of them had never met me before, they were gracious and welcoming. And yet as the evening wore on, I began to feel very estranged. After dinner our hostess lit the logs in the fireplace and asked us to gather in the living room. Flopped on the sofa, chairs, and pillows in front of the fire, we were invited to share our wishes for the coming New Year. One by one, around the circle, each woman spoke—and as the ritual went on, I felt more and more uncomfortable.

"I wish for world peace," the first woman said. Then, after only a slight pause, she continued, "I want to develop a new product line. And I want to lose weight." The next woman began, "I wish to become more forgiving. I wish for a boyfriend. And new client referrals." And so it went around the circle until it was my turn—and I could barely speak. I stammered something vague and abstract about "seeking more balance in my life," and then—when they went out to the garden to light candles—I slinked away in the dark.

Driving home, I tried to figure out what was the matter with me, why I had fled from a group of kind and intelligent women who were openly and sincerely articulating their desires. That's when I realized: I'm a terrible wish snob. It's not that I mean to be. It's that somehow I grew up with a powerful wish hierarchy in place. Under this regime, it's okay to wish openly for compassion or world peace. It's okay, if someone asks you what you want for your birthday, to say you want a sweater or a bracelet. It's okay, if you're having a conversation with your friends, to say you want to find a lover or switch careers or lose ten pounds. But in a ceremonial setting, to openly declare certain desires for personal happiness, and to set them alongside more universal and spiritual goals as if they were all simply part of a continuum: that's taboo.

Recently, while reading a magazine, I came across a letter that John F. Kennedy received from his mother during the last year of his life. "Dear Jack," she wrote, "In looking over my old diary, I found that you were urged on one occasion, when you were five years old, to wish for a happy death. But you turned down this suggestion and said that you would like to wish for two dogs instead."

Clearly, the little boy hadn't yet grasped the hierarchy of wishes, and that's partly what makes the story comic. It presupposes a certain spiritual framework, one in which adults do not merge the categories because to do so is actually a serious matter, a metaphysical breach. And indeed when I dare to say in the same breath, "I want to be spiritually healed and I want to buy a house," I feel a visceral dread, a sinking in my gut, and an impulse to run for cover like a scared rabbit in an open field. It's the feeling that something out there in the universe, some form of the powers that be, is going to swoop down and do me in.

But heck: here I am, living in northern California, the land of Putting It Out There. Which is to say, the land of unabashed articulation of desire, a place where one out of every three people subscribes to the belief that—so long as what we want does not cause harm to others—*the universe wants us to be happy.* And if only we will take the time (1) to discover what it is we really want, (2) to focus and articulate this desire, and (3) to remove the obstacles that arise in the form of certain negative thoughts and habitual behaviors—*the universe will cooperate with us to bring about our goals.*

When I returned to California thirteen years ago, the move was not just a huge geographical shift. I was also trying to shed a way of life that was the opposite of Putting It Out There—a way of life that might have been called Warding It Off or even Making It Hard. Why is it that some of us seem drawn to hardship as if it's a magnet, entranced by the uphill road? Isn't our behavior counterrevolutionary, unadaptive, like fish trying to swim without fins or birds clipping their own wings?

Of mixed Jewish and Catholic heritage, I grew up with an alertness to suffering and a fear of disproportionate earthly happiness that seemed equally reinforced by both traditions.

Consider the Jewish custom of breaking a glass at a wedding. Many people believe that it symbolizes the breaking of the bride's hymen, but some scholars tell a different story. In a village in medieval Poland, a distinguished rabbi came upon a wildly exuberant wedding party. Amid the laughter, the feasting and dancing, the rabbi grew anxious. The joy was so intense and uncontained that it was bound to catalyze misfortune. The solution? Break a glass, in order to restore a proper sense of measure. Create a small disaster, in order to stave off the looming presence of a big one.

That solution makes perfect sense to me. It's a kind of mathematics of existence, a chemical equation: too much undiluted happiness will seed the clouds. When you've been a tribe apart for thousands of years, the stakes are huge. Who knows when your little oasis of happiness will be destroyed again, bringing you endless wanderings, slavery, pogroms, cattle trains? You must remember these things, even when you rejoice. At the Passover feast each spring, when you eat the egg that symbolizes your tribe's new life, you must taste it along with a sprig of bitter herbs, dunked in a bowl of saltwater tears.

At the same time that I was absorbing the long history of Jewish suffering, I was encountering the image of Jesus dragging his heavy cross, the saints and martyrs enduring fire and flagellation, sleeping on nails and consorting with lepers. Baptized a Catholic, when I was confirmed at age thirteen I chose the name Bernadette, in honor of the little wood-gathering saint who encountered the Virgin Mary not far from the French village of Lourdes. I'd come across her photograph once, and it had moved me. Circa 1852, it showed a frail young girl bent under a giant mound of sticks.

Then there was my grandmother Grace, who lived a few blocks away from us in Santa Monica and whom I often visited in her small apartment. With her snow-white hair and fine manners, her violets and embroidery and paper-thin cookies, she seemed the quintessence of old-lady sweetness—but I knew that she carried inside her a secret core of fierceness. As a young girl she had been lovely, with sapphire-blue eyes and a cloud of brown hair. She had grown up in a big house in Chicago in the 1880s, in the sort of neighborhood where people thwacked croquet balls on summer lawns and gathered around the piano on chilly nights, dressed in yards of starched and pleated clothing. She had elegant suitors.

Yet as a young woman she had left it all behind to become a social worker among the coal miners of Alabama. "Tell me the Friday-night story!" I used to beg her, because it thrilled me to think of my dainty grandmother living dangerously. And she would tell me how on Friday nights when the miners got paid they would go to the bar in town and get drunk and rowdy. She'd be in her room in her long white nightgown, in her stocking feet and with her hair brushed loose, and she would hear them on their way home, singing and shouting and breaking bottles. Then she would come to my favorite part of the story: *I'd drag my dresser to block my door, so the men couldn't break into my room.*

The Jews dragging their tents through the desert. Jesus dragging his cross. Bernadette dragging her load of sticks. My grandmother dragging her dresser. Somehow I grew up believing that the recipe for an authentic life was *Drag something heavy*. Later on, when I learned the Buddhist expression "Whatever walks in the family gate is not the true treasure," it hit home for me. Always suspicious of anything that seemed to come too easily, I'm quite sure that if I'd been born with a silver spoon in my mouth, I would have tried to yank it out.

And though I wasn't born with a silver spoon, there were other shiny things that came to me early in life, as if handed on a platter. One of them was California, where I grew up in nearly perpetual sunshine by the ocean: first in southern and then in northern California. Somewhere along the way I internalized the attitude of much of the rest of the world that life in California—despite the always imminent threat of earthquake, flood, and fire—is too easy and therefore unreal. And so as soon as I was old enough to leave home, I moved to the realest place I could find. I moved across the country to another universe: flat, cold, and incessantly gray. The college I'd chosen was south of Lake Erie in Ohio, and in May, toward the end of my first school year, I was sitting at my desk when I became aware of a strange sensation in my eyes. I rubbed vigorously, attempting to remove the foreign object, and then I realized: the foreign object was sunlight. I put my head on my desk and sobbed.

Yet, true to form, I stayed in that gray zone for another two decades. From Ohio I moved to Toronto for graduate school in philosophy. Then, having discovered Zen Buddhism, I moved directly south of Lake Ontario to study at the Rochester Zen Center, deep in the snow belt of New York. In that part of the world, the sky is gray for nearly three hundred days a year—and not a mobile, light-infused gray, but a dense gray in which there is not the least glimmer of light. Whenever the dental assistant lays that heavy gray "gonadal shield" over my belly to protect me from X-rays, I always think of that long, Great Lakes period of my life.

And then, at long last, as though some divine dental assistant had lifted the great, leaden shield of the sky, by some miracle I felt I'd done my time and received clearance to return to the place I loved.

Why is it that some people don't seem to wait for that sense of divine clearance, for some kind of license or permit that falls from the sky, announcing to them, "You've suffered enough. Now you can have what you wish"? They simply move to Hawaii or take up skydiving or buy themselves a horse. They don't seem to operate with the same sense of precarious balance, with the idea that light must follow dark, pleasure is the fruit of pain, and too much fun will tip the scales, attracting calamity. They don't seem to worry about satisfying the prerequisites. If they want Easter, with flowers and eggs and new life, they go for Easter, without the forty days of Lent. If they want sun, they go for sun, without twenty years of snow.

I know I'm not alone. In fact, I know there are more of us than them. Just look in any book of superstitions, and it's clear. From time immemorial, human beings have been wary of good fortune. Not just among the Jews but in every culture there are ancient recipes for disguising joy, for paying homage to suffering in the midst of celebration, for deflecting the envy of gods and neighbors: rub soot on the face of your beautiful child; spit when you get a compliment; throw salt over your shoulder at a wedding; let cider spill from your glass to offset the bounty of your harvest; say "break a leg" when you really mean "good luck."

And so—even though I knew I'd done my time—when I returned to California thirteen years ago, I still felt wary. With my husband and five-year-old daughter, I moved to the wine country, north of San Francisco, where we rented a little house surrounded by vineyards. Out every window the view was rolling hills, great spreading oaks, and the grapevines—turning from green to gold to red and purple with the seasons. The sounds were wind in the trees, the rush of water in the creek, the cry of quails. For the first few months, every time I stepped outside the door, I would find myself thinking: "It's so outrageously beautiful here. Someone is sure to find out and deport us!"

But gradually, when the paddy wagon didn't arrive, I began to relax my guard. Then I went even further. I dared to wish for more. Having reclaimed the beauty of California, there was something else I wanted to reclaim.

The painter Kandinsky once exclaimed in his journal about the happiness contained within the smell of turpentine, and when I read his words I felt them in my body. My mother is an artist, and every house we ever lived in had its painting space, its drop cloth on the floor, its shelves and drawers of tubes, brushes, pads, tinctures, and tools. Painting was as much a part of daily life as eating or sleeping, and my happiest early memories all come with the slightly sour odor of tempera paints and oatmeal paper, the pristine yet slightly earthy smell of a new bolt of canvas, and yes—the intense piney tang of turpentine.

But around the same time that I exiled myself from California, I also gave up painting in favor of writing, which—though it had held equal sway in my life from the time I was small—came harder to me. Somehow, despite many examples of writers who paint and painters who write, I had the notion that one had to choose, and so I did. For a long time after, I had the strange sensation of having paintings in my arms—it was a painful feeling, like a kind of racing pulse that wanted to find its way out of my body and into color and shape. Gradually the feeling dissipated, but in all the intervening years I'd never stopped dreaming of painting, the way one dreams of a lost love.

A love that I would now be reunited with—if only I had space. Our little house in the vineyard was so small—a glorified shack, really—that there was barely room for my daughter's toys, the few props that were the tools of my husband's trade as mask maker and mime, and my own laptop computer and books. Where would I ever put paper, paints, and easel?

That's when I undertook to Put It Out There.

I have no idea where I first heard that phrase—in northern California it just seemed to be in the air. It sounded silly but harmless and cost-free, so what was there to lose? For several months, each morning and evening, I fervently wished for a studio. That's all: no fancy technique, no affirmations, visualizations, mantras, or lighted candles. Just a regularly repeated wish. A wish addressed to whom? I didn't know. I wouldn't presume to bother God with my desire for a studio. And I never voiced my wish aloud or spoke of it to anyone. I just *thought* it, quite intensely, for a few moments each day.

And then it happened. One afternoon, on my way home from a meditation retreat, I stopped to get a cup of coffee. Glancing over the local newspaper, I saw these words: "Free use of studio in exchange for speaking French." *Incroyable!* I thought to myself. Because my father was a French professor, I had lived in France on and off since childhood. I dialed the number, and a few days later I met Carole.

Carole, it turns out, is the Queen of Putting It Out There.

But I didn't know that yet.

I simply knocked on the door of her studio, and when it

opened, there she was, a lean, energetic woman in her early fifties, with large blue eyes and curly dark hair. She was dressed in a loose painting smock, jeans, and wild, multicolored leather shoes. She was painting a large still life with sunflowers, a red chair, and a bright blue hat, and she handed me a paintbrush and pointed toward an easel. "Voilà!" she said, in a way that made me think that might be the extent of her French.

Already, in those first moments, I could see a certain quality of determination—a steeliness that, I was later to learn, is a key component in Carole's ability to make her dreams happen and that gives the lie to anyone who thinks Putting It Out There is strictly for aerie fairies. Though Carole was welcoming, she kept right on painting—which meant I couldn't postpone my own momentous next step. I squeezed out a circle of colors on my palette, stuck my brushes bristle up in their coffee can, and set my canvas on the easel. Then I stared at the blank white square. I stared at it a long time, feeling jittery and slightly clammy, as though waiting for the train to pull up that would reunite me with my lost love. After so many years apart, would I recognize him? Would he recognize me? What if the love was just gone, dried up? What if—worse—it had never really existed? I'd waited for this moment for so long, through years of longing and months of Putting It Out There. But now I just sat on my stool, aware of my heart beating. Finally, I took out a big bamboo brush and tried to loosen up by making swift strokes with water on the canvas. On the other side of the room, Carole was vigorously attacking her sunflowers.

"*C'est vraiment bizarre,*" I began, remembering my side of the bargain. But when Carole said "Huh?" I continued in English.

"It's really strange. Do you know how I found you?" And then I realized it was a good thing we were speaking in English, because I couldn't begin to imagine translating "Putting It Out There" into French—the very idea seems so utterly un-French. For all their joie de vivre, the French are a nation of skeptics. Look at Descartes, who had to think strenuously before he was sure of his own existence! The Gallic shrug, the raised eyebrow, the lips making their various pouty expressions of doubt and disbelief: these belong to a different universe from the one that gives a fig about our wishes.

"So how did you find me?" Carole asked.

When I told her that she was the fruit of my first attempt to Put It Out There, she smiled but didn't bat an eye. She just stood there, dabbing some flecks of orange into the blue of the hat she was painting, and suddenly I felt like Alice having fallen down a hole and found herself face-to-face with a mysteriously authoritative rabbit, waiting for her as though she'd made an appointment.

"*Mais bien sur!*" she said calmly. "For the last twenty or so years, just about everything good in my life has come that way."

"You mean just about everything good in your life has come from Putting It Out There?"

"From consciously wishing, yes."

"Really? Like what?"

"Well, like my husband."

"Your husband? How long have you been married?"

"Fifteen years." Not wanting to get too distracted, she promised she'd tell me the story another time. She'd vowed to finish her painting by the end of the day, and the blue of the hat was getting muddy—

"Okay. But just tell me one other thing that you wished for and got—"

"All my houses."

"Houses? You have more than one?"

"I have four," Carole said. "This one here and three in France."

"Three?"

"*Oui,*" she said, scraping some of the orange flecks from the blue with the edge of her palette knife. "*Un, deux, trois.* You'll see when you come visit me in France."

That was the last bit of French we spoke that day. I couldn't restrain my desire to learn more about Carole's practice of wishing and getting and wishing for more—and her French wasn't up to the task. Fortunately, she seemed to accept that on our first day we might depart from the agenda. She continued to paint without missing a beat, however, and while the water strokes quickly evaporated on my blank canvas, she finished her Still Life with Sunhat and went on to start a new painting.

That was the beginning of a conversation that has continued, intermittently, for the last twelve years.

• • •

"So here you are!" Carole calls out to me now, as I approach the door of her new studio, which is on the ground floor of the house that her husband, Don, recently built for them. Because the two of them have been traveling back and forth so much between California and their three houses in France, I haven't had a chance to visit the new digs. Yet at the sound of Carole's voice, I have a strange sense of déjà-vu, as though when I step over the threshold, I'm going to find her painting that same painting with a red table and blue sunhat.

But it's only a moment's illusion, because for those who truly practice Putting It Out There, time does not stand still. Since I last saw Carole, she and Don have sold two houses in California and built the one they're now living in. They've established an artists' colony in a little village in France and opened a gallery in another village. And from the moment I step inside and look around me, it's clear that Carole's work has evolved—her paintings are looser, more luminous, applied with less paint and more confidence. By the way she answers my *"Comment ça va?"* I can tell that even her French is coming along.

As for me, though the very way I met Carole twelve years ago seemed proof of the power of Putting It Out There, somehow it didn't take. Why? I guess a lifelong habit of skepticism isn't so easily overturned. And maybe it's frightening to think that it might be. Who knows what might emerge from the huge box marked "Don't Dare!" if I managed to open it more than a crack? There really is such a thing as fear of success. Who would I be if I stepped out of my doubts and deferrals, my carefully budgeted sense of possibility? In any case, after that first meeting with Carole, I managed to dismiss it as beginner's luck, a fluke. And though Carole's life—her four houses, her prodigious painting, her devoted husband—was shining testimony to the power of conscious wishing, it was easy for me to label it "Carole's life" and see it as something quite remote from my own.

And then—through a combination of fate and my own leap, headlong, over a precipice—that life of my own came undone.

The community that was the core of my spiritual and emotional life fell apart, and with it my marriage of seventeen years. In a matter of months, I lost my husband, my spiritual mentor, the framework of my life, and many friends. Whenever I think back to this period, what swims before my eyes is the image of hermit crabs. As a child on the beach, I would watch them at low tide— naked, on wobbly limbs, frantically scrambling to find a new shell. I was fascinated by the dramatic insecurity of their existence, by the idea that they perpetually grew out of their homes. That's how I felt during this time: exposed to the elements on a vast beach, a beach littered with the washed-up shards of my past.

Gradually, very gradually, I pieced together the shelter of a new life. My daughter and I moved to a little house not far from her father. He and I learned to navigate our separate lives in harmony. After her initial shock and sadness, our daughter thrived. I began to teach at a local university that offered its own kind of community. Seven years passed. (And here a note to the reader. My daughter, Ariel, is, of course, a major presence in my life. But because she figured so prominently in my last book, at her behest she is a fleeting presence in this one.)

And now, feeling well beyond that time of great upheaval and sheer survival, I'm ready to turn a new leaf.

That's why I'm on my way to Carole's.

Still shaken by my experience among the ladies in Sausalito,

I'm going to take on the wish snob who went slinking off in the dark. I've decided to give Putting It Out There a second try—and this time, I've vowed to stay the course.

· · ·

"I thought we'd make shrines!" Carole says, after I've had a few moments to look around. As always, when I first come into Carole's presence, I feel something akin to the bends, as though I'm coming from a place where it's deeper and darker and harder to breathe, to a place that's light and almost too rich with air.

"I've got balsa wood," she says, always ready to get right back to work. "And this is joint compound. It's what builders use to smooth the seams in Sheetrock, and you can use it to hold almost anything together. It goes on so easily and dries fast, but not too fast, and you can sculpt it and texture it . . . see?" Her hands are covered with the white goo, and she's slathering it on top of the wood. Even when I go a long stretch without seeing Carole, she visits me in my dreams. And when she does, the dreams are in vivid color, and she brings with her a quality of permission, a playfulness that balances on the edge of transgression. In one dream, we each had huge boxes of new crayons and we were about to draw on freshly painted walls. In another dream, we were crossing a body of water, on the backs of ornately costumed elephants.

Permission, crayons, elephants: around Carole, I start feeling the possibility of breaking out of boundaries, doing it in color, and doing it big.

"So, what is it you're wishing for?" Carole asks.

"Well, what I'd really like," I begin. And then I stop. The words seem too big and bright in my throat. "I'd like to buy a house." There. I said it, and I wasn't struck by lightning.

I say it again. "I'd like to buy a house. I'm so tired of perching." And then I begin stammering a sort of defense, though no one has asked me to. "I mean, I like the house we rent, it's a nice little house, we have good neighbors, and there's a pond at the end of the road—but it isn't ours. All my plants are in pots, so we can move at the least notice, and you know the way the price of real estate keeps climbing."

"Owning your own house is good," Carole says when I pause for a breath. "It's so empowering. Did I tell you about my sister?" She tells the story of her sister, whose husband left her for a younger woman after a marriage of thirty years. She was left emotionally devastated, uprooted from the big house that she had shared with her husband, and financially insecure. "And do you know what she did?" Carole asks. "She came to visit me, and we spent a few days just trying to drop below all the fear and confusion and tune in to what she needed and wanted in this new phase of her life. And what came to her was that she had always wanted to live in a little house by the ocean. And she wanted three things to be within a radius of three miles: her little house by the ocean, her sailboat, and her job. So I told her we'd make a shrine—"

"Why?" I interrupt. "What is it about making a shrine?" I have my own thoughts about shrines and their function, but I want to hear what Carole has to say.

"Well, what is a shrine, after all?" she replies, as if it were obvious. "It's a special place where you put something of value, or something that represents what you value. And then, because you've put it there, you pay attention to that something. And when you pay attention, that's when the magic really begins—"

"The magic?"

"Yes, it is magic. But it isn't a magic that comes out of nowhere. It comes because you make a place for it. You move beyond the fantasy in your mind, and you make it visual, you actualize it by making a *thing* of it. Do you know what happened to my sister? She made her shrine in a wooden box, and inside it she placed a tiny white clapboard house, with flowerpots on its porch, the blue sea behind it, and the sailboat bobbing on the sea. Within a year, she had that house!" And then—as though Carole can see that instead of springing into action, I might let myself be lulled by her story, might try to glide by on her sister's coattails, content with vicarious success—she fixes me with her gaze and tells me, "So, that would be a great place for you to start!"

"*Moi?!*"

"Yes, you."

I'd certainly like to start there. I already know exactly what my shrine would look like: it would be in the shape of a little Mediterranean house, the color of apricots, with a red tile roof. It would have bougainvilleas growing over it, potted lemon trees, and a fountain in its inner courtyard. . . .

I can't.

I can't.

I'm just not ready to enshrine my desire for real estate. To declare that I'm expecting favor, blessings in the form of a down payment and the best cut of meat in the house. To me, a shrine—whether large or small—is a sacred space in which you invoke the memory and invite the presence of that which is not "of this world." Having majored in philosophy and religious studies in college, I remember learning that the English word *shrine* comes from the Latin word *serinium,* meaning "box" or "receptacle," and that a shrine is a container of divine power and meaning. It's a threshold, a place where this world and the world beyond meet. The ancient Hindu word for "shrine" is *thirta,* meaning "crossing point" or "ford."

As containers for divine power and crossing points between the visible and invisible worlds, shrines are, indeed, deeply related to the act of wishing. Since ancient times, pilgrims have made long and difficult journeys to shrines, bringing their desire for spiritual transformation and also for concrete and particular outcomes: *may my lover and I be reunited; may I give birth to a healthy child; may my husband recover from his terrible fever.* Shrines can also be "crossing points" between the present and the past, a way to honor the ancestors and commemorate the dead.

Yet even when I think about all the things that a shrine can be and do, I still don't feel ready to make a shrine for the 2 BR, 1.5 BA house of my dreams.

"Well, why don't you just call it a special box, then?" says Carole, searching for a handy loophole. I shake my head. Even if I could forget the ancient link between the two words and pretend that I was just making a box and not a shrine, I would still be begging the question. *What is the true place of our earthly desires?*

As a child I had a disturbing experience. I was visiting my other grandmother in St. Louis at Christmastime, and she took me to see Santa Claus at the department store. We drove to the store, where I stood in a long line of children, preparing my wish for Santa. It was a little puzzling that he wasn't in the room where we were waiting, but I wasn't worried. When you made it to the head of the line, a lady came and took you through a door to where Santa must be waiting. It was always a little frightening to climb into his arms, but I knew I could do it. The slight fear was part of the thrill, and somehow confirmation of his power. At last I was directed through the door into a courtyard, and there I found myself standing alone, at the base of an immense rocket ship. Disoriented, looking for Santa, I would have turned on my heels and darted back out the door, but before I could, a voice thundered from above.

*"What do you want, little girl?"*

What I wanted most of all was a Patty Play Pal, a life-sized doll with dark brown hair, blue eyes, and moveable limbs.

"A Patty Play Pal," I whispered.

*"A what?"* boomed the voice.

"A Patty Play Pal."

*"What's that?"* the voice boomed, beginning to sound a bit cranky.

I fled. I raced back through the door, and before my grandmother could catch me, I had darted clear across one room and into Menswear, where I dived beneath a rack of winter coats. It took a long moment for my grandmother to coax me out, and quite a bit longer to regain my trust. She'd had no idea that they'd given Santa the boot and replaced him with a cutting-edge "Christmas of the Future," 1950s *Sputnik*-style. Though I accepted her apology, I don't think she realized how betrayed I felt. Instead of sitting in Santa's lap, whispering my desire in his ear, I'd been tricked into the most extreme sense of exposure, standing in that cold courtyard under the booming voice. And—though I couldn't have put it into words at the time—as I stood before the rocket, forming the words "I want a Patty Play Pal," I felt a dreadful incongruity. It was dizzying, almost nauseating.

It wasn't until I went to college and discovered a stunning little book by the Romanian scholar Mircea Eliade that I understood such dread. In *The Sacred and the Profane,* Eliade explains that religious experience revolves around a distinction between two orders of reality. He writes, "Man becomes aware of the sacred because it manifests itself, shows itself, as something wholly different from the profane." The sacred is understood to be that which is most real, most powerful—and when it erupts within the context of ordinary, profane experience, it elicits a feeling of awe that is very close to fear. "For religious man," he writes, "space is not homogenous; he experiences interruptions, breaks in it; some parts of space are qualitatively different from others. 'Draw not nigh hither,' says the Lord to Moses; 'put off thy shoes from thy feet, for the place whereon thou standest is holy ground.'"

When I drew nigh to the giant obelisk, stammering my wish for a doll, I had a genuinely dread-ful feeling of violating a fundamental distinction, of bringing my profane desire into a space where it did not belong. And that's what happens now, in a milder form, when I think of making a ritual object to express my desire to buy a house.

The strange thing is, through years of Zen practice, I've tried to let go of the distinction between sacred and profane. For in Zen, one seeks to see all things as equally sacred: from the Buddha himself to a fly skimming by on a summer breeze. As one Zen saying goes, "Outside the ancient temple, a dog is pissing to the skies." In its seeming irreverence, it expresses the fundamentally blessed equality of all things. More than once, it has struck me as the most magnificent sentence in the world.

But what I'm again realizing is that, when it comes to desire, I operate with a very rigid sense of hierarchy. According to its rule, you don't use sacred forms—whether prayers, shrines, or candlelit ceremonies—to express profane desires.

Of course, it's no accident that desire should pose such a challenge for me. In Buddhism, one is usually taught that desire is the root of suffering. The desire to attain liberation from suffering is highly encouraged, along with the desire to purify one's karma and cultivate compassion. But virtually any desire that doesn't appear on this short list tends to be seen as a fetter, a form of enslavement. When one delves in more deeply, it actually turns out that the Sanskrit word *tanha* should be translated as "thirst" rather than "desire" and that the root of suffering is not so much that we crave certain things as that we so strongly identify with and obsess over these cravings.

But none of these distinctions seem to bother Carole.

While I've been thrashing about in them, she's been humming to herself and happily setting out our supplies: balsa wood, X-acto knives, and a can of joint compound. Next to her, I feel like the child of strict parents—as though I was gazing out my bedroom window at the lucky kid on the block, the one who's allowed to be out after dark, to ride her bike with no hands, to tempt fate in all kinds of ways that aren't permitted to me. Where did I get these strict parents who don't even much resemble the parents I actually had? I don't really know. The Jewish/Catholic/Buddhist equation alone can't explain it—because I know other people who share the same tangle of roots but who don't seem to have the same qualms.

What I do know is that, for now, I need to play it safer. If I'm going to claim a measure of transcendence for my desires, then I want to start off with the right kind of desire. If I'm going to appeal to the powers that be, then I want to make sure I'm wishing for something that falls within their purview. I'll make a shrine for the other big thing I'm wishing for: spiritual healing.

"So what happened?" Carole asks when I break the news to her that I'm chickening out on my real estate shrine and going for something more obviously holy. Though Carole herself has a long history of Buddhist meditation, it's been a long time since she was part of a formal community. She vaguely knows that various schisms and scandals have rocked American Buddhism in recent years. "You told me that your community came apart, but you never actually told me why."

"Well," I begin. "It's a sad story—"

"Oh!" Carole says abruptly. "We'd better wait then until you've had a chance to make your shrine and let it begin to work its magic. We don't want those dark thoughts to get mixed up in it now."

Not for the first time, I notice that Carole has an almost allergic reaction to any expression of negativity. And not for the first time, it makes me wonder: What's the shadow side of this positive, powerhouse painter? Whatever it is, right now I'm relieved that it just reached out to put the lid on my story. Though it's been seven years since my community's upheaval, it's still painful to talk about, and the wound, if no longer raw, is still tender. Without a supportive community, it's hard to maintain the same intensity of practice. Without that intensity, I feel estranged from myself, I feel "off," like wine that's turned or an untuned violin.

Yet every time I try to go into a meditation hall, it's as though I'm about to break into hives. There's a wariness that I can't seem to let go of, and the sensation is deeply cellular, like a kind of autoimmune response. When I talk to other people who've fled from chaotic spiritual communities—whether Catholic or Buddhist or some other affiliation—they know exactly what I mean. And to my surprise, I've discovered that many of us have had the same recurring dream. Though the details vary, in essence the dream goes like this: It begins with something irresistibly beautiful—a golden tent, a golden door, a shimmering golden sun. But as we move toward it, we see that we've been drawn to a mirage. It's the perfect metaphor for our spiritual disillusionment, which happened in the very site of what we valued most. For in the dream, the beautiful thing reveals itself to be nothing but cheap plastic—or, in other versions, we stand watching as it turns to dust, to mold, to shit.

"Did you know that joint compound is the secret to the universe?" Carole says to me now, as we begin slapping together the sides of our shrines. No, I didn't. But I'm game. We've cut rectangles of balsa wood for the walls of our shrine, and we are attaching them and covering them with the wondrous white goo.

Carole is making a shrine that expresses her desire to find a gallery in San Francisco that will sell her work. With thin strips of balsa wood, she's making a miniature easel, and on it, she tells me, there's going to be a painting with the words "I want to sell lots of paintings for lots of money." As for me, I've found some thin copper wire, because inside my shrine I'm going to put a miniature birdcage, with its door flung open. The bird has long been a symbol for the soul, and the feeling I have—a very palpable feeling inside the cage of my ribs—is that my soul has gone off somewhere, the bird has flown the coop. Carole feels strongly that I shouldn't leave the birdcage empty, that I should take a plop of joint compound and represent *the bird returned*. Since I seem compelled to represent the emptiness, I add a few faux bread crumbs to appease her, although I know a shrine is not a trap.

As Carole and I lean over our *thirtas,* aligning the walls and smoothing out their texture, Don comes in the door bringing lunch: noodle soup in the raku bowls he's fired in their backyard kiln. Don, the husband she's been with for fifteen years and whom she attracted from six hundred miles away through a brazen act of wishing. I wonder if I'll ever be so brazen as to wish for a man to fill the other big empty space in my life, the space in my heart? As the joint compound dries on my shrine, I shudder at my own greediness and twist the wires to fashion the ransacked birdcage of my soul.

# CHAPTER TWO

# February

## *Arrows: Aiming for Love*

It's Valentine's Day, and my friend Sylvie is already at the restaurant when I arrive. It's a trendy Italian place, and they've put her way in the back, in a dark sort of alcove, where you have to duck as you slide into your chair.

"Look where they put us!" she says, grazing her head against the stucco as she rises to give me a kiss on each cheek. "It's like a woman who arrives without a man has to go into quarantine or something."

Sylvie is French, and though normally vivacious, this evening she's like one of those sourpuss fairy-tale princesses whose desperate father has put out a call to his kingdom: "Her hand in marriage to the one who can make her laugh!" Instantly I assume the role of the determined suitor who's come to lure her out of her funk. I hand her the little gift I've brought her, and when she unwraps it, I feel victorious. It's a plastic figurine of a mustachioed man in a suit. It's called *Hombre Misterioso,* and it glows in the dark. Sylvie cracks a smile.

"Can't we just enjoy each other's company?" I ask her. "Two charming, literate women like us?"

"We're not getting any younger, Noelle," she begins.

"Where is the wine list?"

"I already ordered us a bottle of Beaujolais. You do remember that today was my wedding anniversary."

"*Hélas! Pardonne-moi,* Sylvie." I hadn't remembered. "How long would it have been?"

"Thirteen years."

"And how long were you married?"

"Five years."

Sylvie grew up in a tiny village in the Vendée, which sits just below Brittany, on the Atlantic coast of France. When she was eight years old, her village joined with its neighbor to create the town of Saint Gilles–Croix de Vie with a small burst of fanfare, folk dance, almond cakes, and the cutting of a long satin ribbon. Sylvie had the momentous task of wearing her region's traditional costume with lace cap while bearing an ornate pair of scissors on a velvet pillow. Though I have only heard this story through Sylvie, it is as vivid to me as if I had actually been there: with her chestnut hair and round dark eyes she balances both hat and pillow, walking with a child's solemnity toward the two mayors. Now, as we sit hunched in our restaurant alcove, it strikes me that ever since that celebration, Sylvie's life has been a paradoxical combination of scissors and unions, cutting and joining.

She met her American husband not long after she came from France to teach French literature at an Ivy League college in New England. One of the things that drew them together was their appreciation of *la belle vie,* of sparkling conversation over good food and fine wine, and soon after they married he announced that he wanted to move to the West Coast to become an œnologist. So Sylvie left her plum of a job so that her husband could pursue the divine art of the grape. Not long after they moved, he fell in love with another woman and left Sylvie to fend for herself in a place where she had no work and no friends, and where she was three thousand miles farther away from her roots.

"*Le salaud!*" I say, lifting my glass of Beaujolais to salute her liberation from that bad apple. "Look how far you've come without him!" Since her divorce she's found another professorship, made a circle of new friends, and pursued her love of fine French cooking, theater, and jazz dancing.

But Sylvie is still brooding; and her Valentine's anniversary is hanging heavy in the atmosphere. When I murmur a few comforting platitudes, her frown lines deepen. And when, as discreetly as possible, I inquire whether she'd ever consider becoming more methodical in her quest for love, she looks shocked. "Impossible! Impossible!" she repeats, swirling the wine in her glass, as if simultaneously to release its bouquet and neutralize my offending remark.

It's not that I didn't expect her reaction. Being French, Sylvie is equal parts romantic and skeptic. She believes that true love does indeed exist—but it exists as a kind of naturally occurring miracle, like a spring of fresh water suddenly bubbling up from dry earth. *On ne sait jamais comment l'amour vient aux amants,* the song goes. "One never knows how love comes to lovers."

And no one *should* know! As Pascal said, "The heart has its reasons that reason cannot know." Though the French are an intensely rational people, they believe that there are certain dimensions of life that belong wholly to the irrational, and of these, love is supreme. This belief makes for an interesting mix of hope and resignation. On the one hand, love might suddenly erupt in the most barren heart; on the other hand, there's nothing you can do to give that eruption a jump start.

"Nothing? *Absolument rien?*" I ask.

"*Rien,*" she says.

"What about keeping yourself sort of, you know, ready?"

"Ready," she repeats, without much conviction. "Yes, of course, you have to keep yourself in a receptive state. If you're holding on to the past, if you're carrying a lot of bitterness, you have to let that go. You can't stay locked up in your house all day. You have to . . . circulate."

"Yes, circulate."

"You have to keep up your looks, *bien sur*—"

But Sylvie would never undertake anything so gauche as a strategy. It's not just that the idea is repugnant to her, it's a logical contradiction. By definition, true love is a gift.

"A gift from whom?"

"I don't know. The gods, those Greek ladies in the sky that spin—"

"The Fates?"

"Yes."

"Or just some kind of wonderful fluke?"

"Maybe. But whatever it is, it's something that happens to you. It's not something you make happen." She explains that even if you managed, through some machination, to draw someone to you, the very process would spoil it. It would be like asking someone to tell you they love you. Or bring you flowers. Or throw a surprise party in your honor. There are certain things that need to happen spontaneously, without your conscious intervention, or they don't count.

"You're a Quirkyalone," I tell her.

"*Quoi?*"

"A Quirkyalone. I read an article about them. They even have a website, and there are coffee mugs and T-shirts."

"A website? What is the *content*?" And though she says the word *content* with a tone of disparagement, from the way she's leaning forward I can tell she's intrigued.

"If you go on the Quirkyalone website, there's a test you can take to determine if you qualify."

"And?"

"If you're so deeply romantic that you will hold out for years, preferring solitude to an unsatisfying relationship, trusting that you'll surrender your heart when the great love presents itself, looking down on those who settle for anything less or—worst of all—those who try to go out and find it—"

"*Ah, oui, c'est tout à fait moi,*" she says, sounding both deeply resigned and somewhat comforted to learn she's not alone as a Quirkyalone.

"It's really me, too," I tell her.

"You? You're more of a go-getter."

Though Sylvie's English is perfectly fluent and only ever so lightly accented, there are certain expressions that sound incongruous when they come from her mouth, and *go-getter* is one of them. Plus, the very thought of being a go-getter makes me blanch.

"Oh, come on! I really am not."

"Oh, go on!"

"I'm not!"

Until recently, I've always believed entirely in surrendering to destiny when it comes to matters of the heart. When I was eleven—an age when girls around me were already going boy-crazy—I heard a song that instantly became my default song, the one I seemed to be singing to myself underneath everything else I might be doing. I no longer remember its name or where I first heard it, but its refrain was "Sit in the sun, in the sun, in the sun." Why? Because you can't force good things to happen. But if you just "sit in the sun," before you know it, your love will come.

Still, today, those are the words that I want to believe. That there's no need for anxious scheming. That if we simply allow ourselves to bask in the light of each moment, our heart's desire will come to us.

I met my first love, Michel, in the mountains above a small village in France, where my family had gone for a winter vacation when I was fifteen. I was skiing, and my ski came loose and went flying over a cliff. Before I knew it, a handsome, dark-haired boy took off after it. About an hour later, covered in a fine dusting of snow and with twigs entangled in his hair, he emerged bearing my ski.

As a freshman, I met my college boyfriend while hitchhiking from Ohio to Washington, D.C., for a peace march that turned out to be "the largest human assembly in the history of the United States." His name was Arthur, and he had a great head of wooly hair and wore little round-rimmed glasses that made him look just like the gentle revolutionary he was.

I met my husband, Eliot, at the Zen Center in Rochester, New York, where we sat for hours in a dark *zendo* alongside each other, staring at the wall. Out of the corner of my eye, I fell in love with the straightness of his spine, the way he radiated such a combination of intensity and stillness that it sometimes seemed he might fly through the roof.

This is the way I prefer to meet a man: while I'm absorbed in something else—an escaping ski, a large human assembly, or the famous koan, *Does a dog have Buddha nature?*

But is it possible that, in midlife, one might need to be a bit more proactive? Time grows short, after all, and evolution is no longer working in one's favor. The twenty-year-old flower of a girl can sit in the sun, minding her own business, but her lovely, fresh petals cast a wide net of fragrance, drawing those bees to her nectar. It's not quite the same for the woman of forty, or fifty.

But I do love the stories of lovers coming across each other late in life, and without design. My mother, for instance. She was traveling in Italy and went to hear a lecture, presented in Italian, at the Cultural Center in Venice. A distinguished-looking man with silver hair came up to her and said, *"Parla italiano?"* To which she promptly replied, "No!" That was eight years ago, and they've been together ever since. (Months later, when my mother asked Luigi, "What made you approach me?" he replied, *"Tuo posteriore!*"—your bottom.) Then there's Anne, the friend of a friend, whom I see occasionally at parties. At a recent gathering, I noticed that Anne looked quite radiant, and that she was wearing a ring on her wedding-band finger. Then a tall man with a bearded, El Greco sort of face came to stand by her side, and I saw that he wore a matching ring. Later, our mutual friend whispered to me, "Did you hear how they met? At the bottom of the Grand Canyon! They both just happened to have made it down on the same donkey train. And they looked into each other's eyes and knew."

"*Voilà!*" Sylvie says to me now. "That's what I want. To find my soul mate at the bottom of a canyon, when all I've been thinking about is keeping my little donkey's hooves on the trail."

"Yes, but both my mother and Anne had to wait until they were in their sixties," I remind her. "Is there any harm in trying to give the process a little boost?"

"What do you mean, a boost?" she asks, her eyes narrowing.

And all of a sudden I have a dreadful memory from childhood. It's third grade, the day after our teacher, Mrs. Kenny, has taken us on a field trip to a smelly tuna cannery in downtown Los Angeles. Now we're back in the classroom, hunched over our desks, writing on the theme "My Day at the Tuna Cannery." A question occurs to me about which I have some urgency—perhaps something about the anatomy of the tuna or the spelling of the word *eviscerate*—and I raise my hand and wave it in the air. Before I know it Mrs. Kenny has charged over from her big desk at the front of the room and is shaking my shoulders, hissing, "God helps those who help themselves!"

Though even at the time I was aware that there was something strangely disproportionate about Mrs. Kenny's behavior, I've never been able to get those words out of my head.

I heard them as a kind of curse, and in essence they were. For they were the same curse God spoke when he drove us from the

Garden of Eden. When he announced that, since we had disobeyed Him, He would no longer simply bestow. Once we could just stretch out our hands to pluck a fig, a bunch of grapes, a cluster of dates. We could lounge around all day in the sun, buff naked. But now, because we'd been bad, we would work by the sweat of our brows to earn our daily bread. We would labor in pain to give birth to our children. And we would gnash our very own teeth while writing about My Trip to the Cannery.

Was Mrs. Kenny happy in love? I doubt it. And did she imagine that she was pleasing in the sight of God when she shook the bejeezus out of a young child whose crime was a question about tuna fish?

By the end of the school year I had mostly forgiven her because one day when two Hollywood scouts swept through our classroom, she recommended that I be the one to go on the Art Linkletter show *Kids Say the Darndest Things*. "Why did I pick Noelle?" she said to the class. "Because she doesn't just sit like a bump on a log." As my classmates glowered at me, I tried to process what seemed to me like a very mixed message: one minute I'm scolded for daring to ask a question; the next minute I'm honored for not sitting mutely.

It's another mixed message that I'm trying to process now. For even as one voice sings to me sweetly to "sit in the sun, in the sun, in the sun," another one hisses: "God helps those who help themselves." Is it possible that there's a middle way?

Across from me, Sylvie is gnashing on a bread stick.

"Just look at Albert Ellis," I blurt.

"Where?" asks Sylvie, looking at the table across from us. "There?"

"No, he's not here in the restaurant. He's dead."

"Oh."

"You know, the psychologist who came up with rational emotive behavior therapy—"

"Never heard of it."

"But maybe you heard the story about him, his famous love experiment?"

"No."

I tell her how, at age nineteen, Albert Ellis became concerned that he would be doomed to a life of solitude if he didn't get over his fear of approaching women. So one summer he decided to go to the New York Botanical Garden every day for a month. Every time he saw a woman by herself on a park bench, he forced himself to sit beside her and try to strike up a conversation.

"And?"

"He had to sit in the sun next to more than two hundred women, but he eventually went out on a few nice dates!"

"*Ça alors!*"

"Pretty amazing, isn't it? But you and I would die before we'd try anything like that, wouldn't we?"

"No kidding. Besides, today Mr. Ellis wouldn't need to go to the zoo, he could just sit on a virtual bench at Match.com. Not that I'd be caught dead doing that either, you know."

I do know. Sylvie and I have had this conversation before. I've tried to convince her that I found the idea just as appalling at first, having grown up in an era when the "personals" were those kinky ads in the back of the *Berkeley Barb*.

But then one night, about five years ago, a friend converted me. After dinner at her house she told me, "Come on—just see how it's done." She logged on, and voilà! Within moments, she'd found me a lovely-looking man with shiny black hair who described himself as a bicycle-riding photographer who liked to see foreign films, listen to jazz, and tutor inner-city schoolchildren. He lived about thirty miles away from me, and he had a teenage daughter the same age as mine. His spelling was flawless, he steered clear of romantic clichés (no "hot tubs," "moonlit nights," or "walks on the beach"), he appeared fetish-free (no "freckled only" or "pre-

fer unshaved"), and much to his credit—unlike most of the men—
he wasn't insisting on a vastly younger woman.

Two weeks later, after an exchange of e-mails and several phone
calls, we met for lunch in a little restaurant in the vineyard not far
from where I live. We spotted each other on the street outside the
restaurant, and we walked toward each other beaming, with our
hands outstretched. It was a good beginning, and it went up from
there. After lunch we hiked in a nearby state park, chattering away
as if we were old friends and taking photographs of trees, old stone
walls, and each other. The next morning, when I opened my e-mail,
he'd sent me a spliced-together photograph that made it look as
though the two of us had been leaning side by side against an old
iron gate. "Cute couple, eh?" was the caption. I was charmed.

We continued to see each other for over a year before things
unraveled in the face of our different versions of the future. "I'm
lonely. I'm thinking of buying a dog," he told me one day—and I
knew that was the beginning of the end. He was ready for a live-
in partner, while I thought separate households were good until
our daughters were off to college.

Now I think of him as my beginner's luck—because ever since,
it's been downhill, and often absurd. The second Match.com encounter was with a man who described himself as "someone capable of saying the great Yes to life." We met at a deli, where after
studying the menu for fifteen minutes and then grilling the waitress, he finally scowled and said the great Yes to "the pesto sand-
wich but without the pesto."

Having heard me recount this tale, my third Internet date
brought a large jar of pesto to our first meeting. This I found quite
amusing, but on our second rendezvous he stole a jar of saffron
from a Starbucks store. He displayed it to me triumphantly as we
walked out the door, whereupon I burst into tears. (Had my life
come to this: dating shoplifters?) Not long after that I met a man
who broke into my e-mail. It took me weeks to figure out why I

had the sensation of being watched when I was with him, the eerie feeling that there was some third factor in the connection between us, something I sensed but couldn't name. It was creepy, as though Peter the Pumpkin Eater was trying to keep me in his pumpkin shell—and it all clicked into place when I realized that he had discovered my password and was reading my correspondence. Most recently, there's been a series of men with strange sound effects: Ted who yawned loudly through dinner at a restaurant, then made strange, slightly orgasmic moans during a movie; and a man whose pedometer jingled a cheery tune every hour on the hour, to remind him to get up and walk and thus avert an otherwise imminent coronary.

Is it any wonder I've gotten a bit cynical? As I scroll through the profiles, I do my own instant translation. If, for example, I come upon a man calling himself "Mistah Mom" who specifies "Any woman I go out with must be able to understand my special relationship with my vivacious daughter," I immediately think: "Hmmmm . . . a guy who's enmeshed with his psychopathic kid . . ."

But here we are, in our little alcove on Valentine's Day. Sylvie has placed the *Hombre Misterioso* beside her glass of wine. He's gazing at her now in a steadfast and encouraging way. Her spirits seem to have brightened a bit, and her salmon has finally arrived.

As for me, I'm feeling ready to try something different: between sheer passivity and methodical manipulation, there must be a middle way.

"I told you what my friend Carole did, didn't I?" I ask Sylvie.

"Carole? The one who married herself?"

"Yes."

And Sylvie waves a hand as though dispersing a small noxious cloud of American silliness while simultaneously making that sound of exasperation that sounds like the French word for "beef": *"boeuffffffff!"*

I confess, I would find it hard to do what Carole did. After a long period of what she herself describes as "frenetic, wild-woman behavior," she shaved her head, dressed in white, and gathered her friends around her in a circle. She read the vows that she had written on rice paper, vows that expressed her readiness to settle down and commit to one man for the rest of her life.

Then, a short while after the ceremony, she had a card printed up that described precisely what she wanted in a man and what she was willing to give in return. Wherever she went, I explain to Sylvie, she handed out that card—

"*Pas vrai!*" says Sylvie.

"But it is true! And this was fifteen years ago, long before it became de rigueur for people to openly broadcast their heart's desires—"

"I'd die!" says Sylvie for the third time this evening, pushing her plate away as if the food was poisoned.

"I know what you mean, Sylvie. But listen. . . . Eventually, one day, a friend of Carole's read the card and said, 'I know this man you're looking for!' And the friend got on the phone, reached the man, gave him the news, and invited him to come visit. A few days later, he flew up to meet Carole, and the two of them have been together ever since!"

"*Tu blagues!*"

"No, I'm not kidding. I know Don. They're very happy together. I'll take you to their house—"

"Which house? You told me they had four."

"Their house here, in California, and you can ask Carole to tell the whole story, in vivid detail."

"Well, we'll see," says Sylvie. "When are they ever going to take away these salmon bones?"

And then, as if turning back toward life's more reliable pleasures, she picks up the menu again and buries her face in it. "What shall we have for dessert?"

• • •

If there's one thing that Carole has taught me, it's that Putting It Out There involves rituals but not rituals alone. It also involves a great deal of determination and a sequence of very practical steps. But, alas, at this juncture—despite whatever determination I might muster—I don't feel able to duplicate either the ritual or the practical step, the solo wedding or the card. And after the pesto-minus-pesto, the stolen saffron, Peter the Pumpkin Eater, the strange moans, and the jingling pedometer, I've come to the end of Match.com.

What now?

A few days after my dinner with Sylvie, a friend tells me about her niece who wrote down on a piece of paper what she wanted in a man, then put the paper under her bed. Two weeks later, voilà, he appeared in her life! They're married now. He's a bird photographer, and she teaches Pilates in Marin. Carole would no doubt consider it a form of waffling, but it's an idea that appeals to my chicken heart: a wish at once enunciated, carefully delineated— and then buried.

As a child I loved the magic of things that were hidden, buried, folded up and tucked away: the message in the bottle, the face inside a locket, the secret drawer or door. I loved Pippi Longstocking, and the magic hollow of the tree that yielded bottles of her favorite sweet drinks. I loved stories of amulets and wish stones, worn under collars or hidden in pockets. In junior high, there was a hole in a big cement retaining wall of the school where my girlfriends and I left letters to imaginary lovers, some of them quite obscene. In college, I learned about Pascal and the letter he had sewn into his jacket; it described his mystical experience, and he wanted to keep it near him always: *"fire . . . fire . . . tears . . . tears of joy . . ."*

Now, back at home, I hunt for the book that a friend sent me several years ago, when I was in the worst of my hermit-crab period and couldn't imagine ever being able to love again. ("I know you'd die before you'd ever buy a book like this for yourself," she'd written on the note that came with it, "but what have you got to lose?") I'd never even taken the book out of the brown paper wrapper she'd sent it in. I'd only peeked once to see the title: *Are You the One for Me?* The cover was hot pink and showed the author with a mane of glossy brown hair and a giant toothy grin, as though she'd spent her entire childhood as the star of *Kids Say the Darndest Things.* I shudder again now as I unwrap it, but I'm ready to give it a try. Over the course of one evening, I do a series of exercises until I arrive at this composite picture of my own Man Wanted:

> *He's very intelligent, and witty. He's spiritually oriented, and he does some form of work that he loves. He's had at least one long marriage and been a good father to at least one child. He's handsome, affectionate, and outgoing. He loves travel, foreign films, art museums, good conversation, and hiking. He lives within fifty miles of me. French-speaking a plus.*

It's past midnight by the time I've copied this out on a nice piece of stationery in what Mrs. Kenny would have called "your best Sunday handwriting." Tired but also strangely elated, I heave my mattress up from the box spring, to make a space for my folded-up wish. Is it possible that I've found a way to simultaneously Put It Out There and keep it to myself, to sit in the sun and yet not be a bump on a log?

When I open the local newspaper the very next morning, here's what leaps out at me: "Calling In 'The One.'" It's an announcement for an upcoming workshop that promises: "7 Weeks to Attract the Love of Your Life." I can't help but wonder: Have my eyes fallen on it through purely random coincidence, or is the universe already responding to my wish? I have no doubt what Carole would say—but right now I feel like I could sooner go hog wrestling or skeet shooting than call in "The One" in public. Still, with my inner Carole urging me on, it occurs to me that the workshop might be a way to up the ante if my buried "Man Wanted" should fail to deliver. It isn't happening for another few months, and by then—if I'm really lucky—I'll have found someone. If not, maybe I'll be ready for more forceful tactics. As I jot down the date and the number, I can feel my inner Sylvie glowering.

Meanwhile, in the days that follow, I find myself thinking more about Carole and her wedding to herself—an act that seems unthinkable to me. I'm someone whose cheeks burn red when I open birthday presents in front of my nuclear family—never mind trying to stand in a white dress declaring "I do" to myself before a throng of friends. Still, there is something about it that draws me. It's the idea that something has to happen internally, within one's own consciousness, before it can be confirmed from without. Isn't this like Jesus saying "You can't put new wine in old bottles"? He was speaking in a very different context, and about a very different kind of love. But wasn't he advocating an *active* form of waiting, one in which we transform ourselves into a new sort of vessel for that which we hope to receive?

Waiting: in contemporary culture, it's a highly devalued activity. We want results, and we want them now. We don't want to stand in line, to bide our time, to let the field go fallow. But in the spiritual realm, waiting has long held a place of honor: the prophet waits for the Messiah to come to earth, the mystic waits for divine presence to flare from within. Waiting is both a sign of faith and a deepening of faith, an invitation *to* and a preparation *for* the sacred. In Spanish, the word for "to wait" is the same as "to hope": *esperar*.

For lovers, too, waiting has been granted a special value. It is a test of love, a declaration of fidelity, a way of readying the heart. Though it is often painful, it has its own voluptuousness. In her book *A Natural History of Love,* Diane Ackerman defines the essence of a lover's waiting as "wishing the future to be present.

For a slender moment or string of moments, time does a shadow dance, and the anticipated future is roped by the imagination and dragged into the present as if it really were here and now. The here and now is made to last beyond its mortal limits. What can be controlled this instant, and only for this instant, is magically generalized into a sea of instants in the charted world of the future. The thrill of waiting comes from the pretended breaking of irrevocable boundaries. It is like being privy to life after death."

I'm struck by the way that she equates waiting with wishing in her description of the lover's dance with time. And I'm also struck that, for her, the lover's waiting and wishing don't seem to have any real power in the world. They deliver a "pretended breaking of irrevocable boundaries"—but the boundaries, she gives us to understand, remain irrevocable. The boundaries between present and future, real and pretend, have and have not.

I doubt that Carole would give her stamp of approval to this form of waiting. For even though it's very rich and alive with meaning, it's essentially passive, impotent. Whereas when Carole was waiting, she was not simply trying to imaginatively control the future but to *actually change something* about herself in the present. In having the wedding to herself, she was attempting to let go of her long phase of compulsive dating; she was vowing not to abandon herself to desperation in her quest. And she was betting that in making this change within herself, she was more likely to actually draw someone to her.

When I was younger, I used to find that it was precisely when I made the decision to just enjoy my own solitude that I would suddenly find myself surrounded by romantic possibility. It certainly felt like magic—yet it was a magic that seemed to reward an actual internal shift. I never would have called it "getting married to myself," but in fact it was a way of coming home to myself, embracing my life as it was. In a wonderfully paradoxical sort of way, the movement toward self-containment seemed to be the very thing that drew love to me. It never occurred to me to embrace the paradox as a conscious strategy—but that, it seems to me now, is what Carole did. With her friends as witnesses, she first surrendered her desperation, her "frenetic, wild-woman behavior." And *then* she liberally distributed her card. As for Sylvie and me, I know that neither of us is ready for such an organized plan, but maybe we can find a subtler version.

"Keep the door open and don't want anything," is an expression I've always loved.

If only I really knew how to do it.

· · ·

A week after our Valentine's dinner, Sylvie calls to tell me she's had a series of lovely dreams about being with a man. Her therapist has told her it's a good sign, and she herself feels that something inside her has shifted, that she is finally ready to let the last dregs of bitterness go and open to some new sweetness in her life.

"Well, maybe you and I should do a little experiment," I tell her.

*"Quoi alors?"*

I suggest to her that she adopt a steadfastly interior approach, concentrating on making the old wine bottle ready to receive the new wine. Meanwhile, I will try a combination approach, a mix of internal preparation and external machination—transforming the old bottle and lobbying the winemakers, as it were.

When she reminds me that the husband who left her was a winemaker, I realize I should perhaps have chosen a different metaphor.

How about the arrow?

"Did you know that the root of *wish* is the same as the *ven* of *venison*?"

"Why are you talking about venison, Noelle? Have you lost your mind?"

"Venison—it has to do with hunting. And Venus, the goddess of love, is the mother of Cupid, with his quiver of arrows. So here's our experiment." And I explain to Sylvie that, while she continues to let go of her bitterness and to allow her dreams of lovely men to prepare the target of her heart for love, I'm going to try a two-pronged approach. While readying the inner circle of my heart for Cupid's bow, I'm also going to hone the arrow of my own desire, sharpening its point and learning to direct the arc of its flight. Doesn't that have a nice ring to it?

Sylvie doesn't seem to think so. At the other end of the phone, her voice sounds piqued. "How are you going to do that? You're not going to print out a batch of cards, like Carole?"

"Let's hope I don't have to do anything that drastic!"

"Yes. Let's hope. I don't know if I could really be friends—"

"You're kidding—"

"Yes. I think so."

"You *think* so?"

Pause.

"Sylvie?"

"Yes. I'm here."

"So?"

"So . . . how long do we have?"

"Until next Valentine's Day?"

*"D'accord."*

That night, settling under my covers, I vow to sleep on top of my paper wish with all the fervor I can muster.

# CHAPTER THREE

# March

## *Gold: Gathering Money*

It's March, and the world around me is an explosion of green and yellow. After the winter rains, the hills here turn an almost iridescent green. The acacia trees are shaggy with yellow blossoms, and in the vineyards yellow mustard shoots up among the vines.

In northern California, spring begins at the end of January, with tiny white narcissus poking up through brown underbrush and a fuzz of pale blossoms coming out on the bay laurel and live oak. After twenty years of living in the snow belt, when I first came to the wine country I felt totally thrown by what seemed like the radically premature arrival of spring.

*But we haven't suffered enough,* I'd say to myself, inhaling the scent of jasmine in January as though it were an illegal drug. In our first year, my dread of imminent deportation was closely linked to the lushness of undeserved spring.

Then, one day in our second year, there was an earthquake. A relatively small one—around a 4.2—but strong enough to shake the room we were sitting in and to rattle the teacups on the shelves. My daughter was six then, and she looked up at me, frightened. Comforting her, I felt something deep inside me relax. Ah, yes: this is the hardship of California. Not the prolonged fierceness of winter but the always imminent possibility of a quake. Having grown up in California and experienced countless small tremors, I'd once had an intimate awareness of that possibility, but after so many years away I'd lost it. Now, odd as it seems, in retrieving that sense of precariousness I simultaneously retrieved a sense of balance. I stopped waiting for the paddy wagon to arrive at our door, for the cosmic "Come Due" notice to fall from the sky. In a visceral way, I remembered that in California we pay for the beauty, the sunlight, the mildness of the seasons, by living with the knowledge that at any moment, the ground could give way beneath our feet.

Still, the March lushness surprises me as I drive toward the coast on a long windy road through the hills that remind me of a line from Dylan Thomas that goes: *and fire green as grass.*

In my old white Volvo, I'm on my way to look at a piece of property. I don't have a clue as to how I could ever afford so much as a chicken coop in this county, which, at last count, was the third most expensive in the United States. But—though I still haven't made my real estate shrine, with its little apricot walls and tile roof—Carole has coached me that if I'm serious about wanting a house, I have to get off my duff and go looking. "And not just a drive-by," she says. "You have to get out of your car and look at properties. You have to talk to Realtors. You have to act as if you have the money."

It won't be easy. For almost as long as I can remember, I've harbored a deep suspicion of money.

When I was five, I soaked a bucketful of pennies in blue starch. It was that kindergarten kind of starch, a magical substance. At night before I went to bed, I poured the pennies under my pillow. The plan was this: while I dreamt on top of them, God would take them for the poor in heaven.

In the morning it was a moment or two before I remembered that a miraculous absence lay in wait for me under my pillow. I tried to lift the pillow up from the bed—but I couldn't. I pulled until the pillowcase ripped, the pillow came away in my hands, and then I saw it: a greenish foam of copper pennies congealed in a sour-smelling glue.

I was stunned. The blue starch, which was to be the medium of transformation, had instead been the medium of a ghastly stasis in my bed. The shiny pennies, which I had been gathering and admiring for weeks, had turned on me. Fortunately, my mother was understanding. She didn't scold me for the ruined sheet or pillowcase, or for the mattress that had to be washed and dragged into the sun to air. She explained to me that there were no poor people in heaven, and that God had no need of money.

From that moment on, there was a gulf for me between money and God. I had made a valiant attempt to become intimate with money; I had slept one whole night with it in my bed—and I had been betrayed. I had tried to mix it with my soul's aspiration, in the form of the magic blue starch, and instead the coins had revealed to me their gross material substance. For me, money had fallen out of grace.

When I went to church and heard the words "It is harder for a rich man to enter the gates of heaven than for a camel to go through the eye of a needle," I believed. They took deep root, intertwining with images of Jesus turning over the tables of the money changers, Saint Francis preaching to the birds in his brown robe and sandals, frail Bernadette bent under her load of sticks. In the sixties, when I was a teenager, these images of Christian poverty were readily grafted to the bare feet, the paisley clothes, the yurt, the homemade yogurt thickening in the sun, the plastic bags hung out to dry, the backpack and hitched ride that were the modest emblems of our giant plans to save the planet. Then, discovering Buddhism at nineteen, I was drawn to yet another powerful tradition of simplicity: the monk and his bowl, the raked rock garden, the moon in the hut, the twirling of a single flower that meant release from the suffering caused by desire.

Not long ago, at a friend's behest, I filled out a questionnaire entitled "What's Your Money Personality?" Though I answered no to the question "Would your friends be appalled at the thought of borrowing clothes from you?" I answered yes to all the other questions and came out with the highest possible rating for the "Spiritual Poverty" type. When I read the definition of this type, I recognized myself—along with most of the friends who might borrow my clothes. For us there is a link between being poor and feeling blessed. Deep in our hearts, we believe that to be poor is both a tangible sign *of* and a way to arrive *at* the ultimate happiness: freedom from the tyranny of desire.

"You just have to shift the paradigm," Carole has told me more than once, and I hear her voice now as I drive through the gaudy green and yellow hills. "How can you receive the blessing of abundance when your mind is closed like a fist?"

Wow. It's amazing, really, how deft her question is. How neatly it replaces one worldview with another—so that what, for centuries, might simply have been called "greed" becomes "receiving the blessing of abundance." And what, for centuries, might have been seen as the virtue of self-restraint begins to look more like the absence of gratitude.

As Carole herself would acknowledge, her modus operandi stirs up very strong feelings in the people she meets. There are those who are unequivocally inspired by her vision and energy and even somewhat in awe of her. They want to become a part of her world, and many look to her as a mentor. Then there are those who find her much too aggressive for their tastes, a mover and a shaker, always looking to see how she can "work" a situation to her own advantage. Once, when Carole went to visit my mother in Venice, she scooped up a large box turtle from the Piazza Garibaldi and put it in her purse. My mother was astounded: the turtle belonged to the Italian people! But Carole wanted it, and when Carole wants something she usually finds a way to acquire it. She named the turtle Garibaldi, put it in a plastic bag with some lettuce leaves, a nub of carrot, and a bit of water, and took it back with her on the train to one of her three houses in France.

For myself, as Carole knows, I oscillate between the poles of admiration and resistance, beckoning with one hand and warding off with the other. Carole has never been anything but generous and encouraging to me, holding out the prospect of one adventure after another, and from the first day I met her I knew that she had something very important to impart to me. Yet at the same time, there is something I have always been wary of, some feeling that Carole has taken a pair of rose-colored glasses with thick lenses and fastened them tightly over her eyes.

"Shift the paradigm," Carole says—as though it was as easy as going from low to high gear on a beautiful open stretch of road. As though the new paradigm were perfectly compatible with the belief that existence is suffering, and that suffering arises from enslavement to desire. But the shift isn't easy for me. It makes my world spin on its axis. For what it means—to us Spiritual Poverty types—is that rather than being blessed for our austerity, we're being told to quit kicking the gift horse in the mouth.

"I'm doing the best I can," I tell myself. Though I still haven't made my real estate shrine, I've become very clear that I intend to buy a house. In fact, at this very moment, I'm on my way up the coast, toward the small town of Point Arena, to have a look at a "charming fixer-upper with loads of potential." I've already learned that reading the real estate ads requires the same sort of instant translation as Match.com—which means that "charming fixer-upper with loads of potential" is just a hair's breadth away from "condemned." Sigh. It isn't a very cheering prospect, but the recompense is that I'm going to stay with my friend Lowell, who lives in Anchor Bay, the next town over, in a wood-and-glass house high in the hills above the ocean.

Lowell owes his house, with its beautiful view, to the fluke that in the 1940s his father met a visionary seamstress who had a brilliant idea for transforming the humble brassiere. Lowell's father scrounged for the money to back her, and together they made a fortune, blasting the brassiere out of its homogenous, utilitarian groove into a dazzling spectrum of styles. For Lowell, it's a kind of cosmic joke to have been born to a destiny so profoundly shaped by the underwires, crossed straps, lift cups of his father's brassieres. Thanks to those bras, he's never *had* to work a day in his life.

*But it's not really easy, you know,* Lowell sometimes finds himself saying, like a kind of refrain, like a charm to ward off the evil eye or an offering doled out to the rest of us. When you don't really have to work, it can be hard to make choices, he explains. And without the fire of real need at your back, it can be hard to stay with the choices you make. It's easy to feel that your life isn't justified, that you don't deserve the things you have. And always, you have to face the envy of others—

*Oh, give us a break!*

Isn't that what some of those envious others are thinking at this very moment? Not me. Given my own queasy relationship to money, I have no trouble imagining that it's difficult to be born with a heap of it. And I admire the way that Lowell has carved out his own life from the heap that was handed to him on a silver platter. He's devoted himself to his work as a writer, translator, and editor. He's generous with the people and causes he believes in. And though his surroundings are beautiful, his house is modest—a two-bedroom, wood-framed house, with a whimsical border of broken crockery that lines the path to the front door.

Besides, I know he had a rather melancholy childhood, permeated with the feeling that he and his father came from different planets. Once, when I asked him what his father was like, Lowell told me that in the moment before he died, he gestured toward his well-appointed hospital room and spoke his last words: "I paid for it."

Every time I think of that, it blows me away. Is that the kind of mind it takes to make a fortune? A mind that, on the brink of infinity—whether conceived as eternal life or sheer annihilation—is still thinking *of the bill*? If so, I'm ready to shave my head, put on a sackcloth gown, and declare to my friends my undying commitment to life on a shoestring.

But here I am, driving up to the lovely little guesthouse that Lowell's father paid for. At the sound of my tires on the gravel, Lowell's large tabby cat, Lincoln, emerges, followed by Lowell himself. With his pale skin, high forehead, and prominent glasses, you could easily mistake him for a neurasthenic English poet, the sort who spends his days in a damp, stone ruin of a house, tearing up page after page of his scribbles, then emerges at dusk to be wrapped in the mist of the moors.

But in fact, Lowell is a more robust sort of poet, and after giving me a few moments to settle into my room, he leads me on a brisk hike, just as the late-afternoon sun is turning a violent pink above the sea.

When we return to the house, Lowell grills a halibut on his hibachi, and then we sit by the fire and drink wine.

He tells me he's lonely.

Though we've never discussed it, I think we each wish that something might have clicked between us—but for whatever mysterious reasons, it hasn't. And like Sylvie, Lowell doesn't believe in meddling with fate. He did place a personal ad in a newspaper once, describing his ideal match as "a brilliant and gorgeous" woman at least fifteen years younger than himself. He actually got several replies, and hooked up for a while with "a really cute, redheaded twenty-two-year-old girl." It makes my blood boil to think about it—the chutzpah of men, their fixation on younger women—but I keep my mouth shut. It didn't work out. And he's never been tempted to do it again. He's come to the realization that he's a true romantic, by which he means that it's either his destiny to meet someone or it isn't. Meanwhile, he's jabbing through the bars of the hibachi with his metal skewer, covering the red coals with a layer of ash.

"It just may be that I'm a sort of a monk," he tells me, though he's not at all religious, and he looks despondent when he says it, as if he were going to jail.

The next day, after breakfast, Lowell sits down at his typewriter, Lincoln goes looking for moles in the garden, and I head out to Point Arena for my date with the "charming fixer-upper" house. Before I even get out of the car, it's clear that "loads of potential" does indeed mean loads of disasters just waiting to happen—a slumped porch, a roof with holes in it, collapsed front stairs. Across the street, I hear a parent screaming at a child in the dreadful way that has the ring of chronic child abuse ("Now look what you've forced me to do again!"), and the child is howling. Not an auspicious sign. But, I confess, there's something about the basic shape of the house—two stories and a mansard roof— that, if I squint, makes it look almost French. It reminds me a bit of the house my mother had in Nyack, New York, along the Hudson River. And as I get out of my car and come through the hedge that rings the property, whom should I see but Marie! Marie, whom I met in the third grade, in Mrs. Kenny's class, in Santa Monica.

Over the years, sifting through the chaos of my photo drawer, I've sometimes come upon a picture of the two of us, and my connection to Marie has been frozen in its single moment: we're whizzing in a tiny boat on the manmade lake at MacArthur Park, our faces smeared with frosting from my birthday cake. We're eight years old.

It's slightly more than four decades later, and after an instant of pure shock, we recognize each other and burst into laughter. There is something so absurd about time and how it has simultaneously preserved and demolished our faces.

"Marie!"

"Noelle!" She says my name, and her voice is absolutely the same as it was in third grade: almost comically husky in a little girl, now it's got a certain earthy glamour.

"And this is Peter, my husband," she says, touching the sleeve of the tall man by her side. He has an impressive head of silver-brown hair and the handsome face of a man who's spent years working in the sun and wind. "He's an expert on fixing up old houses," Marie says. "So when we saw the 'For Sale' sign we had to stop. But how amazing to find you! Do you live up here now?"

A few moments later, as we peer through cracked windows, Peter shakes his head and Marie gets more and more excited. "Peter, look! Just what I always wanted. A breakfast nook."

"That's not a nook, Marie. That's a hole where it looks like a huge appliance went crashing through the floor. Look, you can see it—the stove. The floor must have gotten so rotted out from the roof that the stove just fell through it."

"Peter! It's a cast-iron stove! Look at it. It's probably worth five thousand dollars!"

A few hours later, Marie, Peter, and I are finishing a long lunch at the one local restaurant. Peter is looking exhausted, but Marie and I are high as kites. Marie is convinced that the three of us should go in together on the ruined house across from the child abuser. To her, it's absolutely clear and simple: they'll help me with the down, Peter will renovate it—and voilà! We'll be at the cutting edge of a complete revitalization of the town of Point Arena. When Peter points out that Point Arena is foggy eleven months of the year, Marie screws her face into a look of incredulity, as though Peter had just told her the earth was flat. "Peter, *Carmel* is foggy. Point Arena is another Carmel just waiting to happen! And *we* can be the ones to start it!"

Peter shakes his head. He knows that Marie and I are high on our reunion. Having rapidly condensed our life histories, we're as flushed and breathless as if we'd been doing aerobics. I've filled her in on my life all the way up through its unraveling, five years ago, to its current state of relative, if somewhat melancholic, stability. Marie has filled me in on her tragic first marriage to a ruthless Frenchman who abandoned her and their two-year-old son, Julien, in the airport in Paris. Now she's summing up her ten years of struggle as a single mother, after she and Julien returned to California.

She found a job doing PR for a winery. Within a short while, she'd greatly boosted sales. Then she took a job at another winery and repeated her success. I'm not surprised. There's something about Marie's voice, its emphatic, husky warmth, that could convince you to invest in a thousand rotted wine barrels—or in a ruined house in the permanently socked-in town of Point Arena. And speaking of houses, Marie tells me how a wonderful real estate agent led her to the perfect little starter house and encouraged her to pull together a tiny nest egg. "I was terrified. I mean, there I was, a single mother with a little boy. But within just six years, it had doubled in value. Buying a house is just the best way to build wealth, Noelle. You can't go wrong!"

Something about that phrase "building wealth" makes me want to change the topic.

"So, what did you do for your social life after you came back from France? I mean, were there any men in your life?"

"All those years, I never dated," Marie says. "I just focused on work, Julien—and my house. God, I loved that little house! I did get lonely, though. My friends would say to me, 'If you want to meet someone, you've got to put yourself out there. What do you think? A man is just going to come to your door?' And do you know what I'd tell them?" Marie leans over the table and whispers, as if imparting her most important secret. "I'd tell them, 'Yes! A man is going to come to my door.'"

And he did. Peter was the carpenter who came to remodel her

study. The first day he came to her house, she opened the door and saw a tall man with thick, silver-brown hair, a rugged face, and kind eyes. By the time he'd installed a skylight and upgraded her shelving, he'd become a part of Marie and Julien's life. Eventually, he moved in.

As I drive home on the dark, windy road along the coast, Marie's words swirl around in my thoughts. Her story about the house. Then meeting Peter. I like the story about the house—about finding the perfect Realtor, daring to put her tiny nest egg down, and then—voilà!—discovering that her house had doubled in value. But what I like best is her story about Peter. It makes me realize that what I really want is for a man with the aforementioned qualities—intelligent, kind, handsome, engaged in rewarding work, spiritually oriented, et cetera—*to come to my door*. And as long as I'm at it, *I want him to be drawn to me through my writing*. Ever since I was quite young, I've loved the stories of women artists who drew a man to them through their work: Georgia O'Keeffe and her Juan. Marguerite Duras and her Yann. Never mind that Georgia's young man appears to have been a virtual slave or that Marguerite's Yann would disappear for weeks at a time for intense bisexual binges. Maybe the problem was that Juan and Yann were so much younger. I'd be happy with a man my own age, or a few years older. I just want him *to come to my door*. And *to be drawn to me through my writing*. When I get back to my house that evening, I pull the slip of paper out from under my mattress. After making these two revisions, I slide it back under my bed.

• • •

When I wake the next morning, the first thing I see is my birdcage shrine with its open door. It's the first thing I see every morning, since I placed it on the small round table directly opposite my bed. And this morning, its sad emptiness is compounded by the sad aftermath of a dream.

It's a dream about me and Eliot, and it's a dream I've had before.

The two of us are at the Grand Canyon, and I'm feeling very happy because we're just about to go into the restaurant of a majestic lodge that sits on the very rim of the canyon, providing one of the world's most amazing views. But just as we step through the door, Eliot tells me, "Let's go to Gitsi's instead!" And in that moment the beautiful lodge turns into Eliot's favorite diner in upstate New York.

Eliot and I met at the Rochester Zen Center, and we were also neighbors. He lived down the street from me, in a sort of Zen rooming house where he occupied a room so unadorned that once I told him it looked like the room of a blind person. The one decoration was a huge yellow moon that hung from the ceiling, a vinyl moon that he had stitched himself, using a cobbler's awl, as one of his rare theatrical props. He was a mime. He could sit on air, talk on a nonexistent telephone, and swim without water. His needs were so few that, on his tiny income, he had managed to put aside six thousand dollars. This impressed me—not only the stash itself but the way he divulged it. Like a child revealing a secret can of gumballs, he conveyed a mix of pride and amazement at his long self-discipline—with the hint that, in one split second, it could all dissolve into a flood of bright balls on the floor, an orgy of chewing.

Early on, then, I saw that he was both frugal and, in his own way, expansive. After we married, he moved down the street into my house, contributing his yellow moon, his tattered clothes, the rusted red wagon he'd had since childhood, and his six thousand dollars. We set our Zen cushions alongside each other and merged our two extravagant mountains of books on Buddhism. We rose before dawn to go to the center. We returned in the evenings and on Sunday mornings, and signed up for weeklong retreats whenever possible. He performed as a mime in schools, libraries, and shopping malls. I wrote in the mornings and worked as a nanny for a little girl in the afternoons.

It was austere, but it had its own abundance. In the shared intensity of Zen practice, friendships flourish. And in the cracks of a strict discipline, wild laughter blooms. When we and our comrades weren't sitting in the *zendo* or working at our jobs, we told our trickster tales, confessed our great Zen gaffes, concocted lavish vegetarian feasts, and engaged in a constant potlatch swapping of clothes, household goods, and services: one massage in exchange for two loads of fine compost, three homeopathic tinctures, four loaves of fresh-baked bread.

Though by North American standards we lived close to the edge financially, we felt secure in other ways. We were devoting ourselves to "the Great Matter": liberation from suffering. Though we often faltered, gave in to doubt, boredom, or distraction, the quest for awakening anchored our lives. Deep down there was the sense that we were living as we intended to live, that we had made it to adulthood without "selling out."

The telephone rings, jolting me out of my bed.

"Hello?"

"Noelle?"

"Marci?!"

Marci is my cousin. We grew up near each other in Santa Monica, and now she lives in Carmel. Though we've had periods of being very close, I haven't heard from her in several years. "Is everything all right?" I ask.

"Yes. You know me. I'm sorry. I'm just so terrible at keeping up. How are you?"

For the second time in forty-eight hours, I give the nutshell version of my life, complete with hermit crabs. She brings me up to date on her happy marriage, her beautiful teenage daughter, and her newly acquired real estate license.

"Your real estate license?"

The reunions and coincidences are starting to spook me. Marie. Marci. Marci *the Realtor*. I know what Carole would say. She'd say these were signs that my wishes were gathering power, attracting allies, getting ready to hit their mark. She'd clap me on the back and say, "Go, girl!" But instead of excitement, I feel a kind of dread. What am I getting myself into? It's only been a matter of weeks, and already it feels as though *something is happening*. And though whatever it is has been pleasant so far, it's unnerving. As if I'd picked up a magic lantern and rubbed it, and already I could hear a commotion beginning to gather inside it, could see a bit of steam seeping out its spout. Who knows what genie will emerge?

But in this moment what's happening is just my cousin Marci telling me breathlessly about the first little fixer-upper that she and her husband managed to buy. How, when they sold it a few years later, it had doubled in value.

"It's just the best way of building wealth, Noelle," she says.

There's that phrase again—the same one Marie used.

Is *that* where I'm heading?

After I hang up the phone, I sit on the edge of the bed and pull on my clothes in a kind of a trance. Why does that use of the verb *to build* make me so uncomfortable? In my mind, you build a table, you build a fence, you build a house—a little peach-colored house, with bougainvillea vines climbing over the walls.

But building *wealth*?

What comes to my mind is the miser in his tower, stacking his piles of gold. Then a voice calls to me: *Noelle, be careful! For what does it matter if you gain the whole world but lose your own soul?*

When I was living with Eliot on a shoestring, I didn't worry about losing my soul. Even among our Zen friends, Eliot stood out as having few material desires and radiated a kind of innocence. He is the kind of person who, without a moment's calculation, would take his shirt off in a blizzard if he saw someone shivering. And wherever we went, children, animals, and beggars were irresistibly drawn to him, even when he made no effort to attract them. Often, when his image floated before my eyes, it came with the words *pass over*: those words written in chalk on the doors of the Jews in ancient Egypt, so that God's wrath would pass over them. Living with Eliot on a shoestring, I felt beyond reproach and thus safe.

Safe—but from the beginning, there was also something I chafed against. Rochester was Eliot's hometown, and he seemed immune to the dreariness that sometimes drove me to a pitch of desperation. "There are so many different shades of gray!" he would tell me. "It's so depressing here!" I'd explode, as though somehow it was his fault that I'd left the sunlight of California, come to Rochester of my own accord, and fallen in love with a hometown boy.

After one such fit, early on in our marriage, Eliot announced that he had one of the little-known wonders of Rochester to show me. When we went out our front door, I was surprised that he didn't head toward the car. Instead he guided me, through the evening light, down the block and up the stairs of the giant parking structure that belonged to the hospital across the street. We climbed to the asphalt roof and sat down on the newspaper that Eliot had brought with him. "Look!" he said, making a grand gesture toward the sky.

Beyond a red neon SEARS sign, a collection of telephone poles and flat-roofed buildings, I could see the sky turning orange with streaks of red, against which a flock of gulls from Lake Ontario flew, like a kind of wild black calligraphy. Eliot pulled a letter from his pocket. "Look at this!" he said triumphantly. On official letterhead, it was signed by the director of Buildings and Grounds. "The bearer and his wife are entitled to walk to the top of the parking ramp for sunrise and sunset viewing." Through much effort, Eliot had procured the letter after he'd been hounded one too many times by the security man when he'd climbed the parking-ramp stairs to gaze at the sky.

For me that letter was the perfect emblem of my new husband's gift—not for spinning straw into gold but for perceiving straw as more precious than gold in the first place. For Eliot, to view a sunset from an asphalt parking ramp was much more satisfying than to view it from a stretch of pristine beach. He is the kind of person whose mind can range throughout the universe within the limits of his own small room. And though this gift of his enchanted me, as the years went by I sometimes began to feel constrained by it, let down. I began to have the dream about the diner, and sometimes in my dream its ceilings got lower and lower until they turned into a kind of vault.

Now, having bolted from the bedroom, I find myself outside in the yard. I'm still in my pajamas and standing with bare feet on the gravel path. It's a fresh, bright morning, and across the street the people I call the Beavers are already busy sawing wood. They start around six in the morning with their buzz saws—and I've never understood to what end. The wood just piles up around them, looking more and more like a giant, teetering beaver dam. One day, a few years ago, my daughter and I returned from an outing to discover that our large living room window, which faces them, was shot through with BB holes. Several friends felt that I should contact the police at once, but I was afraid to get them even more riled up, and thankfully there have been no further incidents. Still, the first thing I'd do if this house was mine would be to put up a big wooden fence between me and the Beavers. Then I'd install a new living room window—double-paned to muffle the noise of their saws. For now, I consider the cracked window a kind of insurance, should my landlords decide to sell the house. "Oh, by the way," I'd say to any prospective buyers who stopped by for a look. Then, opening the drapes, "There's just a little problem with the neighbors."

That's what it's like when you don't own your house. You actually take comfort in having bullet holes in your windows. You don't build the high wooden fence that you dream of. And you're careful about what you plant in your garden. You don't want to invest too much time, energy, soul, or money in anything that's going to take root in the ground. That's why I've perfected the art of container gardening and have most of my plants in big terra-cotta pots—in case, like the hermit crabs, I have to make a sudden run for new shelter.

Still, when spring comes around, I can never resist the lure of bulbs. The tenant before me planted early-spring bulbs—narcissus, daffodils, tulips—and most of them are already up and blooming. But recently I bought myself a batch of bulbs for later in the season: iris, tiger lily, gladiola. I know it's a little late to plant them—I should have gotten them in by December—but I'm banking on our forgiving climate.

Wrapped in their papery skins, aren't they a kind of wish? You make a place for them, you give them a little care and feeding, but you let them come up of their own accord. And even though you've laid the ground, and added the bonemeal, and watered them every so often, it always seems a kind of magic. The magic, once again, of hidden things. When I scoop that last handful of dirt into the hole, I experience the perfect balance between doing and not doing, between having an intention and making way for the result. If I had to choose between flinging the arrow of a wish into the sky or setting the bulb of a wish into the ground, I'd pick the bulb.

In Chinese medicine they talk about the yin-will, and the yang-will, and it strikes me that the bulb provides a natural image of the yin-will, a feminine way of moving from latent to actual. A bulb is the beautiful potential, gradually unfurling from its womb in the ground, rather than the arrow's sharp yang thrust through the air. In the realm of wishing, is one model more effective than the other? I guess that's what I'm trying to find out, as I sleep on top of my paper wish, keep watch over the open space in my bird-cage shrine, and kick myself out the door to go looking for real estate.

• • •

In mid-March, a week or so later, my neighbor Camille and I are out for a walk, under yellow-green trees that are shaggy with pollen. Camille is a dermatological nurse in San Francisco, and she's bringing me up to date on her latest adventures in skin disease, describing the difficulties of painting an agitated six-foot transsexual with black tar for his/her massive allergic rash to a giant tattoo across his/her buttocks.

"What sort of a tattoo was it?" I ask.

"I don't know. Believe it or not, I think it was supposed to be the face of Bette Midler, but between the rash and the black tar . . ."

All of a sudden, I've stopped in my tracks.

Across the street from us, I feel a beautiful, dark presence.

It's a Jaguar, the old-fashioned kind, powerful and sleek, with its black curves and silver chrome polished to the point that our own faces bounce back to us as we approach. Affixed to the window is the sign FOR SALE.

"Noelle, your face is bright red!"

It's true: my heart is beating hard, my face is flushed, and I feel close to fainting.

What's happening?

I've never cared a fig for cars and have never driven anything but a serviceable clunker. For the last five years I've driven my old white Volvo and never felt the least stigma in doing so—despite being the occasional brunt of jokes and less-than-glamorous demographic profiles. One day last year, as I was driving and listening to NPR, I heard a commentator explain that "the average NPR listener is a forty-eight-year-old Caucasian woman who drives a 1985 Volvo 250 and wears Birkenstocks." Apart from the Birkenstocks, they had me pegged, but it didn't faze me in the least.

But now, having crossed the street, I examine the Jaguar more closely. It's all I can do to keep myself from running my hands over its glossy hood and fenders. From a few feet away, Camille is watching me intently, as though at any moment she might have to pull out her stethoscope and attend to my wildly beating heart.

For the next few days, the Jaguar haunts me like an elusive lover, intruding into my thoughts by day, entering my dreams at night. It hadn't even occurred to me to desire a car, and now, suddenly, I'm obsessed. One night, unable to sleep at 3 A.M., I get up, log on to the Jaguar website, and discover that I am not alone. In one feverish statement after another, people have described "the moment they fell in love"—and because it's mostly men writing, it's a "she" they fell in love with, seduced by her beautiful curves.

But with his powerful haunches, my Jaguar is a shiny black *he*, and the next morning I go to visit him again. Part of me hopes that he'll have disappeared, sparing me from this new torment of desire—but no, there he is, as if waiting for me, with the FOR SALE sign still in place. The only difference is that now a small, hand-lettered sign has been added: "Perception is reality."

What the heck does that mean? I don't know. It sounds like something Carole would say, and I can't help the strange feeling that somehow the statement is meant for me. But when I call the owners later in the day, we steer clear of epistemology and stick to mileage and price. It's four thousand dollars, they tell me. It has a hundred thousand miles on it. Mint condition. We love the car. It's just that our daughter has gone off to college, and we don't have a use for it now. We're heartbroken to sell it, really.

Yes, *that* I can understand.

The next day, when I take my new love on a test drive, he moves like a dream, prowling over the hills, plunging into valleys, making all the other cars disappear from the roads. Maybe perception *is* reality—whatever the heck that means.

Back from the drive, I'm tempted to strike a deal with them on the spot. It's just that, if I'm going to try and buy a house, I'm going to need every drop of savings I have. So I force myself to channel the cautious, forty-nine-year-old NPR listener, and she tells them, "I need to sleep on it." At home, after dinner, I light candles and a stick of incense and, sitting cross-legged on the living room carpet, I throw the *I Ching*. Actually, I've never really learned to throw the *I Ching*. I just sort of close my eyes, formulate my question, and then open the book at random. The hexagram I land on is "perseverance." The verse reads, "Clinging to the white cow, he perseveres and brings good fortune."

The white cow: What could that be if not my old white Volvo, with her square face and broad hips?

*Damn.*

That night, the Jaguar prowls in my dreams in his bright darkness, giving off a greenish night sheen. He prowls like a kind of Aztec animal-god, and the next morning I'm not sure how to interpret his presence. As a dangerous lure, a temptation to be resisted? Or as a kind of annunciation, the presage of something new, a welcome?

If I take him to be the latter, then I need to know this: Is it really possible, this far into my life, to escape from the Spiritual Poverty schema? To stand up to the voices that tell me to stay within the four walls of my room and say, "No, I'm going outside!"

And once outside, in the dazzling light, I'll jump into the lap of the beautiful black beast and he'll lead me, through the jungle of my doubts, to a life more opulent than anything I've ever dreamed of before, a life where *wealth builds,* where it's okay, it's really okay, to make a tower of gold coins.

Lying there in my bed, it occurs to me that what I need, what I really need now more than anything else, is an earthquake, around magnitude 4.2, to topple the very thought of that tower and thus restore some ballast to the sudden, frightening loft of my desires.

# CHAPTER FOUR

# April

## *Shit: Facing the Darkness*

It's April, my birth month, and I'm still driving the old white cow, my Volvo. In the housing department, I've looked at a series of dumps—each more depressing than the last. In the past few weeks I've seen a house whose inner walls appeared to be made of glittered cottage cheese; a house—repossessed from crack addicts— that actually had peepholes on the bedroom doors; and a house with a dead skunk floating in its tiled swimming pool. The house I liked best was the crack addicts' house, but the paranoiac vibes were just too intense.

"You should see some of the houses I've bought in France," Carole said to me when I tried to describe the atmosphere. "Ancient houses that haven't been lived in for decades. The first time you open the door, you're wading through rubble, you're breathing the spores from slimy medieval stone, you're up to your waist in dust and rat poop, and a bat flies over your head." I've looked through Carole's albums, full of before-and-after photos, and the transformations she's wrought are amazing. In the before photos she's dressed like some combination of firefighter, Roman warrior, and surgeon—with goggles, shin guards, and a face-mask. But the images only confirm for me that Carole was born with vastly more than the normal share of pluck and grit. I look at the photos the way I used to read *The Guinness Book of Records* and gasp at some freakish occurrence: yardlong fingernails or a half ton of raw squid consumed in a single sitting.

As for the love department: the paper wish beneath my bed is getting me nowhere.

And if my spiritual healing is under way, it's so subtle that I can't detect it. In fact, my condition seems to be worsening. When I wake in the morning, my birdcage shrine with its few faux crumbs looks emptier than ever. I'm feeling more and more aware of what's missing from my life, and more and more off-center.

• • •

For all these reasons, I'm on my way to Vichy Springs, about an hour north of where I live. Ever since my spiritual community came apart at the seams, this is the place I go to when I feel a special need to collect myself, to rest and regenerate.

On the way, I'm listening to a tape that I found at a yard sale, which is exhorting me to visualize my wishes going up to the sky in the form of pink balloons. I probably shouldn't even try to do such a thing while driving, because I can't seem to get my balloons off the ground. I keep visualizing them on the road right ahead of me, where I'm about to run over them. If nothing else, the exercise is making it painfully clear to me that something is still holding me back, staying my hand, making it difficult to get my desires off the ground. And whatever it is, with each passing day it seems to be growing not fainter but stronger—almost as if my experiment in wishing was provoking an opposing force.

"Wish in one hand, shit in the other, and see which one fills up faster," a colleague said to me recently when I made the mistake of telling her about my experiment.

"*What?*"

"You mean you've never heard that expression before?"

No, I hadn't. Thank you so much for sharing it.

She told me that it was something her father had been fond of saying, whenever she uttered the words "I wish." Now, as an adult, she seemed to find it amusing, but I didn't. I thought it was disgusting, slightly sadistic, and perversely self-validating—a way of shitting in his daughter's hand.

Her open hand.

When we wish, our hands are outstretched, palms up. Anything could fall on them: love, prosperity, mockery, shit. No wonder so many people prefer to keep themselves closed, like fists. Wishing makes us vulnerable—in many ways.

For one thing, it makes us vulnerable to disappointment—to the possibility that the arrow of our wish will miss the mark, that we will overshoot or fall short and thus break the appointment with our heart's desire. How much easier to play it safe and never take that risk—by keeping our desires diffuse, unfocused, unarticulated, undirected.

"Don't get your hopes up," people say. Wishing, like hoping, connotes a vertical dimension. When we wish, we aspire—and thus we can fall. Even though my paper wish is buried underneath my bed, it's my way of aiming high: for that handsome, witty, spiritually oriented, and very intelligent man. And if he doesn't come—soon—there's something about having so explicitly articulated my longing that is going to make me feel both more alone and more foolish than I did when I started.

Then there's the Jaguar. By now I've heard that he's been sold to someone else, and he has completely withdrawn from my dreams—but he didn't leave me unscathed. Something about the way he leapt into my life, ambushing me as I walked, in broad daylight, has left me feeling edgy, jumpy—as though at any moment some utterly new and unexpected desire could stake its claim in my heart. And though he seemed to come to me out of the blue, deep down I'm convinced that something about my three wishes drew him to me, attracting him like an odor. The odor of a receptive female, a woman in heat.

There's something about permitting myself to wish for three things that seems to have opened me to all kinds of wishes I've never even dreamed of before. As if the wishing mind had become a kind of magnet, drawing more wishes to it. And that's frightening.

*Where your treasure lies, there does your heart lie also,* the Bible says. There's both an ancient and a primal link between *what we value* and *who we are.* From the time we're infants, the people around us define us by our preferences: "He loves to be held tight" or "She loves to be swung in the air." As we grow older, the list of preferences morphs and then crystallizes into a kind of essence, becoming central to how we know ourselves, how we present ourselves to others—and even how we're remembered after we die. "He loved to be surrounded by his grandchildren" or "She had a passion for the mountains."

So where does your heart lie when suddenly potential treasures lie all around you? When you can be walking down a familiar street and find yourself accosted by a parked car? It's not easy, in midlife, to discover yourself prone to new and wildly unexpected desires. It's not unlike being a teenager, hijacked by hormones, so that one morning you wake up wanting things you never wanted before—a pair of snare drums or a slimy kiss in the cramped backseat of a car.

*Be careful what you wish for,* people say. I've always assumed the expression meant that we don't really know the consequences of getting the particular thing we think we want, but now I'm beginning to see that there's something about the very act of wishing that's dangerous.

In fairy tales, there is almost always something grave and momentous about the act of wishing. Though wishes can be made very easily—by rubbing a stone or clicking your heels or saying a few words—they are taken seriously, as having a very real power. *"You may have three wishes,"* the genie announces in a booming voice. Or an eerie, disembodied voice announces: *"When you are in danger, you may make use of this amulet once."* There is usually a strict limit on the number of wishes to be made, and this in itself creates tremendous pressure. For even as wishes give rise to certain things, they simultaneously cut off other possibilities—closing doors, creating consequences, sealing fate. If you choose the maiden with skin white as milk, you must forgo the sultry maiden with eyes like black coals. Even worse, it might turn out that your beautiful milky maiden is really a hideous, wart-covered witch! If you replace your shanty with a palace, you might lose something quite precious about your life in the shanty, or suddenly find yourself contending with a retinue of nasty palace guards. The act of wishing is a kind of test, one that poses the questions: Can you choose wisely, or will you make choices that you will forever regret? Can you see through the guise of appearance and choose real happiness?

Then, once you've made your choice, other difficult questions follow. If your wishes are granted, will you be able to make use of them without being carried away by greed, intoxicated by the sudden sense of power, and thrown off balance by the reactions of those around you?

Not long ago, someone sent me this contemporary version of a wish story:

*A married couple in their early sixties was out celebrating their thirty-fifth wedding anniversary in a quiet, romantic little restaurant. Suddenly, a tiny yet beautiful fairy appeared on their table and said, "For being such an exem-*

*plary married couple and for being faithful to each other*
*for all this time, I will grant you each a wish." "Oh, I want*
*to travel around the world with my darling husband!" said*
*the wife. The fairy waved her magic wand and—poof!—*
*two tickets for the* Queen Mary II *luxury liner appeared in*
*her hands. Then it was the husband's turn. He thought for*
*a moment and said, "Well, this is all very romantic, but an*
*opportunity like this will never come again. I'm sorry, my*
*love, but my wish is to have a wife thirty years younger*
*than me." The wife and the fairy were deeply disappointed,*
*but a wish is a wish . . . So the fairy waved her magic*
*wand, and—poof!—the husband became ninety-two years*
*old. The moral of the story: "Men who are ungrateful bas-*
*tards should remember that fairies are females."*

But, of course the wife, too, has been irrevocably hurt by the
wish. What will she do now with the decrepit old coot who just
betrayed her in the midst of their anniversary dinner?

• • •

Usually, when I arrive at Vichy Springs, from the moment I step out
of my car and hear the rushing creek and waterfalls, I feel an almost
instant elation. But this time, breathing in the sulfurous, lightly
lithium-laced air, I feel leaden, sodden, as though I'd already been
soaking far too long in some unsavory tub, and alone in a painful
way. I drag my suitcase over the long gravel path and open the door
to the cottage where no one waits for me.

This is the year I turn fifty. Of all the milestones, people say
that the half century is the time of true reckoning, the time when
you come face-to-face with the gap between whatever it is you
wanted from life and whatever it is you got.

*Fiddlesticks,* I would have said when I was younger—why
make a fuss over the arbitrary importance of certain numbers? But

as my birthday looms, I have to confess that this particular number is adding a strong dose of urgency to my wishes, as though if they don't come true within this next year—

What?

I don't know. I can't really finish the sentence. "For the young, *wishing* has the same currency as *doing* does in middle age," a friend told me recently. She was quoting a line from a play she'd recently seen, and it struck a chord with me. A painful chord. Already I'd been telling myself that if my wishes haven't come true by the time I turn fifty-one—if they haven't crossed the threshold from possible to actual—then it's too late for wishing. I'll have to throw in the towel and fully embrace a life of renunciation. As if to prepare myself, I've been reading a monumental work on celibacy that I discovered in the remainder bin a few days ago. Now, unpacking my suitcase, I place it beside the luxurious queen-sized bed and wonder why I didn't bring something lighter and/or more inspiring. Something called, for example, *The Spontaneous Fulfillment of Desire* or *Your Best Life Now*. The book on celibacy is fascinating, and I can't seem to put it down—but it's full of icky information about eunuchs, semen retention, and nuns kissing crucifixes.

Crucifixes.

Last year at this time I went to Mexico for Easter, to San Miguel de Allende. As Easter approaches once again, I've been having vivid flashes of my week there. And though it was well before I began my experiment in wishing, there has been something strangely insistent about the memories, almost as if they held some kind of secret or clue.

I arrived in San Miguel on the morning of Good Friday, and as soon as I had settled into my room, I set out to climb the narrow, cobblestone streets that led to the central square. Along the way, an old man called to me and showed me an amazing clay object that he was selling *muy barato*, very cheap. He told me that he had made it himself, and though it seemed odd to be shopping on

Good Friday, I couldn't resist. It was a miniature clay beauty parlor for skeletons, with a skeleton hairdresser blow-drying the curls of a row of skeleton customers. I paid him the equivalent of five dollars and continued up the hill with the beauty parlor in my pocket. Arriving at the Jardín, I saw that hundreds of people had already gathered, waiting for the afternoon's procession to begin. Vendors were selling ice cream and shaved ice and popcorn and fruit drinks and chimichangas—big fried taco shells with salsa. Others were selling toys for the children: giant clusters of helium balloons, wooden birds on a stick, jingling pull toys, and bright-colored balls in all shapes and sizes. You'd never know that Jesus was about to be crucified.

When I stepped inside the beautiful pink church that rises above the square, the carnival atmosphere dissolved. I sat down on a hard wooden bench and let my eyes and ears and skin adjust to the cool darkness. Around me I discerned the quiet murmurings of a small group of people; they were performing the stations of the cross. When I suddenly stood up to join their circle, they made room for me seamlessly, without pausing in the recitation of their prayers.

Despite my Catholic upbringing, I'd never participated in the stations of the cross before. And really, when you think about it, could there be anything farther away from making a shrine to a personal desire? Each wooden plaque or box represents a crucial incident in the terrible last suffering of Jesus, and as you move from one to the next, you're participating with him in an experience that represents the absolute annihilation of personal desire. And before each one, you stand, dwelling on the horror, absorbing the image of the god who came in human form and got the very opposite of what any human being would ever wish for. Jesus is mocked. Accused. Condemned to die.

I made it as far as the tenth station, where Jesus is stripped of of his clothes, when suddenly I found myself turning on my heels and bolting back out the door.

Outside in the light, there was the carnival again. The people in bright clothing, the vendors selling their ice cream and shaved ice and chimichangas. A mariachi band was playing in the grandstand, and the children were rushing about with their balloons and pull toys, and birds on a stick. All this while waiting for the procession that gruesomely depicts the Crucifixion, complete with a flotilla of various martyred saints, with droves of *flagellantes,* whipping themselves with leather ropes, with Pontius Pilate and a legion of Roman soldiers, and a bleeding Jesus borne by pallbearers.

It's something that is often remarked about the Mexican people, and on that day I saw it with my own eyes: their ability to hold together, in one embrace, the awareness of suffering and the celebration of earthly happiness, the beauty parlor and the skeletons, the blood of martyrs and the bright balloons. Remembering it all now, I know that there is something inside this embrace that I have not yet fully absorbed and that somehow holds the key to my experiment in desire. Yet when I try to grasp it, it seems too huge, or too deeply embedded to get my mind around. As though I had swallowed a whale, or was trying to remove something as invisible and hardwired as a reflex.

"Don't attach to suffering," a Buddhist monk from Vietnam told me once. And though at the time he didn't know me well, I felt he was seeing through me, all the way down to something that went even deeper than my Jewish/Catholic roots, to something more primal.

When I was small, if I was taken to a park, I would immediately notice who was crying, who was arguing, who looked lonely or poor or had some form of disfigurement. Like everyone, I had my share of childhood sorrow, but it was slight compared to the trauma of many people I've known or heard about. So I don't know where my peculiar attunement to suffering came from, or why it's remained so intense. If I had to choose between being extremely aware of suffering and being blind to it, I'd choose the former, but I'm also aware that being extremely aware of suffering can create its own kind of blindness.

Once, many years ago, I was participating in a Zen discussion group when a woman brought up Viktor Frankl's book *Man's Search for Meaning*. "And wasn't it wonderful," the woman said, "that when he was finally released from Auschwitz, he walked until he came to a meadow full of flowers. And even after everything he'd been through, he felt overcome by the beauty of those spring flowers."

"NO!"

I must have spoken very loudly. Everyone was looking at me strangely, and there was a long, awkward silence. Then someone said, "Well, isn't it funny that you both have such different interpretations of the same book."

"NO!" This time I could feel myself shaking. I have a horror of glossing over. Of adopting an unearned, unfounded optimism—just because it feels good.

"It isn't funny," I said. "And it's not a matter of interpretation. Frankl says as plain as day that, though he knew with his rational mind that he was surrounded by a meadow full of flowers, he was so numbed by the horrors of Auschwitz that he couldn't feel the beauty."

I knew I was not mistaken, but when I got home that night I checked the book. And there it was:

*We walked slowly along the road leading from the camp. Soon our legs hurt and threatened to buckle. But we limped on. . . .*

*We came to meadows full of flowers. We saw and realized that they were there, but we had no feelings about them. The first spark of joy came when we saw a rooster with a tail of multicolored feathers. But it remained only a spark; we did not yet belong to this world.*

*You see!* I felt like going back and shouting to the group. *Shit happens!*

When the woman misremembered the flower passage, it confirmed everything I hate most about a certain kind of smarmy, self-satisfied thinking. You don't just walk out of a concentration camp and find yourself lollygagging in a field of daisies.

And yet a few nights later, a strange thing happened. The book was still lying on my bedside table, and I picked it up and began randomly skimming through it. To my amazement, just a few pages beyond the flower incident, I encountered an episode that had obviously made no impression on me when I first read the book and that had not left the slightest trace in my memory:

> *One day, a few days after the liberation, I walked through the country past flowering meadows, for miles and miles, toward the market town near the camp. Larks rose to the sky and I could hear their joyous song. There was no one to be seen for miles around; there was nothing but the wide earth and sky and the larks' jubilation and the freedom of space. I stopped, looked around, and up to the sky—and then I went down on my knees. At that moment there was very little I knew of myself or of the world—I had but one sentence in mind—always the same: "I called to the Lord from my narrow prison and He answered me in the freedom of space."*
>
> *How long I knelt there and repeated this sentence memory can no longer recall. But I know that on that day, in that hour, my new life started. Step for step I progressed, until I again became a human being.*

How was it possible to have forgotten that second passage? To have been so myopic, so fixated on Frankl's account of the numbness induced by suffering that I was numb to his expression of joy?

The Vietnamese monk who told me "Don't attach to suffering" had lived through horrors, too: bombs, burning villages, imprisonment. Yet he radiated a quality of lightness, gaiety.

How was it possible to attain such suppleness of spirit?

That suppleness is what I glimpsed in San Miguel de Allende on Good Friday. The procession dragging the tortured body of Christ and the martyred saints. And the Jardín overflowing with children, balloons, ice cream, chimichangas, and birds on a stick. There was jubilance in the garden, a jubilance that kept its eyes wide open to the whole of life, utterly without blinders or rose-colored glasses. As the poet Rilke says, in his *Sonnets to Orpheus,* "Jubilance knows, and Longing acquiesces. Only Lament is learning still, nymph of the weeping spring."

Learning still, at the weeping spring: yes, yes.

\* \* \*

Now, outside my window at Vichy Springs, the sun has disappeared behind the low blue mountain with its waterfall and deep, clear pool from which the water spills, all the way down in a stream through the woods to where the cottages are. I change into my bathing suit and robe, and when I step outside I see the sky is full of stars. Following along the lighted path, I make my way to the whirlpool and lower myself in. *Ahhhhhhh . . .*

"Heavenly, isn't it?" a woman's voice says to me. I can just make out the silhouette of a rather voluptuous woman, with a halo of long, wavy hair. She, too, has come here alone, and gradually—as can happen in hot tubs, where muscles loosen and secrets unlock—she begins to tell me about herself. Her name is Lilith. She's recently separated from her husband, and he's initiated a fierce battle to gain custody of their young son. I let her know that I have also experienced a very painful upheaval, and before long we're discussing the challenge of midlife dating. She, too, has ventured out a bit on the Internet—and to our amazement, we discover that we've both gone out with the saffron thief. Only he didn't steal saffron when he went out with her; on their one date, he lifted a packet of clove-scented tea from a café. "The Spice Thief"—wouldn't that be a nice title for a novel, we muse. Her voice is melodious, and in the dark I picture her, with her long, flowing hair, as beautiful and statuesque. Afterward, when she accompanies me to the door of my room, I'm startled to see that her lovely face is covered with a massive wine-colored birthmark. There's something about this discovery that moves me. After telling her good night, I climb into the luxurious bed and—ignoring the heavy book on the bedside table—fall asleep quickly, feeling deeply soothed by the long soak in hot water and somehow blessed by the encounter.

In the middle of the night I startle awake, not quite sure of where I am until I hear the sound of rushing water from the creek outside my window. From somewhere I remember the old superstition that a child's birthmark is caused by a mother's unfulfilled wishes. Lying there between dreams, I can't help but wonder what great wish, or cluster of wishes, would have given rise to the wine-colored birthmark on Lilith's face.

The next morning I rise with resolve, as though while I slept I'd been given a clear set of directions. "Take a book of matches," they begin, "then follow the streambed, and walk until you find a secluded spot, ringed by a stand of poplar trees. There you will gather dry stones and twigs. Shape the stones into a circle, then arrange the twigs and light them. This is your fire ceremony. Ask yourself: 'What is it that needs to burn?'"

As the twigs crack and the smoke begins to rise, I think of Sylvie.

Sylvie who told me recently, "I want to let go of my bitterness. I've been holding on to it for too long now."

And I?

That intense attachment to suffering. It seems too huge, somehow, to bundle up in a single pile and toss into the fire. It's something I'll have to transmute more slowly.

But on a more personal level, there is something I know that it's time to let go of, as Sylvie knew it was time to let go of her bitterness.

It's remorse.

Remorse over the ending of my marriage and the loss of my spiritual community.

Here's what happened in a nutshell:

Over several years, I fell very deeply in love with my Zen teacher, who had also been my therapist for an extended period.

Though he was married, he returned my love.

Then, just as my marriage collapsed under the pressure, he fell in love with another one of his Zen students. Then his marriage collapsed.

In the chaos, droves of students left the Zen community.

Through my own doing, I had lost the husband I loved, the integrity of our little family, the man for whom I'd allowed myself to risk everything, the community that was the core of my life. Because of that experience, I know in my body how it is that people can die of grief. For many months, I found it nearly impossible to sleep at night. Because it felt as though a boulder was lodged in my throat and my chest, it was difficult to breathe and very hard to swallow. I had sharp, intermittent pains in my heart, and I subsisted mostly on liquids and canned peaches. Having never been large to begin with, I lost fifteen pounds and looked like a wraith. I was sustained by the love of my family and close friends, who did not abandon me.

*Re-morse.* "To bite again." That's what the word means at its root, and that's what it feels like. Though I'm well past the period of sheer survival, I continue to bite myself. I know it serves no purpose. I've long ago done the things that I felt I could do in order to set things right with those I hurt most. I've vowed never again to create such havoc. But the remorse remains, like a reservoir that constantly recirculates the same water and never loses a drop.

*Mooooooooooo.*

Across from me, a solitary black cow is grazing in the grass. Her eyes meet mine in a gaze that is utterly vacant of human concern.

She doesn't give a shit if, seven years ago, the pale two-legged mammal standing across from her made a mess of her life.

Wish in one hand, shit in the other.

Shit or get off the pot.

Look at Carole: she doesn't waste her life energy in endless self-torment. She freely acknowledges her "wild woman" period—and it was much wilder than anything I ever permitted myself. She told me that, though she was raising her young son by herself, she had a constant stream of lovers.

But then it came to an end.

One day, she looked in her little boy's eyes and felt pierced by his sadness. She told herself, "I can't go on this way." That's when she shaved her head, began dressing only in white, pared her belongings down to the minimum, and moved with her son from their roomy apartment into a small rented house.

Then she had the wedding to herself.

*Boeuffff,* says my inner Sylvie.

*Yes, but*—I reply.

There was a wisdom in her ritual, *n'est-ce-pas?* Her wild-woman period came to an end. She let something die, in order that something else might be born. She didn't stay stuck, like me, in an endless Good Friday procession, whipping herself again and again.

*Moooooo,* says the cow. Our eyes meet again across the streambed, and then she lumbers farther away from me, toward another clump of grass. At my feet, a black gecko is lying in the mud. I've never seen one holding still before, but he's very much alive. His eyes are bright and darting, and I can see the rapid pulse in his body. Then, the next moment, he's gone. Where he was, I see a black stone. I lean down to pick it up from the mud.

I remember learning about the black stone of alchemy, the *negrita.* The idea that we have to allow the darkness inside us to intensify, to come to the highest point of concentration, before it can be turned into gold. Otherwise there is just a kind of chronic, low-grade negativity, in shades of gray. It serves nothing, creates nothing, can't transform into anything else.

The remorse, biting and biting again.

*Let it go. Let it go.*

A last wisp of smoke curls in the air from my little fire.

I return to the site, stir the ashes with a stick to make sure they've gone out, and throw in my black stone.

Later that day, I take a long soak in one of the very old tubs that are set along the streambed, with a view of the hills beyond. According to the hotel brochure, Vichy Springs is "the oldest continuously operated spa in California." As at Vichy Springs in France, the water is like champagne. Of course, here in California, they say that this makes it "especially good for releasing toxins." I'm not sure if I really believe that, but as I lie in the old cement tub, thousands of tiny gold bubbles fizz on my skin. From somewhere I remember the words of the French philosopher Simone Weil in her meditation on the *Iliad* and its account of human suffering and failure. "Nearly all the *Iliad* takes place far from hot baths. Nearly all human life, then and now, takes place far from hot baths." Yes, but there are days when we are not only near, but immersed in, a hot bath, *n'est-ce pas?* And, given that Vichy Springs is "the oldest continuously operated spa in California," this one is a perfect combination of grungy and sumptuous.

The next day when I get in my car to drive home, the voice of the balloon lady comes on, urging me once again to get those pink balloons up in the air. *Shush,* I tell her, and turn off the tape. Driving home through the green April hills, I just want to stay porous to the mystery of black and gold.

# CHAPTER FIVE

# May

## *Craft: Wishing Well*

It's May, and though it's unseasonably rainy, I feel something in the air that is lightening, loosening, allowing itself to expand. Even as sheets of rain come down through the dark sky, accompanied by eerily green and thunderless streaks of lightning, I'm feeling giddy.

And so far, it's a giddiness that has withstood the storm of numbers into which I've suddenly plunged: down payment, amortization, adjustable rates. At night, the numbers jolt me awake into a state of sheer panic. But by morning, mysteriously, I wake with a sense of lightness and possibility. Despite—or because of?—my descent into the darkness, it seems that one of my pink balloons went up.

On the day I returned from Vichy Springs, I stopped to check my P.O. box before going home and found a letter from my landlords. I had to read it twice before the words sank in: *As we will soon be moving to Utah, and would prefer not to be absentee landlords, we wondered if you would be interested in buying the house.*

What? Was this a trick, some sort of ruse concocted by friends for my fiftieth birthday? Was some practical joker shitting in one hand while I was busy wishing with the other? I checked the postmark and the writing on the envelope, and they looked authentic. I knew I shouldn't be so suspicious, but—despite my constant fear that my landlords would sell the house out from under me—I had actually been under the impression that they were saving it as an investment for their children. Besides, it almost seemed too easy, anticlimactic, to buy the house I'd already been living in for ten years.

Still, I was elated. There was no mention of a price, and I felt slightly ill at the thought of what it was likely to be. But surely, I told myself, there must be something about my intimate connection to the house—the years of scrubbing its floors, hearing its creaks, breathing its dust, and scraping the calcified lime from its toilet bowl—that will translate fiscally? At least my landlords won't have to go through a Realtor, and I won't have to compete with other bidders.

As I pulled in the driveway, my heart was beating wildly. Already the house looked different to me. In the past, I'd always described it as "a little box." But now that I didn't have to defend against its charms, it suddenly seemed to possess the deceptive modesty that I love so much about houses in Mexico. From the street, they don't show much more than a door in a wall. But step through that doorway, and a magical world reveals itself: a courtyard, a fountain, bougainvillea vines.

I stepped through the doorway, and the magical world vanished. The brown linoleum on the kitchen floor was as warped and pockmarked as ever, and the living room window was shot through with bullet holes. Still, I felt in an altered state, a mild swoon of possibility. When I listened to the messages on my answering machine, there was one from Sylvie that said, "Call me!" and one from Marci, my Realtor cousin, wanting to know how I was coming with the "house hunting." Ha! Suddenly the expression struck me as funny. As though I'd gone on safari looking for exotic game and ended up with the gopher in my own backyard.

But how was I going to feed this gopher now that I'd caught him? I'd been around long enough to know that, though he was small, he would have a voracious appetite. Standing there in my kitchen, I thought of "The Rocking-Horse Winner" by D. H. Lawrence. In the story, a little boy is so permeated by his parents' financial insecurity that everything in the house—the furniture, the rugs, the curtains—speaks to him: *There must be more money, there must be more money. . . .*

How was I going to get more money? My start-up salary at the university barely met my monthly expenses. The money from my last book was long gone. I had a few thousand dollars in savings, which was tied up in an IRA. It frightened me to think of dissolving it and having absolutely no cushion for safety. It was all I had in case of emergency. And soon my daughter would need money for college.

*WWCD?* I asked myself.

What would Carole do?

But Carole was off in France again, buying another house, and through the rising din of whispers—*there must be more money, there must be more money*—I couldn't seem to conjure her advice.

I decided to call Sylvie. She had a way of bringing me back to earth whenever I started to spin out, and there'd been a note of urgency in her voice.

But from the moment she answered the phone, I could tell she was levitating. Her voice had lost all traces of its usual melancholy. "I've met a man, Noelle! Imagine! He's actually someone I used to know!" And then she told me that, several years ago, she and a young man named Edward had worked on a play together—about Milena, the love of Franz Kafka's life. There was the spark of something between them then. But to Sylvie, still somewhat fixated on her self-centered ex-husband, Edward seemed "too sweet." Now she told me, in a voice that sounded both giddy and triumphant, "I'm feeling ready for sweetness!" And before hanging up, she told me, "You're next, Noelle! I just know it!"

Ready for sweetness? I don't know. That night I woke before dawn, with the panic rising in my chest again: *There must be more money, there must be more money.* And as I lay there, in the hour of the wolf, it didn't seem to be sweetness that was called for but something steely and sharklike.

When I woke in the morning, I felt released from the panic, but I also felt confused. Was there any sort of law or pattern that could explain the recent turn of events, or was it all simply random? It had been less than two months since Sylvie and I had agreed on our love experiment. Though she had adamantly renounced any overt strategy, she had drawn a new love to herself in record time. Meanwhile, what had made my landlords decide to send me their letter? After all, I'd never made my real estate shrine or appealed to any transcendent power. I'd simply become really clear within myself that I wanted to buy a house, and I'd driven around a bit looking at properties. So were these results a testimony to the power of wishing—or quite the opposite?

If Carole was around, she'd probably tell me, "Wishing releases such a powerful energy that even the smallest dose of it can make things happen." But Carole was far away, and my attempt to imagine her response just wasn't cutting it.

After all, the stakes had suddenly gotten rather high. With my cousin Marci, I'd been negotiating the price of the house with my landlords. We'd settled on $300,000—a "steal" in this part of the world, but still an astronomical sum for me.

And that's why, as I approach the door of the mortgage company, my giddiness is tinged with dread. The strange May rain is coming down in sheets, and in the short walk from my car, I've gotten drenched. It doesn't seem a good omen. Just when I need to look Dressed for Success, I look like the Little Match Girl. Running my fingers through my wet hair, I pause for a moment before ringing the bell and remind myself of my strong points:

Thanks to my Spiritual Poverty mentality, I actually have a very high credit rating. Except for monthly car payments, I've always lived within my means. I also have a regular income.

Is that all?

I'm sorry, what?

Is that all?

Sitting in a stiff leather chair across from the mortgage lady, I seem to have blanked out. She reminds me a bit of the woman I saw on TV a few months ago, the big-haired evangelist who was asking God for the best cut of meat in the house, and I feel ill at ease in her presence. Having just asked me what my monthly income was, she can't seem to get her head around my answer.

"Is that all? Is that your *weekly* take-home?"

"No, that's per month."

Her mouth tightens. She crunches a bunch of numbers on her calculator, and her frown lines deepen. Apparently the ratios aren't good. Even with a 10 percent down payment, my mortgage and taxes will be 80 percent of my income each month. And where on earth will I come up with a 10 percent down payment?

*There must be more money, there must be more money,* the voices throb in my head as I walk back to my car through the rain.

Passing the door of a coffeehouse, I dart in and order myself a hot chai. "Do you want cinnamon, cloves, or chocolate sprinkled on the top?" a young woman with spikes of green hair asks me from behind the counter. All of a sudden I realize I've seen her before: this is the place where I met the pesto-minus-pesto man, well over a year ago. It seems an omen for me now, a reminder—in the midst of my anxiety—to say the great Yes to life. "I'll have them all!" I tell her. Later, driving back home through the rain, I seem to have acquired a new mantra: *Cinnamon, chocolate, cloves . . .*

By the time I pull up to the house, it's dark. I step out of the car and my sensor lights go on. I only recently had them installed, and I love them. In fact, it's begun to disturb me how much I love them. When I walk through my gate at night, they make me feel as though someone is happy to see me, lighting up for me. I bought myself a whistling kettle, too—and it disturbs me how much I like it. It makes me feel as though someone is calling to me, urgently wanting my attention. Though I do have many wonderful friends with whom I am in close contact, I often find myself coming home to an empty house. And as my daughter is often at her father's or with friends, I spend a lot of time in my own company. I've always loved and needed solitude, but the truth is, I'm lonely.

I'm lonely and I'm developing symptoms. Like many people, I've always had a tendency to talk to myself when I'm alone, but lately I notice that I'm actually carrying on a conversation. I'll say out loud, "I'm cold." Then I'll reply, "Me too." That's apparently a bad sign. And though I'm pretty sure that I haven't yet started to have conversations with myself in public, I know it's a slippery slope. Maybe it's time to get a cat. ("Is it time to get a cat?" I ask myself. "Sylvie has a cat," I reply.) And speaking of Sylvie, I'm happy for her—but I'm feeling somewhat deserted, too. Something about the prospect of buying a house is making me feel more alone than ever.

Still wired from my meeting with the mortgage lady, I stay up late switching TV channels and finally land in a place where I've never lingered before: the Jewelry Channel. Two women with southern accents and long, acrylic fingernails are speaking ecstatically about a tray of merchandise. Their voices are like honey, and there is something almost sexual in the way they stroke the jewelry and pronounce the words "freshwater pearl," "dewdrop earrings," "ruby cluster." When a woman calls in to order a brooch, she's congratulated as though she had done something heroic: "Well, aren't you something! You are really stepping up to the plate!" I am transfixed.

Suddenly I understand that the jewelry ladies are not ordinary mortals. They are semidivine. They are initiators, standing at the threshold between the Desert of Spiritual Poverty and the Palace of Consumption, saying "Come in, come in! Buy and be blessed!" And they want me to find the money to buy my house. They do, they really, really do. Lulled by the sound of their voices and mysteriously partaking in their shower of praise, I fall asleep on the couch.

Well before dawn the wind is so strong that the sensor lights go on, shining through the window and startling me awake. Rain pounds on the roof. It doesn't rain in California in May. What's happening to the world? It's the hour of the wolf, the jewelry ladies are long gone, and in their place a man is talking about hair loss. Something seems terribly out of harmony.

*There must be more money, there must be more money.*

When I wake again, it's morning and the rain has finally stopped. Though I don't feel refreshed after my fitful night, I do feel determined. And I've come to a momentous decision: I've got to become more rigorous and methodical about my experiment.

When I began, it seemed to me that there was something inherently fanciful, whimsical, in the art of wishing. Something that would resist any heavy-handed attempt to bring it up to code. I thought of it as something you sort of made up as you went along—inspired by friends, by childhood memories and fairy tales, by ancient archetypes and New Age nuggets. A pinch of this, a scoop of that, sprinkled all over with fairy dust. A concoction with no recipe.

I mean, what have I done? I've made my birdcage shrine. I've slept on top of my paper wish. I've gone out looking at properties. It's true that, nearly as soon as I started, it seemed that "something was happening": there was the encounter with Marie, the call from Marci, the experience of returning from Vichy Springs to find the letter from my landlords. But there's no way to tell whether any of this "something" has been influenced by my actions or utterly random.

When I go to a major bookseller's website and type in the word *wish,* I discover a total of 236,599 books available for shipping. The overwhelming majority of them are books for children. That in itself reveals something profound about the place of wishing in our culture, doesn't it? It's child's play, the stuff of fantasy—not appropriate for serious, hardworking grown-ups. Nonetheless, among the 236,599 entries, there is a short list of books intended for those out of kindergarten, and after an hour or so of clicking and scrolling, I add them to my "shopping cart," do the tally, and submit my order.

Later that day when I go to the post office, I find an ecstatic postcard from Lowell.

"Dear Noelle," it reads, "suddenly love is jumping out at me from everywhere! Can you believe that, since we last met, I've fallen in love with two women?"

So far, the two romantics, Sylvie and Lowell, seem to be coming out way ahead in the love department. "You should be really happy for your friends," I say to myself, tossing Lowell's postcard into the trash bin. "I know. You're right," I reply. And then, looking around to see whether anyone has heard me talking out loud to myself on federal premises, I fish the postcard back out of the bin.

When I get home, I take the plunge and sign up for my "Calling In 'The One'" workshop. I thought I would have to fly down to L.A., but it turns out that since I first saw the flyer, the author has added a "teleclass." It's coming up in just two weeks, and conveniently, I can do it from the comfort and privacy of my own house.

That is, my still rented and increasingly schizophrenogenic house in which there is still no respite from the voices. In fact, the din has been getting worse. For now, against the background of

*There must be more money,* I can make out a new voice. It's the mortgage lady, repeating: *Is that all? Is that all?*

One by one, the wish books begin to arrive. When the last one comes, I spread them all out on the living room floor and consecrate one entire day to an orgy of reading. I go back and forth from one book to the next, reading a chapter here, a chapter there. It's my way of having a kind of wish salon, a philosophy café, a conference, in my living room. If they were in the room with me, we might be able to engage in a lively debate. But as it is, I can't seem to get much controversy going. Basically, they all seem to say the same thing, some with more detail than others: You have to focus, to become very clear about what it is you wish for. The experts vary somewhat, it's true, as to how detailed your wish should be. While some insist that you should form as vivid a picture as possible, others disagree, saying, for example, that if you're wishing for a person to enter your life, you should leave the wish a little "fuzzy." Apparently the fuzziness keeps you from trying to overcontrol the situation, and thus perhaps interfere with the free will of another, unsuspecting person. But basically, they all agree: the first step is to identify and to name what you wish for.

You have to make sure that your wish is not malevolent.

You have to confront the obstacles that have hitherto kept you from making your wishes come true.

And you need to look for proper support—above all, for sympathetic people who will encourage you in your endeavor.

When I go down the list, it seems to me that I've already done just about everything the books advise. But alas, rather than encouraging me, my reading binge is getting me down. As night falls and I close the last book, I'm left with an elephant in my living room.

In every one of these books, there is some place for me where the logic breaks down, and it's usually pretty close to the beginning. It's not that I want it to. Quite the contrary: I want very badly to be convinced. But it's hard, when you've pursued a philosophical bent through graduate school, to simply shed what you've learned. My mind is trained to assess the soundness of arguments, the way a musician's ear is trained to assess the rightness of pitch or a swim coach is trained to assess the angle of a dive. A flimsy argument makes me acutely uncomfortable—as though a gymnast was performing lopsided cartwheels or a singer was way off-key. And again and again, when I read these books, I find some form of faulty reasoning: unproved assumptions, false analogies, insufficient evidence, circular logic.

Take Wayne Dyer, for example. He has a doctorate of education in counseling, and for decades now he's had a huge following as an inspirational speaker and writer. I've never made a study of his books before, but I've always felt warmly disposed toward him. Sometimes late at night on television I've seen him giving one of his very animated talks, with the spotlights shining down on his bald head and behind him a huge colored circle representing the Source. He's always struck me as a witty and wonderful storyteller who is highly articulate, passionate in his beliefs, and sincere in his desire to make others feel more hopeful and more confident. But here's a passage from his book *The Power of Intention*:

> *The field of intention, which is responsible for all creation, is constantly giving—in fact, it knows no bounds to its giving. It just keeps on converting pure formless spirit into a myriad of material forms. Furthermore, this field of intention gives in unlimited supplies. There is no such concept as shortage or scarcity when it comes to the originating Source. So we're looking at two major conceptualizations when we think of the universal mind's natural abundance. The first is that it's perpetually giving, and the second is that it offers an infinite supply.*

No such concept as shortage or scarcity?
What about famines, epidemics, floods, droughts, plagues of

locusts? If "the field of intention" is responsible for all creation and is what gives rise to material form, then what about those naturally destructive elements within the cosmos? Long before we human beings came on the scene with our own powers of destruction, there were giant volcanic eruptions, continent-splitting earthquakes, ice ages, mass extinctions. How can such devastating forces be seen as "giving in unlimited supplies"? And what about entropy, the inexorable movement of all the energy in the universe toward a state that is ever more chaotic and disorganized? How does entropy fit in with the assertion that "the universal mind of Creation is in a constant state of supplying. It never shuts down, it takes no vacations, there are no days off, and it's perpetually giving forth. Everything and everyone, without exception, emanates from this universal mind we're calling intention"?

I don't enjoy finding what seem like major snags in the flow of such encouraging thoughts. I really don't. I'd love to believe that the universe is as entirely benevolent as Dyer purports. But when the logic of an argument seems to break down, I can't swallow it. And that's painful—especially when I feel so drawn to the person making the argument. Reading Wayne's words, I feel a bit like Odysseus, who had to tie himself to the mast in order to resist the beautiful sound of the Sirens' singing.

The truth is, all the authors in my wish salon make a lovely and very enticing music. To a one, they come through as warm, dynamic, generous, and encouraging people. Yet if I spend more than an hour or so in the company of their minds, I feel irritable and depressed. No doubt this is the reason I've kept them at arm's length for so long. As much as I'd like to follow in their footsteps, I don't trust the markers they've laid down for me. In the dark of the night when I really need them, it will turn out that they weren't white stones but only bread crumbs, already eaten by the birds.

What can I do? I want so badly to endorse the optimism, but I feel like I'm surrounded by pages and pages of "thinking lite," and it makes me want to pound my fists on the floor with frustration. And deep down, I still have the fear that somehow I'll abandon Viktor Frankl, standing there in the meadow on the first day, unable to feel the flowers' beauty while someone croons, "Wasn't it wonderful, the way he just walked right out of the gate at Auschwitz and fell on his knees before the flowers?"

And yet—remembering my own myopia, my numbness to Viktor's second encounter with the field of flowers—I make myself keep reading. Of all the books, there's one in particular that I feel most drawn to. It's called *Wishing Well: Making Your Every Wish Come True*. The author, Paul Ka'ikena Pearsall, Ph.D., is a licensed clinical neuropsychologist who teaches at the University of Hawaii.

Hawaii.

There's that magical name again. When you grow up by the sea in California, the far western edge of the continent, it's the place you dream of. When you stand on the beach, it's the place you look toward, the place that beckons you from beyond, with its turquoise water, its blue-green valleys, its breezes that blow like a sheet of silk across your face. For my tenth birthday in Santa Monica, I had a luau. Dressed in muumuus, we wove flowers in our hair and danced the hula and drank 7-Up through straws from a hollowed-out watermelon. That's as close as I've ever come to actualizing my dream of Hawaii, and so it's remained a mythical place to me—the sort of tropical paradise you'd visit if wishes were horses, and horses could swim for thousands of miles across the cold, churning sea.

It seems somehow fitting, then, to learn from Paul Pearsall that in Hawaiian culture the wish has a very special place. Since ancient times, the spiritual masters known as healing kahuna have taught that there is indeed great power in the act of wishing. It's a power that must be used with utmost care to ensure that one's wish is in harmony with the *aina* (land), the *ohana* (family), and *ke Akua* (the transcendent, divine power). Drawing from this ancient tradition, Paul Pearsall's book seems to provide the broadest and deepest context of any of the other books spread out before me. Going well beyond the realm of "how to make your personal desires come true," it actually attempts to offer a science, an ethics, and a metaphysics of wishing. He writes:

> *The best way to understand how a wish works is to think of it as a tiny spurt of energy. Like everything in the universe, our thoughts or intentions are also forms of energy. When we focus our intentions by making a wish, we are creating a tiny energetic shove within the system of which we are all an inseparable part. Because of the power of intentions to be nonlocal, to transcend time and space, they ever so slightly move the cosmos. This is why one simple wish can help swing things a little more our way.*

I'm drawn to that idea of a wish as "a tiny spurt of energy." And though I'm not sure that I could say exactly what it means, I'm receptive to the idea that our intentions have the power to transcend time and space. As to whether they "ever so slightly move the cosmos"—well, I don't know. When my cousin Marci the Realtor called me, when my landlords wrote to me, were these slight movements of the cosmos? I don't dare say that yet. It still seems somehow presumptuous to imagine that the cosmos might exert itself, even slightly, as my personal fiduciary. Presumptuous—and in need of more evidence.

In his own appeal to the skeptical reader, Pearsall makes it clear that, for a more thorough exploration of the scientific research that supports his philosophy of wishing, one should consult his earlier book, *The Heart's Code*. I make a note to do so, but meanwhile I wish that the brief summaries he gives in *Wishing Well* sounded more convincing. Too often I feel that he uses anecdotes, aphorisms, and analogies as if they were proofs.

Still, though I don't yet fully trust his logic, there is something that I trust about him. As he tells it, his own faith in wishing came under the most extreme circumstances: when he was dying of a virulent form of cancer. He writes, "As I lay dying, I experienced my first adult instinct to make a wish and take it seriously. Although I'm not precisely sure of all the reasons why, something made me wish. I am sure now that wishing contributed to the miracle of my survival." This life-and-death context lends a profound sense of gravity and of gratitude to Pearsall's exploration of the act of wishing. He believes that people must take extreme care regarding not only what they wish for, but when, how, and where they wish—as well as how many wishes they make at any one time. More than anything, he emphasizes that our wishes must align with our highest aspirations, our ultimate concerns.

For him the art of wishing has a sacred quality that goes far beyond the fulfillment of merely personal desires.

And yet, and yet—

He doesn't denigrate those personal desires either.

Actually, that's one of the things I like best about him. He doesn't treat all wishes equally, as so many of the wish maestros seem to do. You wouldn't find him writing a sentence like, "Whether you wish for spiritual realization or a face-lift . . ." as though they belonged in the same breath. So in that way, he doesn't trample all over my deep-seated need for a wish hierarchy. But he's not a wish snob, either. He would have been perfectly at home among the lovely women in Sausalito who wished for both world peace and new client referrals. He'll let you have your wish for both spiritual realization *and* new kitchen cabinets—so long as you wish for them properly.

And that means understanding where a wish belongs in time and space.

For him, there are different categories of wishes that exist along a continuum. Their relationship is not rigidly hierarchical but circular. Or rather, he depicts the continuum as a five-pointed star. And he insists that it's important to wish in a certain order around the continuum, beginning with the wish for Serenity, and moving in a clockwise direction. Here, I confess, is one of those places where I balk a bit.

And here is a place where he permits himself a kind of paradox. Though deep down he is very serious about the art of wishing, he also encourages one to have a playful attitude—and even to be silly. The English word *silly,* he tells us, comes from the German word *selig,* which means "holy."

Okay.

Okay.

I know about the wisdom of foolishness, the silly holiness of certain Christian saints and Sufi dervishes and Shakespearean fools and Zen monks and mystics of all persuasions down through the ages. I'm actually a bona fide mystic myself, which is to say, I believe that what is most real and most true is a form of sacred presence that cannot be apprehended through the rational mind. As a Zen student, I've spent years studying koans, those beautiful and amazing teaching stories that defy the intellect, like *Outside the temple gate, a dog is pissing to the skies.* Where I balk is when people seem to be talking out of both sides of their mouth at once. They try to persuade me through rational argument and scientific evidence, while asking me to throw my rationality to the winds.

The truth is, from the beginning of my experiment, I've had to perform what the American philosopher and psychologist William James called "a willing suspension of disbelief." And as I attempt to become more methodical in the art of wishing, it appears that I have to work harder and harder to suspend my disbelief.

But now suddenly, hovering right there beside the elephant in my living room, an angel appears. His name is Leonard. Leonard Angel. I haven't thought of him in years. He was one of my professors at the University of Toronto, and because he also had an interest in Buddhism, I wheedled him into letting me do an independent study on mysticism. He told me something that I came to think of as "Leonard's nugget." One day, as he was struggling over a certain text, he realized that *certain religious beliefs did not need to be taken so much as accurate descriptions of reality as, rather, exhortations to practice.* For example, some Buddhist teachers say, "The last thought that you have before dying will determine your next life." You could get all tangled up as to whether or not this teaching is literally true, but according to Leonard, you don't have to. What's important is that it's a belief that encourages you to pay extremely careful attention to your thoughts, because the stakes couldn't get any higher. If you live your life as though this belief were true, then you're more likely to meet each bump in the road with grace and dignity, just in case it might be the bump that does you in. Then, as your car veers over the guardrail, or you stumble and fall from a roof, your last thought is much less likely to be "Shit!"

It's a relief to retrieve this tip from my long-lost professor. It reminds me that when I encounter an argument that doesn't seem to hold water, I don't have to writhe about and gnash my teeth on the living room floor. Rather, I can ask myself: "If I acted *as though* this were true, would it bring about a positive change in my life?"

Now with Leonard's nugget firmly in hand, I take a deep breath, pull up my bootstraps, and return to working my way clockwise around the five-pointed *Wishing Well* star.

The first wish, according to Dr. Pearsall, is for Serenity. I like that. I like the idea that he begins by invoking a state that's the very opposite of frantic craving. And I like that Serenity seems to naturally encompass the very first wish that I permitted myself to Put Out There: the wish for spiritual healing. As I read on, I'm also pleased to see that under Serenity he includes security, the need for a stable foundation for one's life. Surely that would include my house?

*There must be more money, there must be more money—*
*Quiet! Can't you see I'm trying to be serene?*

In the kitchen, the phone rings. As if granted reprieve, I leap up from the living room floor, and by the time I make it to the kitchen, the answering machine has picked up. I hear a man's voice that I've never heard before. It's deep and resonant, and it sounds both confident and somehow hesitant in an attractive way. The man is saying that he's fallen in love with my writing, and that when he went on the Internet, he discovered that I sometimes work with individual writers, and he wonders if he could come for a consult. His name is Nicholas.

My hand moves to pick up the phone . . . but I don't. I listen to him say good-bye. Did I really just hear what I think I heard? There isn't time to ponder. Rushing back into the living room, I tell the assorted authors: Please forgive me! All bets are on! I hope I haven't offended you in any way or brought any bad juju upon myself.

Then, opening the Paul Pearsall book, I turn rapidly to the instructions for how to wish. I know I'm doing this out of sequence, but I can't wait. I turn to page 154, "How to Wish Well" and follow the eight-fold path, which tells me to:

1. "SD-SU-CD—Sit Down, Shut Up, and Calm Down." I'll try. But it's hard, my heart is pounding.

2. "Pick a wish target." This means to "connect *and* resonate with nature by looking at something alive." Hmmmm . . . something alive. How about that elephant in the living room? He seems to have gracefully bowed out. How about the bulbs that I planted outside my bullet-riddled window? Yes, that will do. I go and press my face against the glass.

3. "Close your eyes."

4. "Breathe deeply and abdominally."

5. "Place your left hand over your heart."

6. "Press your right hand gently but firmly on your left hand."

7. "On exhaling, whisper your wish."

8. "Use eight short words."

*Please, oh please, may this be the man.*

PART TWO

# Raking It In

*In which, as I set out
to explore the ancient history
of wishing, my own wishes
surprise me by beginning
to come true*

# CHAPTER SIX

# June

## *Magic: Tracing Primal Roots*

Summer has finally come with its ten thousand grasses. A friend once told me that in a restroom in France, she happened to see a map of the world's most allergenic places—and there was our county, surrounded by vibrating yellow lines that marked it as a cosmic hot spot for pollen. That's where I am right now, smack in the middle of those vibrating yellow lines. Since I can't bear to be inside on such a beautiful morning, I'm out in the yard sneezing my head off while simultaneously trying to (1) learn something about the nature of magic, and (2) make a new shrine.

It's very hard for me to concentrate on either task, however, because ever since I got the phone call from the man with the confident/hesitant voice, my mind has been spinning. Can it be true? Is he the One? And if so, should I cancel this evening's workshop on Calling Him In?

The day after I got his phone message, I called him back. We fell easily into a long conversation. He told me that for a long time he's been wanting to write a book on a subject that's close to the theme of my last book, and it seemed that we had many interests in common. We talked for nearly an hour, and then he made an appointment to come and see me on the first Saturday afternoon in June.

That would be the day after the day after tomorrow, and already I'm jumping out of my skin.

When I woke up this morning, I knew that I needed to do something to keep myself grounded, and that's why I chose my two morning tasks: one to focus my mind and the other to occupy my hands. For the latter, I decided to buckle down, take Carole's advice, and make a real estate shrine. However, I'm not making the shrine as I'd originally planned, the miniature Mediterranean house with its apricot walls and red tile roof. Since I'm now hoping to buy the house that I'm already living in, it seemed to me that I no longer needed to work so hard to envision it. Instead, I'm going to cut to the chase and just make a shrine to money.

Inside a little wooden box, I'm gluing gold coins, and I'm cutting a one-dollar bill into a pile of miniature dollars.

*You're what?*

That's right.

Just a few short months ago, I would have been incapable of such an act. Blatantly mixing the sacred and the profane. Putting cold, hard cash inside a *serinium*.

But today I'm repeating a line from Paul Pearsall: "When we wish, we make an intentional regression back to the ancestors." I like that. It sounds so much better than those other mean things I could say to myself, like:

*Mammon worshipper.*

*Now you're really mixing up God and Caesar.*

There's also a way that Paul Pearsall's phrase appeases my rational, critical mind. Instead of seeing myself as being childish and greedy, I can see myself as a kind of anthropologist, consciously choosing to embrace the ancient ways of my own tribe. For the act of wishing is inextricably bound to the art of magic. And magic takes us as far back as our species can go.

Among the books I've brought with me to the picnic table is *A History of Magic* by Richard Cavendish. "Magic is as old as man," he writes. "It is found as far back as evidence of human existence runs and has influenced religion, art, agriculture, industry, science, government, and social institutions. The western tradition of magic was born in the Roman world at about the same time as Christ, but its ultimate ancestry is veiled in the mists and cloudbanks of prehistory." So, even as I sit here, defacing a piece of postmodern American currency, I'm wrapped in the mist of primal humanness.

And deep within that mist I recognize: sharp teeth.

We've come to think of magic as child's play, a motif for innocuous movies, or an amusing diversion for birthday parties—complete with sequined wings, wizards' wands, and rabbits coming out of hats. But fundamentally, magic emerges from a fierce—and often desperate—will to power. As Cavendish puts it, "Magic is an attempt to exert power through actions which are believed to have a direct and automatic influence on man, nature, and the divine."

Our modern magician has lost the ambition to exert such power in any truly significant way. He's a kind of jokester, performing extravagantly useless acts. He can make water come out of his ears and discover a dove inside a hat—but that won't make the rain come down or bring new life to a barren womb, and no one even imagines it should.

But for our ancestors, magic was another story.

Those hairless apes. Every day of their lives they faced mortal danger, whether lightning, fire, flood, drought, starvation, disease, lions, tigers, bears, wolves. They had big brains, but they did not have fur, fangs, claws, bristles, scales, venom, or even camouflage to protect them. Magic was their attempt to gain an edge, to grasp a measure of control in a brutally unpredictable world. The magician's powers were directed at what mattered most: the birth of a child, the growth of the crops, the hunting of animals, the destruction of enemies, the casting out of disease. Our ancestors couldn't afford to be shy about informing the gods and spirits of their earthly desires.

It's strange, really, that we've come to think of "magical" as the opposite of "practical." For when we say "magical thinking" we mean precisely a kind of thinking that is not grounded in the physical reality of life on earth. We mean a childish kind of thinking that puts faith in invisible powers and ceremonial acts, rather than in a methodical exploration of the natural environment. We mean a superstitious kind of thinking that is the very enemy of science. When we encounter those rare indigenous cultures where magic still thrives, we might be fascinated and entranced, but we tend to be condescending. How pathetic, if a child is ill, to daub her forehead with a shaman's feather rather than giving her penicillin.

When we emerge from "the mists and cloudbanks of prehistory" into the realm of science, then magic—and with it the art of wishing—loses its sharp teeth. If you want your crops to grow, why bother with an elaborate ceremony to cajole the gods into granting your wish? It's science that will grow your garden: the application of certain principles, deduced from careful observation of the environment, with predictably repeatable results. And where science reigns, magic withers and becomes debased—leaving us with the modern magician, the jokester who can make cards slide up and down his sleeves.

But do they really belong to separate worlds, the shaman's feather and the penicillin? The crop dance and the field of botany? Yes—and no.

Another book beside me is *Magic, Science and Religion* by the anthropologist Bronislaw Malinowski. Leafing through the beat-up, dog-eared copy that I haven't read since my comparative religion class in college, I'm aware that this time around I'm reading it in a radically different way. Because this time I'm not just looking at another culture as if in a glass museum case, rather I'm looking for clues to my own life, for my own experiment in desire. And Malinowski does not disappoint. Having immersed himself in the life of the Trobriand Islanders of New Guinea, he insists that we moderns have badly misunderstood the role of magic in traditional cultures. For they never use magic to *replace* the practical knowledge that they have gained from centuries of observation of their environment. Rather, they use it *in precisely the place where their practical knowledge leaves off.*

He writes, for instance, that the "natives" wouldn't dream of planting a garden without recourse to magic. For they know that various kinds of disaster, including "blight, unseasonable droughts, rains, bush pigs and locusts" would destroy an unconsecrated space. But, he asks, does this mean that "the natives attribute all good results to magic"? Absolutely not. And the next passage seems so momentous to me that, leaving my shrine with its glued coins to set in the sun, I dash inside to get myself a notebook and a pen. These are words I want to absorb through the physical action of writing:

> *If you were to suggest to a native that he should make his garden mainly by magic and scamp his work, he would simply smile on your simplicity. He knows as well as you do that there are natural conditions and causes, and by his observations he knows also that he is able to control these natural forces by mental and physical effort. His knowledge is limited, no doubt, but as far as it goes it is sound and proof against mysticism. If the fences are broken down, if the seed is destroyed or has been dried or washed away, he will have recourse not to magic, but to work, guided by knowledge and reason. His experience has*

*taught him also, on the other hand, that in spite of all his
forethought and beyond all his efforts there are agencies
and forces which one year bestow unwonted and unearned
benefits of fertility, making everything run smooth and
well, rain and sun appear at the right moment, noxious insects remain in abeyance, the harvest yield a superabun-
dant crop; and another year again the same agencies bring
ill-luck and bad chance, pursue him from beginning till end
and thwart all his most strenuous efforts and his best-
founded knowledge. To control these influences and only
these he employs magic.*

*Thus there is a clear-cut division: there is first the well-
known set of conditions, the natural course of growth, as
well as the ordinary pests and dangers to be warded off by
fencing and weeding. On the other hand there is the
domain of the unaccountable and adverse influences, as
well as the great unearned increment of fortunate
coincidence. The first conditions are coped with by
knowledge and work, the second by magic.*

It takes a long time to get the passage down, and when I do my
hand is aching slightly but I feel a great relief. It's as though two
tectonic plates that had been rumbling, jostling each other, finally
released their built-up pressure and settled back into place. The
pragmatic and the magical, the practical and the wishful. Now I
know how to respond to those people who say, with indignation,
"I don't wish. I make plans." I can see the way to reconcile the
split. To have my cakes and eat them, too.

Of course, what Malinowski describes is what I've long observed in Carole. She never "scamps her work." If there's something she longs for, she makes her shrine—and then works like a
dog. She paints long hours; she trudges through waist-high dust
and bat droppings to renovate her medieval homes; she prints up

a card and distributes it liberally to find her ideal husband; she places an ad in the newspaper for "free use of studio in exchange for speaking French."

Though Malinowski's distinction isn't really new to me, he provides a broader and deeper context for understanding the connection between wishing and doing. He further delineates the boundary, within traditional cultures, between sacred and profane. And in so doing, he fleshes out the meaning of making "an intentional regression back to the ancestors."

For Richard Cavendish, too, the magical and the practical are intimately linked. According to him, magic arises as a response to the "mysterious" elements that affect our earthly existence: a strange shift in the weather, a change in the herd's patterns or sudden bend in a bowstring. He, too, provides me with a passage that I feel compelled to transcribe on the page facing Malinowski's, so the two can send sparks back and forth:

*Magic tries to control these mysterious agencies. It is far more concerned with what "works" than with why or how things work. In magic, if the right procedure is followed, the desired result will occur: if it does not, then the correct procedure cannot have been followed. The correct procedure is the one which experience associates with the desired result. Ceremonies were held every year in ancient Egypt to make sure that the Nile would flood. They were held at the time when the Nile was due to flood in any case. Similarly, primitive societies which conduct rain-making ceremonies hold them at the beginning of the rainy season, not in the middle of the dry season. The ceremonies are man's contribution to the right order of things, which includes the seasonal renewal of rainfall. To omit them would be to disturb the right order, and the rains might not come.*

*Against this background, the simplest reason for*

*believing in magic is that it works: not always, but often*
*enough to inspire confidence. The Nile normally does*
*flood, the rains usually do fall.*

Thousands of miles and thousands of years from ancient Egypt, don't we find this same dynamic in the magical worlds of Harry Potter, where the laws of cause and effect are just as exacting as those of the ordinary, workaday world? And isn't there something profoundly, if oddly, reassuring in the tyranny of rules that Harry Potter encounters in each fantasy realm? As Cavendish says, "In magic, if the right procedure is followed, the desired result will occur." Of course, in Harry Potter's world, so long as you followed the right procedure for rain making, you might not have to wait for the start of the rainy season, as Cavendish's real-world magicians do—and that's a radical difference.

Together, Malinowski and Cavendish are helping me see that, at its root, magic—and thus the art of wishing—arises in the place where human power and powerlessness meet. If your fences break, if your seed is dried or washed away, you don't throw up your hands and wish. You tie back the fence posts, you search for new seed, you dig another garden—but where your human knowledge and effort can carry you no further, *there* is where you plant your wish.

"No!" many people would say. "*There* is precisely the place where you keep pushing, so that your knowledge and effort may carry you through the next edge." But given that we will always arrive at a new edge, it seems to me that there is something profoundly wise and eternally relevant about the moment of putting down one's hammer and making oneself receptive to another kind of power.

As Malinowski writes of his prototypical "primitive" man: "He never relies on magic alone, while, on the contrary, he sometimes dispenses with it completely, as in fire-making and in a number of crafts and pursuits. But he clings to it, whenever he has to recognize the impotence of his knowledge and of his rational technique."

If what Malinowski says is true, then when I wish in the mode of the ancestors, I adopt an attitude that is both confident and humble. I commit to doing everything within my human power to make something happen—while also recognizing that my human power is limited.

And it is right there, on that boundary, that I place my shrine.

My shrine, which is starting to look pretty spiffy. The gold coins are holding in place, and the pile of little green bills is growing. The summer breeze is blowing in the leaves, and while my fingers are busily cutting and pasting, my mind returns to its very new but already deep groove of Nicholas.

It wasn't until I hung up the phone that I realized his name rang a bell for me. I went back through my files, and there it was: a letter to the editor he had written in the local newspaper, praising my last book not long after it came out. Rereading the letter, I remember having wondered, in a fleeting sort of way, Who is this man? And will I ever meet him?

Suddenly I'm struck that, even before I put the paper wish beneath my bed, our connection through words and paper had already begun. And that in itself seems auspicious. For almost as long as I can remember, there's been a magical link for me among paper, writing, and love. As a girl, I had a little wooden sewing chest with drawers that were meant to hold spools, thread, needles, and buttons. But I used the chest as a kind of oracle. On tiny pieces of paper I would write the names of the boys I liked at school: *Scott, Michael, Justy.* I'd put one name in each drawer and then, closing my eyes, I'd open and shut the various drawers until finally one drawer seemed to tell me, "I'm the one." I'd open my eyes, take out the paper, and discover the name of the man I would marry.

Now I'm surprised to learn that even then I was following in the ways of the ancient ancestors. According to Cavendish, writing was long held to have magical powers. For who else but the gods could turn the breath of speech into tangible, permanent marks? Among the humans, only a chosen few knew how to make these marks, which were seen as vessels of mysterious power. Inscribed by priests on rolls of papyrus, tablets of stone, lumps of clay or shining jewels, words were used to repel bad fortune and bring good luck.

So far I seem to be having good luck with words on paper. But meanwhile, my "Calling In 'The One'" teleclass is just a few hours away. Should I cancel it? Will I be jinxing my link to Nicholas? Then again, if he is the One, what's the harm in taking a multimedia approach to Reeling Him In?

*Achoo!*

I sneeze violently again, and—not for the first time this morning—the tiny bills scatter. The breeze lifts them and they swirl in the air full of pollen.

"*À tes souhaits,*" the French say when somebody sneezes—"to your wishes." We say "God bless you" because of an ancient belief that when we sneeze we are expelling an evil spirit. Now that I'm making a proper study, I've learned that there are fundamentally two modes of wishing: expelling and attracting. And in either mode, an act of wishing can bring about consequences that are beneficial or harmful.

If I'm working on a money shrine and getting ready for a workshop called "Calling In 'The One,'" then it seems obvious that I'm wishing in the mode of attracting and that the cosmic consequences are likely to be relatively harmless, no?

Alas, as I learn more about the ancient art of wishing, I'm discovering that it's not quite that simple.

In the magical view of the universe, everything is interrelated. The very possibility of magic is rooted in a world of fluid boundaries, a world in which spirit and matter, animate and inanimate, are not separate, so that thoughts, words, and dreams are as real as things and deeds; a prayer can seed a cloud and make the rain come down; a curse can make a person sicken and die; and even stones have souls.

And because wishing is not child's play but an act of true potency, a wish sets off a chain of consequences within this interrelated universe. Inevitably, some of these consequences will be unintended—and if the wisher is not very careful, some of them could be harmful.

This cautious view is rather foreign to our modern way of thinking. When contemporary people say, "Do you believe in magic?" they're almost always talking about happy outcomes. If I had a dollar for every time my students use the word *magical* when they're writing about a pleasant experience—a candlelit dinner, a sunset walk—I'd have my down payment in no time. But when people really believe in the power of magic, then they also believe that magic can be bad—really bad.

Cavendish writes, "Human beings have a primitive and persistent reluctance to believe that things happen by chance and, where everything strange is magical, harmful events are readily put down to evil magic. In the ancient world magic was credited with extraordinary powers over nature." Drought, disease, miscarriage, flood, and famine: all could be explained as the result of "black magic."

In cultures where magic is truly alive, the magician is a formidable figure, worthy of respect and even awe—but also vulnerable to the envy and suspicion of others and even to vicious and systematic persecution.

In our own era, something quite remarkable is happening. Science itself is beginning to dissolve many of the boundaries that it first delineated. Boundaries within time and space, boundaries around what we call "objects," boundaries between mind and body: all have become more fluid. And this means, in a strange way, a reversion—based on new understandings—to certain beliefs and practices that used to be understood as magical.

Among these simultaneously new and ancient notions is that of "action at a distance," the idea that an act of consciousness— whether a thought, a prayer, a spell, or a curse—can somehow travel through time and space, bringing about changes in animate or inanimate things, even across vast distances. Though it remains a very controversial field, it is fair to say that a growing number of distinguished scientists are looking quite seriously at the notion of "distant intentionality" or "nonlocal mind."

Alas, not everyone who is drawn to the field has purely benev- olent intentions. If thoughts can indeed induce change in both an- imate and inanimate objects, then it does not take a great leap of the imagination to grasp the potentially destructive power of thought: the possibility of making a bridge collapse or a soldier keel over without the least trace of ammunition. For those whose vocation it is to think up ways of causing injury to others, "dis- tant intentionality" represents the ultimate gold mine, the crème de la crème of stealth weaponry.

But even when our motives are entirely innocent of malice, when we approach the realm of nonlocal mind we must proceed with utmost caution. At least that's what the modern maestros of wishing say. For again—whether they're invoking the ancient world of magic or the realm of modern science—to experiment with the power of wishing is to posit a world of fluid boundaries, a world in which thoughts, things, and events do not occur in iso- lation. Thus Paul Pearsall writes that when you attract something toward you, you are drawing it away from somewhere else. If you are trying to send something away from you, then you are send- ing it somewhere else. And in the book *Be Careful What You Pray For,* physician Larry Dossey points out that if you are trying to get rid of something in your life, then you must be aware that you are asking for the destruction of that thing. Even if your wish seems entirely innocent, it actually involves a degree of violence. If your wish is "May I be cured of this illness," then you're asking that whatever is causing the illness—a virus, a bacteria, a group of wayward cells—be destroyed.

If I look at my loneliness along these lines, it takes on colors and contours that I haven't seen before. If I'm seeking to draw a lover into my life, then—following Larry Dossey's reasoning—I'm seeking to kill off my loneliness. When I put it that way, it seems sad—because deep down I know that I'd be killing it off before having ever become truly intimate with it. I've learned how to bear it, but that's not the same as having fully experienced it.

And if I follow Paul Pearsall's model, then I'd have to acknowledge that in drawing a lover toward me, I am pulling him away from someone else, from some other actual or potential lover that he might have. And if I'm trying to cast off my own, not-fully-embraced loneliness, then I'd have to acknowledge that I'm sending it toward someone else.

Suddenly it's as though I'm walking through a minefield. I've become so aware of the potentially lethal consequences of my every move that, like a Jain, I feel I should wear a cloth over my face to keep from inhaling insects. And I begin to have more appreciation for Paul Pearsall's counsel that the first wish on the star should be for serenity.

Presumably, if one begins from a state of serenity, one is less likely to make a wish that scatters a wide range of unseen, negative consequences. And fortunately, under the category of serenity, Pearsall includes security. Under security he includes having a "stable, material platform." For me right now that means release from the voices that continue to hound me:

*There must be more money, there must be more money.*

The mortgage lady called last night. Because my credit rating's high, they'd like to be able to come through for me—but I must come up with a bigger down payment.

Now, outside at my picnic table, I'm amassing another pile of little green bills. This time, I'll try to keep them from going up in thin air. I know it's a crime to cut legal tender, but if anyone questions me, I've done my research and I've got my answer ready: "Don't you know anything about *imitative magic*?"

The Venus of Willendorf, the cave paintings of Lascaux and Chauvet: these are among the most ancient human artifacts ever found on earth. They are wishes made into palpable things, and they embody the principle of imitative magic. If I make this voluptuous woman, with her round belly, I will draw fertility to me. If I paint this stag with his antlers leaping over the rock, I will have a good day of hunting. Cavendish writes:

> *Animals were painted in sanctuaries deep inside caves to give man control of the species. Pictures of animals wounded by weapons were probably meant to help the hunters wound and kill them in real life, and would have helped them on the most practical level by giving them confidence. Or some of the "wounds" and "weapons" may have been sexual symbols intended to promote the fertility of the species and so secure an adequate supply of game. Delineation in pictures is part of the magical technique of mimicry, which works on the principle that if something is imitated with sufficient concentration and vividness it comes into being in reality.*

Here it is again: the ancient link among wishing, Venus, and venison. Certainly it's been sobering to realize that wishing may give rise to a chain of unintended and potentially very negative consequences. Yet I also find it strangely comforting to remember that, at its root, "to wish" is anything but frivolous. Sexual love, fertility, hunting: these are life-and-death matters. *Life and death,* I repeat to myself, gathering the tiny green bills that my sneezes have driven deep into the cracks of the picnic table.

When the moment for my teleclass arrives, I am sitting on a stool beside the telephone in my kitchen. I have my newly purchased copy of the book *Calling In 'The One'* beside me, and I am tingling with readiness. When I signed up for the class several weeks ago, we agreed that the time would be from five to six-thirty and that Katherine Woodward Thomas would initiate the call to me and the other presumably far-flung and lovelorn participants. Five minutes go by, ten, fifteen . . . and the phone doesn't ring. Half an hour goes by, and as I sit here alone with my feet dangling above the brown, pockmarked linoleum floor, the silence around me is growing louder. What does it mean when your call doesn't come for Calling In 'The One'? Half an hour goes by, and though I'm in the privacy of my own kitchen, I feel somehow foolish and exposed, like a jilted bride. If I hadn't been reading so recently about the dangers of "blowback" from negative wishing, I'd be tempted to plant a fork or blacken a tooth in Ms. Thomas's radiantly confident author's photo. I settle for leaving a crabby message on her answering machine and then decide to go for an evening walk to calm my mind.

Rather than heading down to the pond, I choose the steep curving road that leads from my door to the top of a very high hill. Our neighborhood gaggle of wild turkeys is out and about, and a family of deer is feeding under the live oak trees. The sky is going from pink to red, a sliver of moon is already visible, and halfway up the hill I see a man in spandex just ahead of me, huffing beside his bike. His buns are buff, his hair is salt-and-pepper gray. Could it be that the call didn't come because he is the One and I was supposed to cross paths with him at precisely this time? He tosses an empty water bottle to the side of the road, and there's my answer. Spice thieves and litterbugs need not apply.

When I return to my house, my answering machine is blinking. The first message is from Katherine Woodward Thomas, with whom I've hitherto had one brief phone conversation. "Oh, sweetheart," she gushes, "I'm so, so sorry. Didn't you get the e-mail I sent out yesterday? It told you to call another number. I'm afraid I won't be having another free teleclass for quite some time, but I could give you a discount rate of $219 on my nine-session class that's starting up. Let me know, and meanwhile much love to you, sweetie . . ."

Delete.

The second message is from my mother in Italy, telling me that though it's 3 A.M. her time, she has a wonderful piece of news for me. I call her back, and when she answers the phone she can barely contain her excitement. From the midst of a deep sleep, she suddenly woke remembering that before she first moved to Europe, she had put aside a stash of money in a savings account in case she ever needed to buy a car. That was nearly two decades ago, and the compound interest has surely grown. Since she no longer plans to buy a car, she'd like to give the nest egg to me.

My mother is a woman of modest means who has always lived frugally. As she's been retired for some twenty years now, I never imagined that there could be a hidden stash of money. Though it's not yet the 10 percent I need to appease the mortgage lady, it gets me more than halfway there. Once again—as when I came home from Vichy Springs and found the letter from my landlords—I feel as though I'm cheating somehow. As though it's not supposed to be this easy. Is this how it feels when wishes come true?

Wednesday night is "Garbage Eve" on my street, and as I roll the garbage can to the curb, I'm in a kind of daze of amazement. The moon is shining brightly now, glinting off the trees' leaves and making the metal garbage can look almost magical in its sheen, like an amphora in one of Aladdin's tales. Then suddenly there's a jolt of anxiety. Is it possible that somehow my wish wires got crossed, so that my intention to Call In the One is yielding not the man but the moolah? That old sense of measure, proportion, kicks in. It's just not possible to have so much good fortune at one time: a check on its way to my mailbox and a man on his way to my door.

Or is it?

Ever since Nicholas called, my hopes have been rising and falling. My mind spins its web of fantasies: What if he really does turn out to be the flesh-and-blood manifestation of my paper wish? But then I remind myself: "Noelle, you don't know anything about him! He could be twenty-five. He could be eighty-five. He could be married with six children. He could be extremely short, fat, and bald."

· · ·

Three days after my thwarted teleclass, the moment arrives.

The doorbell rings.

My heart is beating hard, and by now I've parted, unparted, and reparted my hair a thousand times. "Short, fat, and bald," I'm repeating to myself, like a kind of spell to ward off disappointment.

Then I open the door.

*Short, fat, and bald. Short, fat, and bald—*

He isn't short, fat, and bald. I seize up for a moment; it's as though I was braced for a cold shower and then discovered it to be deliciously warm.

He's lovely! He looks just about my age, and he's tall and slender, with intensely blue eyes and thick light-brown silvery hair.

We sit down at my dining room table and talk about the book he wants to write, about the inner wisdom of children. It's an inspiring idea, somewhat like Plato's idea that we come into this world with a full reservoir of knowledge within us, and that the task of the parent or teacher is to draw it out. But, I confess, it's hard to concentrate. Mostly what I'm aware of is that this lovely man has come to my door, and that he's been drawn to me through my writing. Somehow, by the end of the session, I've gleaned that he has one child—a son about the same age as my daughter—and that he's single. Before he leaves, he blurts out, "I like you! Could we be friends?" Though he's writing about the wizened sage that lives within us all, there is something open and childlike about him that I find utterly touching. I take his hand for one long moment as he goes out my door, and then I watch him drive away in a very battered red car that is covered with what appear to be inflammatory political bumper stickers.

# CHAPTER SEVEN

# July

## *Grace: Seeking Divine Favor*

July is hot in the wine country. The iridescent green of spring is long since gone. The hills are a goldish brown, and in the vineyards the grapes seem to be hiding their juice under a thick coating of dust.

Almost every afternoon, I walk down to the pond at the end of the road. When we moved into this house, we didn't know that the neighborhood came with a pond. The first time I discovered it, walking down the road with my daughter, it felt like a dream, as though we'd opened a door or stepped through a wardrobe and found a secret world-within-a-world.

Though I've now spent seven summers swimming in the pond, the surprise has never quite worn off. Every time I round the last bend and see it sparkling there, with its rim of bulrushes and its rope-swing tree, it seems a little miracle to me. Quite a few of my friends turn their noses up at the pond. They think it's too murky to swim in. And the truth is, I'm often the only adult in the pond, paddling around with a swarm of the neighbors' children and a variety of dogs.

But the man who came to my door loves the pond. The weekend after his first visit, he drove up to see me again and I took him down to see the pond. Within moments he had taken off his shoes, rolled up his jeans, and waded in. I felt as gratified as though I'd actually remembered to put "pond swimming a must" on my paper wish! There's only been time to go twice since then, but amazingly enough, it seems that the miracle of my wish-come-true has already yielded the start of a routine. We wade out to the little island that's right in the middle of the pond, ringed with stones. We lie there, soaking up the sun and reading various books that we've brought along in our knapsacks. I usually just bring one, but at any given time, Nicholas is reading the most eclectic combination of books I've ever seen: *The Portable Nietzsche, Theater Games for the Classroom, The Feminine Face of God, Backpacking in Chiapas,* and *How to Get Control of Your Time and Your Life.* He loves to read aloud to me, moving from one book to another. I've never met anyone whose thoughts can fly so quickly from one zone of the universe to another and back again. I find it amusing, inspiring, and endearing—but after a while the vast jumble of both form and content makes me feel that I'm on the brink of going insane. That's when it's time for us to slide into the water and splash around or climb onto one of the wooden rafts and float, sometimes accompanied by somebody's very wet dog.

It pleases me that Nicholas is so delighted with it. Not only because it's something we can share but because—as I grasped soon after meeting him—he has chosen a hard life for himself. For years he's worked with a rough population of students, ranging from emotionally disturbed and outright delinquent youth to men court-mandated for anger management classes. More than once he's been physically attacked in the classroom, leaving him with two painful shoulder injuries that flare up periodically. Currently he teaches in Oakland, in the inner city. It's a year-round school, so he'll only get a few days off at the end of the summer. Though his passion is early-childhood education and he longs to teach a kindergarten class, he hasn't yet found a position. So he's teaching a junior high school class, and in the summer—when all the other kids are out wandering the streets—it's harder than ever to keep the students still and focused in their seats.

Nicholas's father was in international finance, and so—between regular stints in the USA—Nicholas grew up in Jakarta, Cairo, and Barcelona. Sometimes I try to picture him, this blue-eyed, cosmopolitan man, surrounded by his mostly African-American students, many of whom have rarely left Oakland.

The third time he came to see me, Nicholas brought a stash of family photographs. I was amazed at what I saw: such proud and somehow golden-looking people. Even generations back, they don't have that awkward, uneasy look that haunts so many old photographs. Nicholas's family goes back to the *Mayflower* on his mother's side, and on his father's side he's descended from a long line of slaveholders. His family still owns the property in North Carolina where the plantation once stood. Apparently what remains now is a scattering of smaller outbuildings, in disrepair. Once, when Nicholas was visiting there, he came across a list of slaves owned and slaves sold at auction. When he returned to California, he posted the names on a website that was created to help Americans of African descent trace their roots.

Not long afterward, he received some disturbing information from different parts of the country. It seems that one of his forefathers was such a cruel man that the memory of his cruelty had been passed on for generations. "My great-grandfather used to tell me how he was forced to hold a hot coal in his mouth as a child of five, simply because he had taken a peach from the master's orchard," one elderly man wrote from a nursing home. "His tongue was badly burned and his distorted speech was mocked for the rest of his life." And a woman wrote that she had grown up being told how her great-great-great-grandfather had been forced to watch while the master performed "unspeakably nasty deeds" with her great-great-great-grandmother. "You and I are probably cousins," she wrote, "but alas it's a kinship born of shame and sorrow." On some very deep level that I've never even heard him speak about, Nicholas seems to feel that he owes a giant debt.

Among Nicholas's odd jumble of books is *Religion and the Rise of Capitalism* by the British economist R. H. Tawney. Though it's not exactly my idea of summer reading, I find myself irresistibly drawn to it one afternoon as I lie beside Nicholas on our small sandy island. Leafing through it, I quickly discover the reason why. After only a few pages, it's as though I'm being handed a missing link, a vital clue for my experiment in desire. *Shift the paradigm,* Carole said, as though to go from spiritual poverty to divine prosperity was as easy as shifting gears. Tawney's book is really all about the shifting paradigm, about the move from "blessed are the poor" to "favored are the elect."

John Calvin taught that human beings are inherently sinful. It is through God's grace alone that certain people—"the elect"—are chosen, predestined, for salvation. And though no human effort can induce God's grace, this is no excuse for human idleness. Far from it. Those who are elect have the responsibility of living in a godly way. Their conduct is subject to a very rigorous discipline, one that extends to every facet of their lives: spiritual, moral, practical—and, yes, financial.

Here's where that dazzling shift in the paradigm comes.

Though Calvin himself was fairly austere, his successors were ingenious about bridging the ancient gap between God and Caesar, soul and money, the rich man and the gates of heaven. They were the first to relax the ancient laws of usury, the making of money with money. But at an even more radical level, early Calvinism, Tawney writes, "no longer suspects the whole world of economic motives as alien to the life of the spirit . . . and it is perhaps the first systematic body of religious teaching which can be said to recognize and applaud the economic virtues."

*To recognize and applaud the economic virtues:* isn't this a world away from Jesus warning that it is easier for a camel to pass through the eye of a needle than for a rich man to enter the gates of heaven? I'm starting to realize that when I find myself struggling with such conflicting ideals as *spiritual poverty* versus *building wealth,* I'm actually reenacting a struggle between the medieval Church and its Protestant reformers.

As I delve deeper, I'm reminded of what a strange combination of pride and humility lies at the Calvinist root of the American soul. For as fate would have it, the new "economic virtues" were the very ones most likely to promote financial success: thrift, sobriety, moderation, horror of idleness. And so it was that as white Anglo-Saxon Protestants flourished in the New World, they were inclined to see their own worldly prosperity as a sign of their chosenness, a gift of God's grace. That they worked hard to live in a way that befit the grace of their "election" tended to make them feel all the more entitled to its tangible rewards: money, houses, land. And for some of them, slaves.

But what a radical shift of the paradigm this is, indeed.

And how far from earlier understandings of grace!

*Grace.*

To me it is one of the loveliest words in English. With its one syllable, *grace* has always seemed onomatopoetic to me, as light and quick on the tongue as a flutter of bird wings. And that's how grace is often described, as a fleeting experience—like a breeze, a visit, a dove flying in and then out of the room. An ephemeral experience, light as a feather, that is simultaneously heavy, overflowing with meaning and value.

It was Saint Paul who first used the Greek work *charis* (the root of *charisma*) to refer to the divine favor of God, present in the body of Jesus Christ. This presence offers itself through gifts of the spirit: peace, hope, forgiveness, generosity. . . . Through its long and convoluted history, grace has retained a connotation of *presence,* of divine power made manifest: whether in events, actions, objects, or experiences. Yet—perhaps because it is one of the most elusive concepts in the history of religious thought—it has often been at the center of dogmatic and utterly graceless battles. And in my own life, the mystery of grace has at times become its own kind of struggle.

• • •

From the time I was quite young, perhaps eight or nine, I felt susceptible to a certain kind of joy that seemed to come from nowhere. It was very quiet, not earthshaking, but when it happened, it utterly altered the atmosphere. One of the first times I experienced it was in a tiny village in Brittany where my family was visiting. The village was in the region of Finistère ("Land's End"), once believed to be the very edge of the flat earth. On the foggy afternoon that we arrived and went to stand on the beach, I felt permeated by a powerful and ancient fear. I knew that this was the place where the devil was said to have leapt off the earth and into the endless sea, a place that for centuries had represented the human terror of being nowhere, of facing the unknown. That night I fell fitfully asleep in the little farmhouse hotel where we had rented a room. In the morning, just at dawn, a rooster crowed. Hearing the sound, I experienced that everything around me—my parents sleeping in their bed, the glass of water on the windowsill, the green grass outside in the pink light of sunrise, the waves crashing beyond—was in the right place, at the right time.

After that, there were other moments. And along with the moment when the rooster crowed, I saved them one by one, like jewels in a box. Mysteriously, over the years, they began to exert a powerful pressure on me. Though they had been moments of a deep and peaceful joy, they began collectively to make me suffer. They were so rare and came so unbidden—like windfall, or shooting stars. I didn't know how to make them come, to make them last, to link them together.

By the time I was a teenager, I felt they wanted something of me—but I didn't know what. I felt they held the key to the meaning of life, yet they just lay there, shining in their box. As Philip Lopate writes in his essay "Against Joie de Vivre": "To know rapture is to have one's whole life poisoned. If you will forgive a ridiculous analogy, a tincture of rapture is like a red bandana in the laundry that runs and turns all the white wash pink. We should just as soon stay away from any future ecstatic experiences which spoil everyday living by comparison."

I wouldn't have described my own experiences as "rapture" or "ecstasy." They were quieter than that, less flamboyant. But they seemed to be revealing something absolutely true about the very bedrock level of existence—and that is why I couldn't stay away from them. That is why, in their very sweetness, they did indeed begin to poison the rest of my life. And early in my first year of college, the tension became unbearable.

One day I leapt onto my bicycle and rode, as fast as I could, through the campus and its surrounding fields to the rectory. I pounded on the door for a long time, until at last a scowling woman came and opened it a crack. "I need to see a priest," I told her. "The rectory is closed today," she said, and shut the door in my face. I rode home through the cornfields feeling so desperate that, if there'd been a cliff anywhere in that flat part of Ohio, I might have thrown myself over it.

Through some extremely fortunate fluke—or gift?—of timing, about a week later I saw that a young monk from Thailand was coming to the college to offer a class in meditation.

His instructions were very simple: cross your legs, keep your back gently straight, focus on your breath as it leaves the nostrils. At the end of the first session—which lasted only twenty minutes—I knew that I had found what I'd been looking for, with increasing desperation, for so long.

On my way back to the dorm, I walked through the student center, where a group of young men were playing a game of pool. A bright wooden ball came flying off the green table, across the room—and into my hand. I just opened my palm, as I was walking by, and the ball flew into my hand.

YES! Following my breath, I had found my way to where the rooster crowed, and everywhere I went was the right place at the right time. I climbed the stairs to my room under the eaves, and when I walked in the door the first thing I saw was a tiny art-gum eraser sitting in a pool of light. It was absolutely luminous.

Years later I came across this story of the Buddha's early life.

When Prince Siddhartha was still a boy, a plowing festival took place in the countryside. It was a scene of great gaiety, with music, dancing, and teams of oxen yoked to brightly painted plows. While his nurses and companions got caught up in the festivity, the young prince sat for two hours, unmoving, under the shade of a rose-apple tree. Alone, with the breeze blowing through the leaves of the tree, he had an intense experience of the sweetness of life, a sweetness that filled him so completely, he had no need for any external diversion, no need for anything but to be present.

When I was first getting to know Eliot, he told me about a morning when, upon waking, he heard the birds singing and realized: "I'm not responsible for making the birds sing!" Like young Prince Siddhartha under the rose-apple tree, when Eliot heard the birds he had an experience of the intrinsic perfection of life, its wholeness, givenness, already-there-ness, apart from any act of human will or effort. An experience so fulfilling that—even in its fleeting, ephemeral quality—it dissolves the ache of need, of wanting, and thus blesses us with the knowledge of eternity.

It's just such experiences that I would define as grace. And they have absolutely nothing to do with practical usefulness—indeed, their sweetness, the joy they impart, is inseparable from the way that they obliterate all sense of need, all ache of desire for things to be anything other than what they are.

Even as I grasp the historical links, at some level I will always remain astonished that grace could ever have been associated with material favor. It seems to me to belong to a different dimension of reality entirely.

Like the money my mother gave me for the house. Without question, it has been a welcome windfall, an entirely unexpected gift. And it has certainly shown me something about the power of wishing. For if I hadn't dared to wish for a house and begun to take concrete actions to bring about that wish, I doubt that my mother would have ever remembered the little nest egg she'd stashed away.

Though some people would dismiss my mother's gift as just "a lucky break," a random fluke, others would seize upon it as a prime example of divine participation in our earthly affairs. Whether the latter ascribed it to God or the Universe or Source, they would see my mother's stash of cash as having come to me through the participation of some form of more-than-human power. They would see it as a concrete manifestation of divine favor.

As for me, I feel truly agnostic on this point. Even as I marvel at the timing of my mother's gift, I'm also aware that it came to me through a host of very nitty-gritty factors. Factors that are a world away from the rose-apple tree or the rooster's crow, and that require a completely different kind of language to describe them—a prosaic, social science kind of language.

For instance: I've read a bit about the history of home owner-ship in the United States, and I've learned that after World War II there was a great push to make housing more affordable. Home ownership became the basis for passing on wealth, from one gen-eration to the next, within the middle class. But these advantages were primarily preserved for the white middle class; for people of color it was vastly more difficult to obtain a mortgage. As Tawney writes, "Few tricks of the unsophisticated intellect are more curi-ous than the naïve psychology" of the person who celebrates his own success "in bland unconsciousness of a social order without whose continuous support and vigilant protection he would be as a lamb bleating in the desert."

My mother's means are modest, and she has practiced the virtues of hard work, thrift, and generosity. But she—like every member of the white middle class in this country—has also benefited from a system that is shot through with dreadful inequities, a system that leaves so many lambs bleating in the desert. And that's why it's very hard for me to see my mother's gift as being of the same order as divine grace. Though I do indeed feel blessed by it, it seems a world away from my jewel moments.

And Nicholas?

He's chosen to live among the bleating lambs.

Or more precisely: he lives in a rooming house, about forty-five minutes south of where I live. I drove down there last week. It's an elegant rooming house—spacious, with hardwood floors, paneled walls, and a beautiful view of hills and trees and the town below. But it's a rooming house. There were heavy pieces of furniture somewhat arbitrarily strewn about that seemed as though they might have been abandoned by an array of former tenants. In the kitchen there were notes taped to various surfaces and appliances: "Do NOT run the dishwasher after 10 p.m." "Remember to sponge the counters: ANTS!!!!" And when Nicholas showed me his room, what struck me was that in its cluttered, fanciful, and above all *provisional* quality, it seemed like the room of a very young man. An Indian bedspread hung from the ceiling, posters were tacked to the walls, and piles of books and papers were strewn across the narrow bed. It wasn't a room I felt like lingering in. It confused me, made me feel like a college girl visiting my steady guy in his dorm. Coming down the stairs, whom should I run into but a student of mine! Bert. A young man in his twenties. He was as startled to see me as I was to see him.

"Professor Oxenhandler?"

"Bert? What are you doing here?"

"I live here."

"Oh."

"That settles it," I thought. I won't be visiting my new fifty-one-year-old boyfriend in his dorm again.

We'll lie on the island, in the middle of the pond at the end of my road, the breeze rustling through the leaves, the dogs paddling in the water around us, his books piled high on the sand: *Indigenous Peoples and the Struggle for Restitution, The Sufi Guide to Ecstatic Dancing, Plumbing for Dummies, The Portable Plato.* I might not be able to talk to Nicholas about my frantic drive to purchase a piece of real estate. But I can talk to him about anything else under the sky. I can talk to him about my jewel moments.

. . .

Sadly, since the upheaval of my community, I haven't experienced a single one. And it's strange. Here I am, in the seventh month of my experiment in desire. Already, the folded-up paper wish beneath my bed has done its part and brought a lover to my door. And so long as my money shrine continues to exert its magic and bring me the last chunk of the down payment, it looks as though the house will one day be mine. Yet the wish about which I had the least doubt—the wish for spiritual healing—is the one that still eludes me.

In my heart of hearts, I know that the treasure house from which the jewel moments come is never far away. But I feel like the character in one of Iris Murdoch's novels who says, "I know God exists, but I don't believe in Him." I know that a state of pure, undiluted happiness exists, but I'm not in touch with it. And the worst part of it is, the not being in touch is just a kind of dull, background ache. It doesn't intensify into the fever of longing that once propelled me to leap onto my bike, drive through the cornfields, pound on the rectory door . . . and find my way to the monk from Thailand.

*Knock and the door shall be opened.*

I've always believed that to be true, in the spiritual realm.

But what happens when you can't seem to muster up more than a tap?

• • •

"Here's a quote for you," Nicholas says. We're still on the island, and with my face pressed against the warm sand, I have no idea what corner of the universe he's browsing in—whether he's been consorting with the aborigines of Australia or learning about the virtues of copper pipe. But it turns out he's been leafing through a history of modern mysticism, and now he reads aloud these words from Simone Weil (the same French philosopher who observed that most of life takes place far from hot baths): "The danger is not lest the soul should doubt whether there is any bread, but lest, by a lie, it should persuade itself that it is not hungry."

I've come across this quote before, but it's different hearing it now, when I'm actually in the danger zone.

*By a lie,* she says.

Could it be that these are the words I need to unlock the sealed-up, double-bolted door? I've been taking the absence of intense longing at face value, as though—through the excruciating experience of my community's upheaval—my soul had irrevocably altered, atrophied. And for the first time I realize how literally I've thought of *having a soul,* as though it were a physical organ that had become diseased. I've thought of it as a kind of liver that got so overwhelmed by toxic substances that it could no longer cleanse itself. Scarred, misshapen, it just sort of hunkered down, in a small corner inside me, producing that dull ache.

If a Zen master bellowed at me, "Bring me your sick soul!" I couldn't do it. It doesn't exist. I know that. But I don't know it deeply enough—yet.

• • •

The next morning I wake up, as I do every morning, looking straight into the emptiness of my birdcage shrine, with its pathetic sprinkling of faux crumbs. But this time it's as though someone had left a message for me inside the emptiness. The message reads: *You must look for God exactly there where you lost him.*

That's a line from the German mystic Meister Eckhart. I first came upon it long ago, and I haven't thought of it in years. Through what mysterious alchemy of dreams has it returned to me now? I wonder. Or is this one of the ways that wishing works, by reawakening memories, retrieving messages from our own inner storehouse?

But even more important at this juncture: How would I put Eckhart's counsel into practice?

It's hard for me to go into a Zen space. The incense, the tatami mats, the dark round meditation cushions, the chants . . . everything brings up such painful memories—and *memories* doesn't even seem like the right word. It's a cellular kind of recoil I feel, as if I'd grown allergic to the very atmosphere where once I used to feel so deeply calmed and held, as if a safe and peaceful cove had turned into a churning open sea.

If I don't feel able to return *exactly there,* then where might I go to get close enough?

Maybe Spirit Rock. It's a beautiful Buddhist meditation center about an hour away from where I live, and I've been there on a few occasions. Because it's not Zen, I don't have quite the same knee-jerk reactions—and I do feel a genuine connection there. Jack Kornfield is Spirit Rock's director, and just before my own community came apart, I wrote a letter to him, asking for guidance. Though he didn't really know me very well, he responded swiftly and compassionately. Since then, we don't see each other often, but we've stayed in touch.

And so—as though pulling the leash of a still very recalcitrant camel, the kind of camel whose legs keep buckling back down into the sand—I make myself look at the calendar from Spirit Rock that arrived in my mailbox the other day, along with a sheaf of bills and my weekly coupon from Bed Bath & Beyond. There's an event coming up with a monk named Ajahn Jumnian. He's the abbot of a forest monastery in Thailand, and he comes to visit once a year. When I went down to hear him once before, I thought he was the most radiant man I'd ever seen. This time, I note, Jack will be translating for him. It seems like a good conjunction of circumstances—but it's not happening until October.

•  •  •

Then one afternoon in late July, after picking up a few summery items at the drugstore—deet, citronella candles, flip-flops—I decide on impulse to go into the little beauty salon next door and have my nails done. I've had precisely one manicure in my life—at a little Korean hole-in-the-wall in Manhattan, where a stony-faced woman hacked at my cuticles and gave me a nail fungus that hung on for months. I haven't tried again since then, but something draws me into this place—maybe it's the gold bodhisattva in the window, wreathed with a garland of paper flowers and holding a little hand-drawn sign that reads, "Come in! Everything for you very lovely. Nails, eyebrows, and more!"

Once over the threshold, I feel as though I've entered another world. Three men in business suits are leaning against the front counter and talking, with great animation, in what I imagine is Vietnamese or Laotian. One of them smiles and nods at me and motions me to go back to where three dark-haired women are chattering softly among themselves, waiting for customers. One of them gestures to me to sit down in the chair near her. She seems to be middle-aged but has a girlish face, and the name on her pink smock is Patty.

"Is your name really Patty?"

"No. In Vietnam my name Phuong," she says and laughs. "But too hard for American people."

She has me choose the color of nail polish I want, and then she takes my hands in hers and dips them into a bowl of warm water. I see that the tops of both of her hands have been badly burned.

Though the skin has healed over, it's dark and raised up like a little cushion on each hand.

She sees me see them and says, "Very ugly. My hands are very ugly."

"The war?" I ask.

She doesn't reply.

As she gently, gently trims my cuticles and files my nails into smooth ovals, I ask her a few questions about herself. She tells me that she has to work every day, seven days a week, because her husband is old. He's an American, eighty years old, and when she tells me that she came from Vietnam seven years ago to marry him, I get the feeling that maybe she was a mail-order bride.

Looking into the big mirror before me, I see that hanging on the wall next to her framed cosmetology certificate is a postcard of a temple.

"What is that temple?"

"City of Ten Thousand Buddhas."

At the sound of those words, it's as though twenty-five years compress to an instant, and I am back on a Greyhound bus, traveling south from the northernmost boundary of California.

It was just after Pol Pot's regime had fallen, and the bus was filled with Cambodian refugees. For the many hours that we were on the bus, they were silent. And when, at one point, we all filed off the bus for a rest stop, I found myself looking into faces whose eyes held a look I had never seen before. It's very hard to describe such a look, except to say that it must be what consciousness looks like when it has been forced beyond the limits of what it can bear. From sheer habit of terror it remains silently vigilant, but with every particle it seems to scream: *Let me be something without nerves or eyes or beating heart, something hard and impenetrable as rock.* Is it any wonder that, among the survivors of the Killing Fields, there were so many cases of hysterical blindness, of eyes that—in the absence of any physical disease or injury—simply stopped seeing?

Among the stonelike faces, there was only one whose eyes managed to meet mine. It was the face of a young woman, her long dark hair tied back with a ragged piece of string, and she spoke a few words of English. When I asked her where they were going, she told me, "City of Ten Thousand Buddhas." I gave her the little crystal-drop necklace I was wearing and a card with my name, address, and phone number, but years went by, and I never heard from her. Since then, though, I've been vaguely aware that the City of Ten Thousand Buddhas is not far from the wine country, but I've never known quite where, and the name has not come up.

Now Patty takes down the postcard to show me, and when I look on the back I see that it's in Talmadge, a tiny town near Ukiah—very close to Vichy Springs. "Most of life takes place far from hot baths," the philosopher said. Yes, but sometimes life surprises us with its juxtapositions, its overlaps and strange proximities.

• • •

Two days later I drive through an imposing archway and enter the City of Ten Thousand Buddhas. It's a strange setting. Nestled up against a line of beautiful hills in the background, its numerous buildings are a jumble of architectural styles, from 1940s functional to faux Tudor. It's clear that the grounds are lovingly tended: there are rows of mature trees, flowering shrubs, and a reflecting pool, around which white peacocks are gathered. But the property is a former state mental hospital, and—despite the fact that, in bright painted letters, the buildings bear names like Instilling Goodness and Developing Virtue—there is some heavy institutional gloom that lingers.

A friendly man greets me in the front office where I sign in. "So are there really Ten Thousand Buddhas here?" I ask.

"Oh yes!" he says. "Even more. You must see our Jeweled Hall of Ten Thousand Buddhas," and he points northward out the window. As I thank him and turn to leave, he says, "You know, in

Buddhism 'ten thousand' stands for infinity. If you want to, you can read more about Venerable Master Hua and what Ten Thousand Buddhas means to him." He hands me a booklet called *Propagating the Dharma: The City of Ten Thousand Buddhas,* and I step outside.

Apart from two people with shaved heads and monks' robes sweeping leaves, I don't see any people about. Maybe there's a service going on in the Jeweled Hall of Ten Thousand Buddhas? Following the signs, I make my way to a giant concrete building that looks like a former gymnasium. Passing through the narrow foyer to the great hall itself, I'm surprised to find that it's completely empty—empty of living beings, that is. For like a kind of honeycomb, the walls are lined with thousands of gold Buddhas, each one sealed in its own little alcove behind a giant wall of glass. On a sea of red carpet, hundreds of brocade cushions are lined up in rows. Because I'm so used to the sparseness of Zen, the atmosphere is strange to me, both gaudy and eerie. The rows of Buddhas in their cubbyholes make me think of petrified monks in catacombs, or fetuses floating in glass jars.

But when I sit down on a cushion and open my *Propagating the Dharma* booklet, I'm amazed to learn that in fact Master Hua was a disciple of Hsu Yun, one of the most revered Zen masters in modern history—and a man often quoted by my teachers at the Rochester Zen Center. Without realizing it, I've come to a Zen center! How on earth did a disciple of Hsu Yun, from the faraway Nanhua Monastery in Caoxi, China, ever find his way to a small town near Ukiah, California? In the booklet's account, Master Hua doesn't provide too many details: "'Ten thousand births and deaths and hundreds of difficult ordeals' is a perfect description of my life. I underwent countless hardships to establish the City of Ten Thousand Buddhas. Don't let it be destroyed. When I came to America, I made a great vow: I wanted to be a sculptor who would mold living Buddhas."

Carrying this great wish, when he arrived in California he

wanted to see his wish represented by thousands of Buddhas, sculpted in wood and gilded in real gold. Surrounded by them, I can't help but think of those dreams that I and others had in the wake of our spiritual community's upheaval. Those dreams in which something gold shimmered in the distance, beckoning. But then, as we approached it, the gold turned to plastic, tin, shit. Now here I am in the place where a man took his golden dream and worked tirelessly to make it real. A man who traveled for thousands of miles, who crossed the ocean, enduring innumerable sufferings, to make this shining place of refuge.

And though the gaudiness of the temple is strange to me, the silence is familiar. It's not the silence you would hear in just any giant empty building. It's the silence of a space where hundreds, even thousands, of people have poured themselves out in prayer and meditation, and it is palpable.

*You must look for God exactly there where you lost him.*

Sitting on a cushion in the middle of the red sea, I let the silence expand inside my ears, my chest. Those people I rode with on the bus so many years ago, the young woman to whom I gave my necklace and my phone number: Did they contribute the weight of their suffering to the intensity of this silence? Did something transmute for them, become to some degree lighter and more bearable? Did they find a measure of consolation? My own disillusionment is such a tiny thing alongside theirs, and yet the silence doesn't seem to care. It is simply there for anyone who has ears to hear. It is so huge and so intense. It has the sweetness of a balm and the heat of fire. And though I know that it doesn't need to be tended by anyone—*unborn, undying, uncreated,* we say in Zen—I am grateful to those who have tended it here, and whose presence now, if invisible, reverberates around me.

. . .

On my way out the door, I pass by a table of books for sale. Among them is a booklet with the title *Guan Shi Yin, Bodhisattva Fulfills*

*Every Wish.* Stuffing a few dollars into the glass donation jar, I go out into the sun, onto the steps, to read it.

Guan Shi Yin (sometimes spelled Guanshiyin), who can be either male or female, is the Bodhisattva of Compassion, also known as Kwan Yin or Kanzeon. According to the Venerable Master Hua,

> *Guanshiyin Bodhisattva uses kindness, compassion, joy, and giving to save all living beings. He saves beings from the seven difficulties, responds to two kinds of seeking, has fourteen kinds of fearlessness, speaks Dharma in nineteen ways, and has thirty-two response bodies. If childless people seek sons or daughters, their wishes will be granted. These are the two kinds of seeking. Therefore, in a Guanyin recitation session, any vow can be fulfilled and any result can be obtained, because Guanyin Bodhisattva responds to all requests. You may seek to leave the home-life, to remain a lay-person, or to become a Buddha. Guanshiyin Bodhisattva has great kindness and compassion, and will not disappoint you no matter what you ask for. He'll definitely fulfill your wishes. Therefore, during the Guanyin session, you may seek whatever you like. Whether you seek a son, a daughter, wealth, or long life, you will be able to obtain them.*

I'm amazed that a man who took in refugees from Pol Pot's genocide would write with such confidence of wishes—including earthly wishes—that the Bodhisattva of Compassion will "definitely fulfill." If he were still alive, I'd love to ask him, "What about the people who perished? Did they forget to wish? Did they not know how to wish properly?"

He concludes the passage with these words: "Worldly riches, honor, and glory all come to an end, but non-outflow happiness is endless and infinite. Let's recite Guanshiyin Bodhisattva's name more in order to realize an everlasting fruition."

*Guan-shi-yin,* I repeat to myself as I make my way home. *Guan-shi-yin.*

And though I try to focus on everlasting fruition, there is something else that I find myself compelled to wish for. It's a big dose of outflow happiness—with days off and extra money—for Patty/Phuong with her burned hands and her old husband, Patty/Phuong who sent me to the City of Ten Thousand Buddhas.

Is the bird of my soul flying back to me? I don't know. It seems too soon to tell. But when I glance at my beautifully polished nails, I feel like the prey of some benevolent trickster spirit. Not in a million years could I ever have imagined that from the place where I went for a manicure I would be led to the temple's thundering silence.

# CHAPTER EIGHT

# August

## *Guides: Discovering Their Presence*

It's August, and we're baking. The gold of the hills has gone so dry and brown that in the late afternoons it looks on the verge of spontaneous combustion. Though their light summer clothes—shorts, sandals, and sundresses—give people an air of gaiety, there's a feeling of dread in the air. A dryness like this seems too early in the season. And for a prospective home owner, it's taken on new consequences. I've been told that once I pull together the last chunk of the down payment, the final step will be signing up for house insurance, and I've already made a dozen calls. But each time I have to tell them my zip code, they tell me, "Sorry. The fire danger is too high."

Meanwhile, from Italy, a disturbing letter has come from my mother's partner, Luigi. It seems her blood pressure has been dangerously high, and more than once she's had fainting spells. Once she even had to be taken to the hospital in an ambulance. When we call him on his cell phone, he sounds over the edge with anxiety. He's been told that the fainting spells are little strokes, and though he doesn't say it directly, he seems to feel that we should bring her back to live with us. He still goes to work every day as a judge in a neighboring town, and his own health is rather frail. He is very attached to her, but it frightens him to have the sole responsibility for her care. We don't know what to do. She is so very attached to him, and to her life with him in Italy.

Not long after the letter from Luigi, I get the news that a dear friend of mine named George, a filmmaker who lives in Santa Cruz, is ill. He's been diagnosed with prostate cancer, the disease his father died of.

In my mind, there's an obvious cause-and-effect connection. I'm being punished for wishing. The recent bouts of good fortune have tipped the scales and caught the jealous gods' attention. Now they're responding with a force that is not just equal and opposite but outright punitive. They're sending waves of sorrow to drown out my little sparks of hope.

When I put it like that, of course, I see the irrationality. The way children blame themselves for their parents' misfortune, I'm attributing to myself a far greater power than I actually have. Yet it's amazing how visceral the conviction is that the recent strokes of luck—Nicholas's call, my mother's gift—have caused the other shoe to fall.

The other shoe.

How often do we live our lives cringing in its shadow?

Recently my colleague Greta moved out of the tiny apartment she'd been living in and bought a beautiful and spacious house with the man she loves. For weeks she'd been telling me, "I feel so anxious. I keep waiting for the other shoe to fall. I think it's the midwestern part of me. If you dare to want too much, it makes you stand out—and then something's going to happen to tamp it down." Then Greta's car was stolen, and she felt an immense relief. She'd paid her dues, provided collateral, and thus appeased the monster of misfortune—for a while at least.

If she lived in another time and place, she might not have had to wait for the other shoe to fall. She might have staved it off in the ancient human way of assuring one's good fortune didn't tip the scales: through sacrifice.

This is the other, primal meaning of Putting It Out There. The most ancient altars are just a slab of stone under the sky. On that slab, you place an offering: a chunk of meat, a bowl of oil, a living creature. In this way, you try to assure a certain balance in the universe, and thus keep the other shoe from falling. If there's something you want—to have rain for your crops, to be safe from your enemies—you have to pay for it. And you're better off paying for it before, in a ritualized way that you yourself can perform. Rather than cringing in perpetual fear of the gods' retribution, you offer the first fruits of the season, the heart of the stag, or even the beautiful child.

What I see in myself and so many people I know is that we still operate with certain primal assumptions in place, yet without fully acknowledging them—and this gives them even more power. We live as though we were indeed under the constant gaze of jealous gods, yet without the means to appease them, to satisfy their blood lust and calm them with hymns of praise and thanksgiving. It's the worst of both worlds, really.

But perhaps it accounts for why some people don't feel free to fully pursue their wishes until they've endured a terrible bout of suffering: a catastrophic illness or accident, a natural disaster, or the death of someone they loved. Years ago I met an American woman who seemed to be living an idyllic existence in France. She played the flute, her husband played the violin, and she told me that for years they had dreamed of leaving Manhattan, moving to one of the beautiful *villages perchés,* those villages perched high on a hill in southern France, and making music together. It wasn't until their teenage son died suddenly from a seizure that they finally gave themselves permission. Hearing her story, I wondered how many people who seem to be leading their dream lives are actually recovering from a devastating blow of misfortune.

Lacking rituals of expatiation, we rely on illness and other forms of catastrophe to earn the fulfillment of our wishes. Not everyone, of course. Look at Carole, with her made-to-order husband, her four houses, and her life devoted to painting and traveling. If she's making up for some giant sorrow, she's never told me about it. I've known her for a long time now, and I still don't really understand how she pulls it off. She just seems to assume her right to earthly happiness. But maybe the real question is, Why aren't more of us like Carole? For so many of us behave as though it's only when the worst has already happened and the biggest possible Shoe has already dropped that we can scuttle out from the narrow ledges we've been hiding under and dare to stake a claim. Only when we've paid our debt to the god of tragedy do we feel fully entitled to comedy's happy ending.

Isn't this the theme of those organizations that grant the wishes of people facing various forms of disaster? Through suffering we become uniquely deserving of life's earthly rewards. Desires that might otherwise be seen as silly, frivolous, inflated, greedy, or extravagant—to ride with Madonna in a stretch limousine or throw a pitch for the Red Sox—become purified of any negative connotation. This is especially true if the suffering person is a child, and in recent years a network of organizations has sprung up to grant the wishes of children facing such tragic circumstances as life-threatening illness.

When fate has denied a giant wish—like the wish to be healthy, the wish to stay alive—then lesser wishes gain a new weight and authority. In brochures for organizations like Make-A-Wish, the list of wishes fulfilled is presented in boldface like a sacred litany, a recitation of miracles: **Tanika got a belated birthday party at the Oakland Zoo; Julio got a shopping spree at the local mall; Chinasa got a complete makeover at Macy's.**

In a very different context: even the condemned man gets to have his wish for a last meal fulfilled. And no matter how modest or predictable the menu, it always has an oracular ring to it, as if it, too, should appear in boldface: **chicken-fried steak, a twice-baked potato, and key lime pie.**

To the one granting wishes in the face of tragedy, on the edge between life and death, a special power also accrues. As it says in the Make-A-Wish brochure: "We can't promise Make-A-Wish kids that they'll get better, but we can make a child feel, for a brief time, like the most important person on earth!" What the brochure *doesn't* say is that, in doing so, we get to feel at least somewhat important ourselves. But doubtless the wish granters are having a very innocent wish of their own fulfilled: the wish to feel less helpless in the face of catastrophe.

I've been thinking about these things because something mysterious has been happening, something I hadn't consciously felt ready for. For though my experiment in desire is still very much in process, it seems already to be expanding, pushing outward to include others. And while I always knew that eventually I wanted to move beyond the petri dish of my own life, I didn't imagine that it would happen so soon, so spontaneously—and while two of my own wishes were not yet fully realized.

Just last week I got a rather desperate call from one of my students, asking if I could possibly come down to the university and meet her in my office. Liz is a returning student, a woman in her sixties, and though I've never once heard her give way to self-pity, her life story has been one tragedy after another. For several years now she's been working with me on a memoir about her eldest son's death from cancer. Her middle child is a daughter, but she and Liz have a difficult relationship, one that has recently been exacerbated by Liz's anxieties over her daughter's teenage child. A few years before Liz's eldest son died, her younger son received a massive head injury in a car accident. He can't speak, he has great difficulty walking, and he has lived with Liz ever since. Last Thanksgiving, in the middle of the night, a serious fire in their apartment building consumed almost all their possessions.

On this early-August afternoon, Liz was seated in the chair across from me and we were trying to reconstruct some crucial chapters from her memoir that had been lost in the fire. Suddenly I found myself saying, "Liz, forgive me. This is going to sound like a complete non sequitur. But I just have to ask you: If you could wish for one thing, what would it be?"

Liz had been chattering away, but now her voice grew quiet and grave. "I would wish to be reconciled with my daughter," she said.

Then the fire alarm sounded and Liz gave me a look of panic. "Don't worry," I told her. Though I knew it was a drill that had been scheduled months ahead of time, in Liz's presence I felt slightly unhinged by it. We stepped out into the hall and there was Kent, her brain-damaged son, sitting on a chair outside my door. Liz and I each took one of his arms, and with his braces clunking we made our way down the stairwell. Somehow I couldn't shake the superstitious feeling that Liz, like a magnet for emergencies, had triggered the piercing wail of the alarm.

When I got home that night I went to the same bullet-ridden window where I'd wished that Nicholas would be the one. Pressing my face against the glass, I just stood there for a while, thinking about Liz and wondering how it is she finds the strength to go on, and with so little apparent bitterness. Then I followed Paul Pearsall's sequence of steps. I looked out at the bulbs that I had planted in the spring. The irises had long ago drooped and turned brown, but the tiger lilies were in full orange bloom, and the pink, red, and yellow gladioli were flamboyant as showgirls. With my hand on my heart, I repeated these eight syllables: "May Liz and her girl make their peace."

. . .

Meanwhile, how I'd love to be able to swoop into Nicholas's life and grant him a wish or two. In secret I've wished that the perfect job may come for him soon: the kindergarten class he's been longing for, in a well-run and well-funded school. Though he rarely complains, the current situation seems intolerable to me. It's hard enough to teach inner-city teens in the summer's heat, but to make matters worse, the principal seems to be running some kind of scam, gathering money from the state but withholding salaries from his staff. For weeks now I've been convinced that Nicholas should quit, but I only told him so once, in a sort of subtle way. Though he didn't resist, I felt I shouldn't press too hard. I know he feels responsible to his students, and after an extended period as a substitute teacher, he's relieved to have something steady—even if the money hasn't been coming in.

The other day I had an impulse to pull my folded-up paper wish from under my bed. Reading it over, I saw that Nicholas fulfills absolutely everything that I wished for on the list: he is indeed very intelligent, spiritually oriented, outgoing, and handsome. He's had one long marriage, and he's a devoted father to his son. He does love teaching, if not his current job. And he likes hiking, travel, and foreign films. He doesn't speak French, it's true—but he did spend his adolescence in Barcelona, zooming around on a motor scooter among its towers and archways and gardens and cafés. He went to an American school and didn't learn either Spanish or Catalan, but I know he keeps their Romance music in his heart, and that's good enough for me.

The one thing I forgot to wish for was: a man who is solvent.

Though Nicholas's salary as a teacher—when he gets it—is comparable to mine, the money seems to go through his hands like water. It's not exactly clear *where* it goes, given his beat-up car, his thrift-store clothes, and his reading glasses with one missing lens. But there are all those books he buys: *The Feminine Face of God, Backpacking in Chiapas, How to Get Control of Your Time and Your Life.* . . . There's the monthly out-of-control bill for the cell phone he shares with his son. The regular donations to Save the Whales, Protect Battered Women, Abolish Corporate Personhood, and Support the Indigenous People of Chiapas.

Every time I suggest that we might go out and eat at a restaurant, he ponders for a while and then tells me, "Well, I could possibly afford a burrito." But here, among all the lovely restaurants in the wine country, I get tired of eating burritos. And sometimes, I confess, I feel like I'm back up on that parking ramp "for sunrise and sunset viewing." I think of the little, low-ceilinged diners where Eliot was always most at home, and I can't help but feel that the wish fairies are having their sport with me, being literal in that maddeningly fairy-tale way: "You asked for a golden coach with red velvet seats? You shall have it. But guess what? You forgot to ask for a horse to pull it. So sit back and admire the pavement!"

In real life, as in folktales, it frequently happens that something gets left out of a wish—and then returns to haunt or taunt the wisher in some way. It's easy to see this return as a form of negative judgment, a punishment for the greed of wishing. But recently, when I brought this theme up to a friend of mine, he offered a refreshingly different view.

"You could consider that the missing piece of your wish is telling you something," my friend Paul said. "Because that flaw, that omission, is a place where you're still unconscious. It's a place where you have a blind spot, or where there's something you take for granted. That's why it's so important to really know oneself well before wishing, right?"

Paul's words helped me to remember why some of us who grew up Christian were discouraged from making prayers of petition. It's not just that it's greedy or bossy to ask God for specific things—it's risky, because as humans we see through a glass darkly and thus can't ever fully know the implications of our wishes. Since God is omniscient and knows us better than we know ourselves, it is wiser to ask Him simply to do what is best for us, and thus protect us from our blind spots and our flaws.

I guess I'm lucky that the flaw in my wish has so far resulted in nothing more ominous than a man who lives in a rooming house and dines out on burritos. But what does it mean that I forgot to wish for a man who was solvent? Perhaps it's an indication that money still doesn't rank very high on my list of values—or at least it didn't six months ago, when I wrote out my wish on a piece of paper.

Though I can't go back and revise my wish, now that I'm in the thick of buying my house I find myself hoping that some of my newfound worldliness will rub off on Nicholas. I drop hints about the great programs that are apparently available for inner-city schoolteachers, and I sometimes slip brochures about great deals for first-time home buyers inside his book bag. But I've been trying not to be too pushy. At fifty I've made a vow that I hope to keep, which is not to try to change the people I love, especially those my age or older. It just seems reasonable to expect that when you meet people at this stage of life, what you see is what you get. And what you see is mostly the result of very deeply rooted patterns that aren't likely to change without massive intervention. As it is, I find it hard enough to let go of some of my own rather recently acquired patterns, even those that Nicholas's presence in my life should have made obsolete. Like keeping up both sides of a conversation with myself or feeling a rush of tenderness when my sensor lights go on or my teakettle whistles.

• • •

One evening when we come back from the pond, Nicholas's cell phone rings. It's the principal from an elementary school letting him know that a kindergarten class has suddenly opened up. It's what he's been wanting for years, and I let out a whoop of joy.

But when he comes over the next day, he tells me that three of his colleagues at the middle school have begged him to stay on through the calendar year and he's given in to their pleas. In the short time I've known Nicholas, one of the things I've noticed about him is that he has a tremendous need to feel needed, to respond to the urgencies of those around him. Knowing how miserable he's been in the current situation, I could cry with frustration. "You're fifty-one! When are you going to give yourself permission to have the life you want?" But I bite my lip and keep my silence.

And the truth is, I've been feeling very preoccupied by other matters. From Santa Cruz there's been even more ominous news about my friend George. It turns out that he's had his diagnosis for quite a bit longer—at least a year—than he let on when he first told me about it. And, though he grew up as a skeptical Jewish intellectual, it appears that through the influence of a close friend, he's discovered Christian Science and has decided to forgo medical treatment for his cancer. Meanwhile, my sister has gone to Italy to see how our mother is doing. Her reports are disquieting. Luigi seems to be going over the edge with anxiety about our mother's condition, and he's made it clear to my sister that he can no longer care for her. But it's excruciating to think of my mother being separated from the home she's made for herself in Europe and from the man she describes as "the love of my life."

. . .

After receiving a series of distressing e-mails one evening, I wake up the next morning and find I can't stop crying. It's a feeling that I'm standing over a dark hole that leads down, down, into an endless whirlpool of sorrow.

I call a wise friend of mine, and somehow she manages to make out what I'm saying through the flood of tears. There's a pause, and then just when I'm expecting her to say something profound about the nature of impermanence, she asks me, "Did you ever use that coupon I sent you?"

"For the hot springs, in August?"

"They have a cool pool. I think you should go there."

. . .

An hour later I'm lying in the shade at a spa that is close to where I live. It's very expensive, which is why I've never come before, and it's beautiful. Surrounded by potted palms and birds of paradise and, mercifully, no one I know, I lie there, trying to keep my thoughts from their obsessive worry grooves. What's going to happen to George? Should his family and friends do some kind of intervention—now, while there's still time—to make him see a doctor? And what about my mother? Should we try to bring her back here? How will we ever wrench her away from Italy and her beloved Luigi?

I don't yet have the energy to swim, so I decide to dip into the wading pool, which is shaped like a clover leaf.

To my chagrin, I see someone I know. Her name is Irene, and she's the "life coach" of a close friend. We met at a party once, and she told me that she leads creative retreats for women. She takes them to beautiful places—like Santa Fe and San Miguel de Allende—and they paint and explore and play. At the party we'd briefly discussed the possibility of my coming along as a writing teacher sometime, and I'd sent her a packet of information about myself and my workshops. She'd never responded, and actually I'd felt a bit miffed about that.

I'm not in the mood to say hello to her—or anyone—and I pull my visor down low. Irene is with a friend, and as they bob up and down in the water, they're saying words aloud to one another:

"Glee!"

"Beauty!"

"Adventure!"

*Oh, shut up,* I feel like saying. *Go away.* And I fiddle with my fake headset to make it look as though I'm turning the music up louder.

Then Irene turns to me. "What about you?"

"What?"

"What are you wishing for?"

How strange that she would ask me that. She doesn't seem to

recognize me—and even if she did, she doesn't know anything about my experiment in wishing.

"Ease of mind," I say.

"Ease of mind," she repeats. "And?"

"Health for those who are not well."

Suddenly the tears are streaming down my face again, and Irene is floating beside me, like one of those mythical sea creatures who appear to sailors in distress. Though my attempt to hide is breaking down, I'm still feeling an enormous reluctance to remind her that we've met before. I want to get out of the pool, go back to the chaise, and bury my face under a pile of towels. But she is floating beside me with such kindness that I force myself to speak her name. "Irene?"

"Have we met before?"

I remind her of where and in whose presence we met, and I ask if she ever received the packet of information I sent her about my writing workshops.

"Oh, yes. I'm sorry," she says. "It came at such a hectic time for me. Between two trips." Then she pauses for a moment and tells me, "You know, I'm leading a group of women to Hawaii in a few months. Is there any chance you'd like to come and be the writing teacher?"

*Hawaii?* Did she say *Hawaii?* The beautiful name, full of vowels, that springs up like a flower whenever I hear the word *voyage?* The mythic land, the wish place that I've never believed really existed in time and space?

She did.

She's never led a group there before, but she's found a remarkable spot on the Big Island. It's usually used as a yoga retreat, and it consists of Balinese-style wooden huts set in a tropical garden right on the ocean. She's rented it for one week in November, and she's gathering a group of women. The proceeds will be donated to SeaWolf, an organization that works on behalf of dolphins and whales. So far a painting teacher has signed up to come, but there's not yet a writer.

Only a moment ago I felt as though I was standing over an endless dark whirlpool of sorrow. Now, though the sorrow has not vanished, a door has appeared. And Irene herself is standing in the doorway, a goddess of the threshold.

What to make of this apparition? Is it *just a fluke, a lucky break,* as the voice of my inner skeptic says? Or is it a sign—as another, more hopeful voice says—that *help is there for us, so long as we go out to meet it*?

I know what Carole would say. She has no trouble believing that life is constantly providing us with magical helpers—if only we keep ourselves receptive and don't give in to doubt or despair. Nor does Carole believe that they only come to us in our extreme states of need and despondency. By her lights, the magical helpers aren't snobbishly hierarchical about offering themselves: they'd as soon fix the flaws in an old house as comfort a broken heart.

When Carole first fell in love with a little house in France, she didn't grasp the enormity of its structural flaws. Having bought it rather impulsively on a bright summer day, she returned the following spring to set about the task of renovation. For three weeks she camped out by herself: sleeping on a mat on the hard stone floor, picking her way through knee-high piles of debris, enduring the outdoor toilet, which flooded the back garden every time it flushed, trying to get used to the bats that flew through the holes in the walls at night.

She'd come expecting warm spring weather, but it rained without stopping—and the house as yet had no heat or hot water. Two friends from California arrived to help her, and though she greeted them with exuberance, she wasn't prepared for how helpless the three of them would feel. The house was in infinitely worse shape than she had realized.

The final straw was Carole's discovery one morning that underneath the large stone tiles that formed the downstairs floor in wildly warped and undulating patterns there was: nothing. The tiles had wonderful character, and she had pried them up with great optimism, expecting to find old floorboards on which to reset them. Instead she found that the tiles had been resting on several feet of several centuries' accumulation of dust.

Feeling completely overwhelmed, she sat down and cried.

But Carole isn't one who helplessly cries for long.

Looking up, she saw the mantel on the fireplace, where she had placed a laughing Buddha, a crumbling plaster Virgin Mary from the local flea market, and a pouch of rune stones—an essential divination ingredient for ancient Celts and contemporary northern Californians.

She threw the runes.

They told her, "A messenger will arrive with good news at a turn in the road."

"I'm going for a drive," Carole told her friends.

She got into her car, and with no particular sense of where or why, she began driving until she came to a house by a stream. In front of the house she saw a man standing by a small van. Painted on the side of the van were the French words for "Chimneys. Sandblasting. Stonemasonry." Carole stopped the car. She leaned her head out the window and asked, "Do you speak English?"

"Of course!" the man replied.

Moments later, she jumped into his van and they went off to the masonry to look for supplies. In the days and weeks that followed, Gerard Vergouw became an indispensable ally—driving Carole around to hunt for stones, tiles, and wood beams; teaching her how to barter with the locals, guiding her and her friends through the restoration of the crumbling walls and ceilings, and doing a great deal of the work himself. "He was a gift from the gods," Carole says.

And now here I am, floating in the turquoise water with what appears to be my own gift from the gods: not a mason but a mermaid.

• • •

It's evening when I return from the spa, in a completely different state from when I left home in the morning. When Nicholas calls, his voice sounding frayed and exhausted from another day of wild kids in a hot, stuffy classroom, I hesitate a moment before telling him that, as I stood over a dark whirlpool of sorrow, a beautiful helper appeared and offered me a trip to Hawaii. But he sounds happy for me when I tell him, and before we hang up, I remind him that in two days we'll be going on another kind of adventure. My friend Lynn is turning fifty, and she's throwing herself a party. The invitation I received announced that the birthday bash would culminate in a "shamanic journey."

Neither Nicholas nor I have ever had such an experience, and despite our shared predilection for Far Eastern mysticism, we're both game for something more indigenous. After years of trying *not* to attach to the mind's endless parade of vivid images, we're curious to see what it's like to actually cultivate an inner vision.

• • •

The party falls on a beautiful Saturday, clear and sunny but with a slight breeze blowing through the dry August leaves. After a sumptuous birthday picnic, friends make offerings to Lynn of poems and songs. Finally, just as evening falls, we're ushered into the den for our shamanic journey.

Lynn's teacher does not fit my stereotypical notion of the shaman as a brown-skinned man with a shock of black hair and a geometric pattern of blue lines etched across his high cheekbones. She's a slightly plump, middle-aged woman with gray hair tied back in a bun, and she is not sporting any feathers, bones, shells, tattoos, or ritual scarring. She has the manner of a Montessori schoolteacher, and she asks us to form a big circle around the room, to sit down in a comfortable position on the floor, and to begin by breathing slowly, deeply. When we've done so for a while, she passes out scarves and asks us to wrap them around our eyes. In order to fully enter the inner world, we need to withdraw our senses from the world around us.

Then she asks us to envision a place—real or imagined—that we associate with a feeling of calm and safety. It needs to be a place where there is some sort of opening into the ground, an opening big enough for a human being to pass through. I know exactly where my place is: Vichy Springs. More specifically, it's the grotto where the warm, gold water bubbles up from deep below the ground. Having visualized the grotto, I remember to add the small hand-lettered sign that reads, "The water from this spring is at least twenty-five thousand years old."

"Now that you've found the opening in your special place, go in," our birthday shaman is telling us. She's begun to beat a tall feathered drum, softly.

The evening light is dark in the den, and a plume of smoke from the incense is curling upward.

I enter the grotto. Though I've always been phobic about enclosed spaces—caves, elevators, and anything remotely resembling a vault or a mine shaft—I dive headlong into the gold water. Like Alice in Wonderland, I find myself spinning down a long, dark passage, which is remarkably not wet. Down below, I find to my relief that it's not dark or scary. I seem to have landed in a green meadow, surrounded by great spreading trees that feel vaguely southern.

"When you've entered your special place, take a few moments to breathe and settle in. Feel the ground beneath your feet. Look up and down and all around you. Smell the smells. Hear the sounds."

I do as she says, and the vaguely southern feeling intensifies. I've never been farther south than Missouri, but there's something in the dense humidity of the air, the perfume of the trees' leaves, that makes me think I'm in Alabama or Mississippi. How did I land in the Deep South by way of Vichy Springs?

"Now, in your mind, begin walking. See if you can find a path."

The drumbeats get louder.

Along the edge of the meadow, I do see a path. It's a well-trodden trail of red dirt that runs along the meadow, then takes off into the woods.

"As you walk along this path, keep your mind and spirit open. Be ready to meet your guide. A special being who understands you at a very deep level and who has something to impart to you. Something that is going to help you as you enter the next phase of your life."

Even as the drumbeats get louder, they seem to be receding, sending me deeper and deeper into my waking dream.

I'm walking through the woods now, breathing in the dense, perfumed air. I'm feeling both excited and wary, as if at any moment I'm going to meet . . . a lion, a tiger, a bear? Most likely a bear in these southern woods. Or some kind of portentous bird.

"What if nobody comes?" one of the birthday guests asks.

"They will. Just be patient, trust."

I continue to walk, trusting.

The drum continues to beat.

Nothing is happening.

No one is coming.

Ever so subtly, I peek out from under my bandana. Beside me Nicholas is obviously having a very intense experience. Though he's still sitting cross-legged, his body is rocking back and forth. He's breathing heavily and moaning slightly. I readjust my bandana and go back into the darkness, back to the middle of my southern woods.

What will I do if no guide comes for me?

I'm sure we're going to have to share our experiences in the circle when we emerge from wherever it is we've plunged. Should I make something up?

A jaguar—my beautiful black Jaguar, that's what I'd like to encounter. And it wouldn't exactly be cheating, would it, because I've already established a kind of relationship there . . .

But, listen.

Something or someone is coming.

I hear footsteps, a rustle of leaves . . .

I see a flash of red . . .

It's Aunt Jemima!

It's her, unmistakably. With her red bandana, her white, high-buttoned dress with its long skirts falling in folds around her wide hips. What is she doing here? I haven't thought of her in ages. I rarely eat pancakes. Is this politically incorrect? If it is, I can't help it. I did not intend to see her. She was the farthest thing from my mind. But here she is, coming toward me.

She looks happy to see me. She's beaming. She's stretching out her hands to me. One hand holds a ladle, and from the ladle a golden syrup is pouring.

"Once you've met your guide, then ask your question."

I'm not sure I have a question. I'm just so stunned to see her.

I go up to her and kneel at her feet.

She anoints my head with maple syrup.

The disciples are glowering.

What disciples?

The glowering disciples I carry inside me. The ones who scolded Jesus when, in a moment of celebration, he let a woman pour a pitcher of precious oil over his head.

Now, this is a moment of golden abundance.

*Take it in. Take it in.*

Beside me Nicholas's moans are growing louder.

The drums are getting louder, too, calling us back.

I want to stay with Aunt Jemima, but around me other birthday guests are coming to.

"Thank your guide, and return."

I thank Aunt Jemima and, slipping back through the opening, move through the bubbly gold waters of Vichy Springs and find myself back at the birthday party.

Welcoming us back to the living room, the shaman lady hands her feathered talking stick to the woman beside her and asks that each person say a few words about finding a guide in another dimension of time and space. As we go around the circle, I'm struck that each person has had an encounter with an animal guide. And though quite a variety of animals has been sighted, they're all of distinctly noble ilk: eagle, bear, wolf, whale. No slugs or gophers here.

Beside me Nicholas is looking pale and rather shaken. When the talking stick is passed to him he tells us that he met a snake, a very large snake. It wrapped itself around him and squeezed, until his innards felt uncomfortable.

"Are you in a constricted place in your life?" the shaman asks.

Nicholas and I exchange a look.

"Well, yes—"

"That's what your guide seems to be telling you. Something is squeezing the life out of you, and you're allowing it to. You've got to resist it. You've got to give yourself some room to breathe."

*Hallelujah!* I feel like shouting. I've always had a horror of snakes, but I'm impressed with the perspicacity of this one. I make an effort not to look at Nicholas, so as to hide the "I told you so!" gleam in my eyes.

Then it's my turn.

"Noelle? Did you encounter a guide?"

Should I fib and tell them I saw a beautiful black jaguar?

"Aunt Jemima," I blurt.

Everyone falls off their *zafus* with laughter.

Except for the shaman. "The dark Madonna," she says. "She's a very important archetypal figure. Did she say anything to you?"

"She just poured golden syrup on my head."

"She anointed you."

"And what does that mean?"

"Just let it sink into your dreams. . . ."

• • •

That night, well before dawn, I'm awakened by loud groaning. Nicholas is sitting up in bed, clutching his stomach. "I feel like I have a terrible hangover," he says.

"But you only drank one small glass of champagne."

"I know."

"It's the snake, squeezing your insides."

But before I can offer any further unsolicited interpretation of his totem animal, he's lurching off the bed and down the hall to the bathroom to vomit.

I bring him cold washcloths, bubbly water, and a mash of ginger root to calm his stomach, but nothing seems to work for long. All night he's in and out of bed, padding up and down the hall, retching in an agonizingly loud and rib-wracking way.

• • •

In the morning when I open my eyes, I feel as though I'm lying beside a shipwrecked sailor. He looks like a bag of bones that have been tossed and turned on the waves of a ravaging night. He's out cold, and snoring in a ragged sort of way.

Poor thing.

I slip out of bed, pull the covers up around him, and go into the kitchen to make breakfast.

Pancakes.

Aunt Jemima is clear about that. Never mind that I haven't made them in years; she won't cut me any slack. As I begin mixing flour, sugar, baking powder, I hear her sort of humming. I heat up the oil, pour the batter in, and the humming turns to a chanting. I can't quite make out the words, but it's something about

Nicholas. About the plantation in North Carolina. And his cruel great-great-great-great-grandfather.

"He has to stop punishing himself."

"What?"

Nicholas has walked into the kitchen and is standing there like a wraith, with dark shadows under his eyes and his hair standing up in points. I know that I'm taking advantage of his ravaged state, but I feel like I'm channeling my black Madonna: "Pick up the phone. Call that principal. Tell her you want the job."

"But I'm not awake yet. I need some tea."

"Pick up the phone. Dial the number."

He picks up the phone and goes outside with it, to avoid my imperious gaze. When he comes back in the door a few minutes later, I can see the relief in his face. "They'll give me the job! They'll give me the job!"

Piling a stack of pancakes onto his plate, I notice that—despite my best intentions—I'm not feeling the least bit guilty about having just made a blatant intervention in my midlife lover's plans.

• • •

Later, when we decide to go down to the pond, Nicholas doesn't seem to remember that he usually lugs a mountain of books. He just walks beside me empty-handed, in a kind of trance. When we wade through the shallow water to the island, he sinks, facedown into the sand, and falls asleep.

Spreading my towel out beside him, I try to imagine how we might look from a sort of archetypal, shamanic point of view: a spent snake strung out in the sand, while beside him Aunt Jemima stretches luxuriously, then reaches for a bottle of golden cocoa butter she keeps in her beach bag and rubs a big dollop into his pale skin. She rubs with a circular motion, round and round, and as she does so I'm reminded that circularity—receiving and giving back, receiving and giving back—is crucial to the art of wishing.

In folktales, in myths from around the world, over and over there are twin dangers that accompany the wish fulfilled. One danger is that the wisher becomes stuck, fixated, holding on so tightly that he squeezes the life out of the object of his wish. This is the famous story of the emperor who became so obsessed with the song of the nightingale that, in his greed, he nearly lost it forever. It's also the story of the golden egg, and the long chain of people who got stuck to the goose who laid it.

The other danger is that the wisher seems to fall through the object of his wish into a well of endless desire. Rather than bringing him satisfaction, his wish come true spawns a state of infinite wish-come-true greed. This is the famous story of the fisherman and his wife. Having learned that her husband caught and then released an enchanted flounder one day, she insists that he go back and ask a favor of the flounder. The flounder complies, but as the days go by the fisherman's wife keeps wanting more and more. It's not enough that their miserable shack has turned into a comfortable cottage—she wants to live in a castle. Then she wants to be queen, wearing a jeweled crown. When finally she wishes to command both the sun and the moon, the flounder says no. "This is too much!" he thunders, and the fisherman and his wife find themselves back in their miserable hut.

Both of these dangers come from a mentality of scarcity. Because there is not enough, I must hold on, hold on to what I've got. Because there is not enough, I must grab for whatever else can be had.

But Aunt Jemima represents the very opposite mentality. With her voluptuous body, her broad smile and sweet gift, she belongs to a throng of female figures who represent free-flowing abundance. Whether black or white, whether found on syrup cans or a cathedral's stained glass, such figures represent the bounty of an unconditionally loving mother. It's no wonder that I found Aunt Jemima at the other end of an inner spring, for such loving mothers are often associated with a life-giving liquid, whether water, milk, or nectar. In Europe, one finds again and again that a church that is dedicated to "Our Lady" is built on the ancient site where a pagan goddess was once worshipped for her gift of a bubbling spring. In Asia, too, the goddess of compassion often comes with a pitcher that never runs dry. Though these mother figures may represent distinct forms of bounty (Our Lady of Perpetual Mercy, She Who Hears All Sorrows), fundamentally they represent infinite generosity, the fulfillment of every wish.

In every culture the act of wishing invokes a retinue of helpers, a kind of cottage industry, a hive of industrious workers whose function it is to make wishes come true.

The male counterpart of Aunt Jemima and her boundless generosity is the roly-poly man, whether Santa Claus with his laugh like a bowl full of jelly or the Chinese Hotei, whose round belly, when rubbed, makes wishes come true. The roundness of such figures, both male and female, connotes the circular, continuously regenerating nature of their generosity; such figures appear to be happy because they give and to give because they are happy.

Along with those whose help comes through their amplitude, there are those who seem best able to help because they are small. These are the dwarfs, fairies, and elves who can pop up in unexpected places—squeezing through cracks, hiding in keyholes, hitching rides in a pocket—in order to save the day.

The animal world provides its helpers, too, in the same range of big and small. In myths and fairy tales, there are the great fish who carry lost travelers over the sea, the deer who give up their own bodies for food, the birds who carry secrets in their beaks or lead the way to a hidden treasure.

Of all the benevolent animals, my favorite is the Hindu elephant god, Ganesh. With his squat, voluptuous body, the spilling folds of his belly, his bejeweled trunk, ears, and legs, he belongs to the category of roly-poly, all-giving purveyors of happiness. Whether his posture is loafing or dancing, he's at ease; unhurried and unworried, he has all the time, food, and wealth in the world, and nothing makes him happier than to share it. Ganesh is known as the remover of obstacles, and he himself once faced the major obstacle of losing his head! One night his mother, the beautiful goddess Parvati, had asked her handsome young son to guard her door. When her husband, Siva, returned and found Ganesh standing there, they got into a scuffle and Siva chopped off his head. Parvati was furious and demanded that Siva make her son whole again. So Siva sent out his attendants, and they brought back the first available head: that of a magnificent elephant. From all appearances, the once handsome young man was perfectly happy with his great new pachyderm head.

Whether human or animal, large or small, there are two basic personalities to be found among wish granters. There are those who seem to give purely through the joy of giving. And there are those who seem more mercurial about their help, prone to mood swings, more or less dominatrix: the fierce genies, the bossy fairies, the reluctant oracles, the gods and goddesses who will grant your wish if you show them a slavish devotion and don't waver from their instructions by so much as a hair's breadth.

To make someone else's wish come true is to have a certain power over that person. For the one who makes the wish come true has something that the other lacks, whether knowledge, physical force, social prestige and connections, or material resources. There is thus an inherent imbalance in the equation from the beginning, and it's an imbalance that is prone to continue even after the wish is fulfilled. For to grant a wish is always, to some degree, simultaneously to confer a debt. Myths and fairy tales are full of stories of some powerful being who granted a wish and then came back to exact some form of payment: love, obeisance, a share of the treasure, a firstborn child.

Even in the utter absence of malevolence, to grant someone else's wish is an act that's thick with implications and consequences. Along with whatever sincere and empathetic pleasure there may be in fulfilling another's wish, there is simultaneously the experience of oneself as an agent, an initiator, a capable and expansive benefactor. This is one of the reasons why it feels good to make someone else's wish come true; in the more mundane sphere, it is also one of the reasons why volunteer work has a significant antidepressant effect. To bestow something upon someone else is a very effective antidote to feeling unworthy and deficient.

There is nothing ignoble in the reality that the one who gives also receives. But whenever there is an imbalance of power, that power can be abused. And though in the moment of granting another's wish there may be absolutely no strings attached, those strings have a way of appearing later on in the scene. The desire for recognition, for gratitude, the inability to accept that the one whose wish we once granted no longer seems to need our help: these are some of the ways we can get caught in a tangled web.

"Be careful what you wish for," we say—and the need for caution extends to the one who grants another's wish as well. Indeed, even more so. For it's hard enough to know what is truly best for ourselves, let alone for others. Perhaps, if we hadn't intervened, they would have discovered a deeper, more significant desire. Perhaps, if we hadn't intervened when we did, they would have discovered the gift of their own patience and been amazed by their own ability to aim the arrow of a wish.

What blowback will come to me from pushing Nicholas to make his move? Something dreadful perhaps. But right now, lying beside me on the island, he's looking distinctly less like the strangled victim of a giant snake. As if my thoughts had awakened him, he opens his eyes, smiles, and anoints me with these words: "You're my very own bitch goddess." And though he's the one who's slathered with cocoa butter, I feel a golden glow from head to toe.

# PART THREE

# Holding It Lightly

*In which, as I move
through a modern history of
wishing, my journey expands
in new directions*

# CHAPTER NINE

# September

## *Thoughts: Tapping Their Power*

It's early September, and though the intense, dry heat will linger for weeks, autumn is near. Even before the first yellow leaf falls at my feet, my thoughts turn. Their scale shifts, and the dense closeness of summer gives way to a broad horizon. Suddenly I have a craving to learn about distant planets, other species, kings and queens, plagues and battles, great inventions, and major revolutions in art. Meanwhile, the pressing questions of personal life begin to shrink, becoming like those small brown nuts that the squirrels are suddenly busy burying in my yard. Perhaps I'll dig them up and chew on them some winter's day.

Which comes first, and which matters most: The waning light that reveals a widening horizon, or our own expanding thoughts? The world around us, or the world inside? It's one of the great philosophical questions of all time, and it has everything to do with the act of wishing.

*If wishes were horses, then beggars would ride.*

Though it sounds like a nursery rhyme, it comes from a place that is a world away from the magical thinking of children. In this place, there's a radical gap between matter and mind. And in this gap, matter reigns supreme. The mind is powerless over matter unless it obeys the material laws that govern material reality. And unless it understands those laws, the mind is utterly ineffective in altering that reality. A mind that fails to acknowledge its subservience is a mind that makes itself vulnerable to matter in its grossest form.

*Wish in one hand, shit in the other.*

It sounds like a curse, but at root it's just a harsher way of declaring the radical gap. It represents a distinctly modern understanding of the relationship between mind and matter, and it's one that spells death to the art of wishing. On the vast screen of human history, it's definitely a minority view, a brief blip. For thousands of years human beings have granted primacy to the invisible and eternal world of thought.

In ancient Indian philosophy, for example, matter is unreal. It is *maya,* illusion. Suffering arises because we identify with the illusion: this is the reason for extreme ascetic practices. Pushing past pain and deprivation, the yogi aspires to transcend the illusory bonds of matter and to identify as pure consciousness. Only then, released from the illusory fetters of the material world, can he know the bliss of absolute freedom.

For the Greek philosopher Parmenides, Thinking and Being are One. There are not two orders, two dimensions of reality, but one alone: an invisible and eternal reality that underlies and gives rise to everything that may be seen or known. Whether a wish, a dream, a yellow leaf: all partake of the same essence.

For Plato, too, everything in the world around us is real by virtue of its participation in the timeless and unseen world of Ideas.

In the Bible, the material world emerges from a divine conception. "Let there be light," God said, and there was light. "Let me have some company," he said. And there were human beings.

Once, when I was a child, I asked my father, "Where was I before I was born?" He replied without hesitation, "You were an idea in the mind of God." How comforting that was, so much more comforting than certain modern beliefs. That we evolved from ancient slime. Or, as the existentialists say, that each of us is simply "thrown," at birth, into a particular set of circumstances, a random web of "givenness." Is it any wonder that people adhere to the belief in intelligent design? Nobody wants to feel like an unwanted child, an accident of nature, a fluke of circumstance. It's so much more reassuring to feel that we were wished into being.

• • •

How I wish I had some ready comfort to offer Nicholas one late-September night, when he wakes up in the midst of a dream, grief-struck. Though most of the dream's content evaporated the moment he opened his eyes, it left him with a flood of undiluted emotion. And without his having uttered a sound, the emotion woke me.

He tells me that it was a dream about his childhood friend, and it was one of those dreams that is like a visit, and leaves you saturated with the sense of someone's presence, even if you haven't seen that person for years. When Nicholas was sixteen and had just gotten his license, he took his best friend, Josh, for a drive and got into a terrible car accident, in which Josh was killed. He and Josh had known each other since kindergarten and had traveled around the globe to stay in touch. Everyone who knew them well had come to think of them as twins. The accident was not Nicholas's fault: they were sideswiped by a drunk driver. But Nicholas has never been able to forgive himself. Though I already know that the accident has cast a long shadow over his life and left him with profound survivor's guilt, I've never seen it quite so clearly before. Weeping soundlessly beside me in the dark, he tells me that he's anxious about the new job that starts in just two days—the kindergarten job that he's been wanting for so long. When we try to get at *why,* he keeps getting vague, going blank. Until finally he sits up and says very clearly, "Since Josh died, I've never really felt that I deserved to have a life."

What can one say in the face of such a revelation?

It's like seeing a meteor's sudden streak against a dark night. Like hearing a sudden clap of thunder, a cloud cracking open in the sky.

"You can lie down again now," I say.

I put my arm around him, being careful not to press too hard against those two bruised dents on his shoulders, and we nestle back into sleep. The magnitude of his revelation is still reverberating, but somehow it has brought a freshness to the air around us, like light rain.

· · ·

When I wake up a few hours later, it's still night, and Nicholas is sleeping. When he isn't recovering from a nightmare, an illness, or a shamanic snake, Nicholas sleeps more sweetly than any man I've ever known. He doesn't snore or thrash about or steal the covers. He sleeps quietly, soundly, yet so responsively that if I stir or make a sound, he murmurs in response, a little "oh," or "mmmmmm." Tonight, though, after the intensity of his dream, he doesn't seem aware that I've awakened. In the moonlight seeping in through the blinds, I look at him.

How much easier it is to see through another's self-limiting thoughts than to see through our own! Like the hazy ring that surrounds a planet, our thoughts form the atmosphere in which we know ourselves and through which the universe appears. I can look at Nicholas, asleep beside me in the moonlight, and see an extremely intelligent, articulate, passionately energetic man, a man who could be anything he wanted to—if he would let himself. Since I'm not looking through the dense, grief-engendered ring of his self-limiting thoughts, it's not hard to see the vast possibility that surrounds him.

But when it comes to my own cloud of self-limiting thoughts: it's thick, dark, convincing. And, especially when I wake in the middle of the night, it's made of worries. Thick, dark, convincing worries that ceaselessly engender more thick, dark, convincing worries. With my rational mind, I know that worrying is a futile activity, but somehow this knowledge never seems to help when my need is greatest.

Lying there in the dark, I am flat, passive, semi-undressed, swaddled in sheets, victim of the mild form of paralysis that affects the motor nerves at night and helps prevent sleepwalking. Conditions are perfect for feeling helpless, stuck, and overwhelmed in the face of every dreadful thing that could conceivably occur.

Like Mark Twain I could say that I have suffered a great many disasters in my life, most of which never happened. But there, precisely, is the rub. The paradoxical, self-reinforcing power of worrying. If you're a first-class worrier, you are constantly imagining scenes of disaster. Then, because for the most part those scenes don't happen, you tell yourself that it's your worrying that warded them off, that kept the other shoe from falling. And so you go on to imagine the next scene of disaster.

*Worry in one hand and shit in the other, and see which one fills up faster.*

Like wishing, worrying is a form of magical thinking, one that springs from the deeply held belief that our thoughts can affect what happens in the world around us. But worrying, it seems, is the shadow side of wishing. For it begins not with the vision of something desired but of something feared, something to be repelled. And whereas desire is a powerful form of fuel for actually making something happen, fear is less so. Rather than energizing us, motivating us to take action, it tends to deplete us, to make us feel helpless, overwhelmed, lying there flat on our backs in the darkness.

Lately what I'm worrying about is my mother. I wake up in the middle of the night and lie there imagining a thousand frightening scenarios. The apartment where she and Luigi live is close to the train station in Padua, and the neighborhood is swarming with desperate-looking immigrant men. When they first moved into their apartment, there was someone who kept trying to open the door with a key, and Luigi had to change the locks. Luigi still works and is gone for hours at a time, leaving my mother alone in the apartment. Though he's charming and affectionate, he's also prone to sudden fits of anger and abrupt departures. I imagine her left suddenly alone in the midst of a crowded street full of pickpockets. I imagine her alone at night in the apartment when suddenly a key that is not Luigi's turns in the lock. I imagine her getting out of bed, fearful, and suddenly fainting.

•  •  •

One day in the bookstore, while browsing idly, I come across a set of Jack Kornfield's tapes on Buddhist psychology. I pounce on them as though they were the very thing I'd been looking for. And almost as soon as I begin listening to them, I realize that the timing is really quite perfect. For not only does Jack provide a wealth of antidotes to the self-constriction of my worrying mind, but he also provides the vast horizon that my autumn thoughts are craving.

Unlike its Western counterpart, Buddhist psychology never split itself off from its metaphysical foundation. In Buddhism, to study one's own mind is simultaneously to study the ultimate nature of reality, for the two are not separate. Indeed, as it says in one of the most ancient texts of Buddhism, the *Dhammapada:* "Our thoughts make the world." On the level of our own daily existence, this means that when we change our thoughts we change the world we live in. As Jack says, "Buddhism is an ancient method of thought control."

*But it's not the only ancient method of thought control!* I find myself wanting to say back to Jack's voice—because in the West, too, there is a long tradition. And when I finish listening to the tapes, I set out to prove my case, as if responding to a challenge.

For Socrates, who lived in the fourth century B.C., happiness (*eudaimonia*) does not depend on external circumstances or material resources but on one's capacity to know what is good and true and to act accordingly. The philosopher's task is to lead the mind through its habitual patterns of deluded thinking to this life-altering knowledge. Having accomplished this for himself, he then becomes a compassionate "gadfly" for others, pestering them to break through their false and limiting preconceptions so that they, too, can discover the ultimate happiness of the human soul.

Following Socrates, there is a great lineage of Western thinkers—including the Epicureans, the Stoics, the Cynics—who devoted themselves to understanding how to lead a good life. Though there are significant differences among them, they share a common belief that *it is within the realm of thought that we have the power to cultivate true happiness and to bring ourselves into alignment with the ultimate nature of reality.*

Transmitted through the centuries, this ancient belief continually reasserts and reinvents itself in different forms. For example, it lies at the heart of the nineteenth-century American movement that came to be known as transcendentalism. For Ralph Waldo Emerson, its most influential proponent, the physical world is a product of one mind, one spirit, and it is within the power of each one of us to align with that great underlying will, or consciousness. How do we do so? By mastering the pattern of our thoughts. Henry David Thoreau was Emerson's close friend and fellow transcendentalist, and he was not a radical idealist: "I want a world that I can put my foot through!" he once exclaimed. But Thoreau, too, put great stock in the power of thought. "As a single footstep will not make a path on the earth, so a single thought will not make a pathway in the mind," he wrote. "To make a deep physical path, we walk again and again. To make a deep mental path, we must think over and over the kind of thoughts we wish to dominate our lives."

This core belief in the power of thought lies at the heart of Christian Science and other varieties of "New Thought"—such as Religious Science and the Unity School of Christianity—which drew inspiration from the transcendentalists (though the compliment was not always returned). This belief also lies at the heart of what has come to be called New Age thinking. In both its ancient and its modern manifestations, it is optimistic and empowering. Human beings are not at the mercy of gods or fate, because the secret to true happiness lies within each individual's mind. But here is a major difference: where ancient philosophers from both East and West tended to equate happiness with the mind's ability to *transcend* external circumstances, New Age thinkers tend to celebrate the mind's ability to *transform* those circumstances.

*Create your own reality,* they say.

Where does this exhortation come from?

When ancient beliefs in the primacy of the inner world and the power and freedom of thought are revived and then mingle with the spirit of American pragmatism, a new kind of practice emerges. In this practice, *the nature of our thoughts can actually make things happen in the world around us.* And what happens in the world around us confirms the truth of the practice. In other words, *if it works, it's true.* If changing the nature of my thoughts can both make me feel better and change the material circumstances of my life, that's all the proof I need that my thoughts are in alignment with the truth.

In the belief that thoughts can make things happen, there is a strong element of magic. It's from this mingled, magical matrix that New Age optimism arises. From its deepest roots to its newest shoots, it is radically eclectic. In both its pragmatism and its resistance to any absolute outside authority, this create-your-own-reality approach to life is ready to draw inspiration wherever inspiration may be found—whether from the Buddha or Benjamin Franklin, Plato or Norman Vincent Peale, Albert Einstein or Madame Blavatsky, Mary Baker Eddy, or . . . Larry Wilson.

Somewhere in my quest, I came upon a book called *The Aladdin Factor*. Compiled by the authors of *Chicken Soup for the Soul*, it's a compendium of encouraging anecdotes and aphorisms on the theme of "how to ask for what you want." It includes a story from a man named Larry Wilson who was having a dreadful time trying to make it as an insurance salesman. Though it was excruciating to admit defeat, he decided to quit. In his darkest hour, a friend gave him Victor Frankl's *Man's Search for Meaning*—and the book turned his life around. It made him feel that he could, indeed, succeed in the insurance industry by making a few simple "belief changes." The first was that he would never again allow a single sale to be the measure of who he was and what he might become. The next involved a rather ingenious method of reframing. At the time, the average commission from each life insurance sale was five hundred dollars. Because it took about twenty calls to yield one sale, it dawned on him that he could think of each call—whether successful or not—as being worth twenty-five dollars.

> *This is how I changed the belief game. I would call on Mary, and she wouldn't buy. Instead of putting her on my back, I'd mentally say, "Thanks for the twenty-five dollars." I would do the same thing with the next eighteen prospects. . . . When I got to the twentieth prospect, and he bought, again I would say, "Thanks for the twenty-five dollars."*

Before too long, the twenty-to-one ratio became ten-to-one, while the average commission doubled to one thousand dollars. At which point, Larry Wilson writes "I could hardly wait to go out and say, 'Thanks for the twenty-five dollars!'"

Imagine using Viktor Frankl's revelations, forged in the crucible of Auschwitz, to boost your insurance sales! I'm honestly not sure which is the greater distortion of Frankl's legacy: to omit one of his two flower stories, or to glide, without the slightest hitch, from *Man's Search for Meaning* to man's search for moolah.

Yet even as Larry Wilson makes me want to gnash my teeth, there's a question I find myself compelled to ask: What if time were no barrier, and Larry Wilson and my great-grandfather had chanced to meet?

*Nahhh! She von't buy anyt'ing!*

In the early 1900s, my great-grandfather came from Russia to St. Louis, and for a while he tried to make his way as a door-to-door salesman. When my father was a little boy, he sometimes accompanied his Grandpa Lutsky, and what he remembers is this: His grandfather would walk up to a door, extend his finger to ring the bell, and then suddenly announce, "Nahhhh. She von't buy anyt'ing!" Then, without ringing the doorbell, he'd take my father's hand and they'd walk back down the steps.

This is the stock from which I come.

I have one memory of sitting on my great-grandfather's lap, on a rocking chair in a nursing home in St. Louis. I remember him looking down at me, stroking the top of my head as we rocked. It's a tender memory, and I know that I will always keep the tenderest spot in my heart for men like him, for all the world's door-to-door salesmen who just can't bring themselves to knock on the door.

But what if Larry Wilson had been able to sit down with my great-grandfather and teach him to replace the mantra of "Nahhh. She von't buy anyt'ing!" with "Thanks for the twenty-five dollars!"? For it does seem obvious that Grandpa Lutsky's negative thoughts would be self-fulfilling prophecies. Perhaps that was part of the lure for him: better to fulfill his own negative expectation than to be open and vulnerable to the unpredictable wheel of fortune.

In her book *Kitchen Table Wisdom*, the physician Rachel Naomi Remen tells a story about her father, who had always held the firm belief that the family struggled under an unlucky star. "The luck of the Remens," he would say whenever anything bad happened. Then he won fifty thousand dollars in the state lottery—more money than he'd ever had all at once in his entire lifetime. Surely this would give her father a new perspective, Rachel thought. But no. At first he was afraid to redeem the ticket, convinced that something would go awry. When he finally claimed the money, he stashed it away against some future emergency and swore Rachel and her mother to secrecy—lest anyone take advantage of them. What Rachel saw so clearly then was the way that the habit of anxiety could turn anything—even a stroke of pure good fortune—into another burden. "I saw that the luck of the Remens was homemade," she writes. "Until then, I had believed that we really were unlucky. I have lived off my windfall from that lottery ticket ever since."

Like my great-grandfather, Rachel Remen's father was of Eastern European Jewish stock, and both of these men seem to have lived in a different universe from the positive thinkers, the affluence affirmers, the manifest-your-dream, create-your-own-reality believers, and all those expecting radical favor, blessings, and the best cut of meat in the house.

• • •

"Would you like to come over and watch *The Secret* with me?" my neighbor Rosemary calls to ask me one afternoon in mid-September. And I say yes without realizing how absolutely apropos the invitation is. For though I'm dimly aware that this little online film has something to do with the power of thinking, all I really know is that it has spawned a giant underground cult. Rosemary herself watches the film three times a week and considers it an essential part of her own spiritual journey. Lately she's been thinking about taking its message out to the wider community, especially to people in difficult circumstances: in hospitals, nursing homes, perhaps even prisons. My curiosity has peaked.

Evening comes, and Rosemary and I sit on the sofa in her tiny studio apartment, with her laptop open on the coffee table before us. She clicks the mouse, and *The Secret* begins.

A blob of red sealing wax appears on a piece of parchment, along with a quill pen writing the words "The Secret" against a wash of turgid colors as an overlapping fugue of voices whisper "The Secret" in several languages. Though one of my friends has warned me that the film is "a really weird combination of inspiring and tacky," I'm not quite prepared for how hokey it seems. Yet at the same time, I can't deny its powerful building of suspense. It seems that at some point in the vague but not too distant past, an attractive, blond middle-aged woman of undetermined but English-speaking extraction who lived near a beach found herself in desperate circumstances. She was exhausted from work, her relationships were in turmoil, and her father died. Just when it seemed that she might go over the brink of despair, help came. One day she found a note, scrawled in her daughter's handwriting, begging her to heed the wisdom of the Secret.

And what is that Secret? It's apparently been around since time immemorial (shots here of stone tablets, pyramids, sandy feet in sandals), but it's inherently so potent that the powers that be (men in armor running with torches, men in suits sitting in boardrooms) have tried to suppress it. But now, a team of contemporary experts—including a couple of philosophers, a metaphysician, a visionary, an investment trainer, several writers, a quantum physicist, and a feng shui consultant—are here to share it loud and clear. As one of these experts puts it, the Secret can be expressed in three simple words: *thoughts become things.* How do they do so? Through *the law of attraction:* when we think about something, we attract that something to us. As metaphysician Dr. Joe Vitale explains: "It's like the universe is a catalogue, and you're saying: 'I'd like this experience.' 'I'd like this product.' It's really that easy." And indeed, much of the film is a kind of infomercial for the power of the Secret, as one after another expert gives testimony to what can be ordered through the great catalogue of the universe: whether a fancy car, a \$4.5 million mansion, good health, or "a wife to die for."

The film ends, and there's an awkward silence. Rosemary is someone I admire deeply, and I know how much the film has come to mean to her. But I honestly don't know what to say. I murmur something like "I can see why people are so drawn to it" and then make my way along the dark road back to my house. Feeling distracted and confused, I have to work extra hard to avoid the deep trench where last year I slipped and broke my metatarsal. For even as I feel repelled by the film, I also feel stirred, revved, as though someone had given me a shot of some sort of energizing, confidence-boosting drug. Though I still haven't quite pulled together the down payment for my little house with its bullet-riddled window, I feel like charging out on a white steed and moving right into a Tudor mansion.

I'm truly shocked at the film's blatant materialism. And I'm irked by what seems to me its pseudoscientific language. The various experts invoke the law of attraction, the principal of *like attracts like* as if it were a law of physics, as inexorable and predictable as gravity, momentum, the rising of heat, or the leveling of water. Yet if I look around at the natural world, it seems to me that *like often attracts unlike*—whether we're talking about male and female, or negative and positive electrons, or predators and prey. And even magnetism—the central metaphor used for the law of attraction—is actually an example of like attracts unlike.

In essence, it seems to me that "the Secret" is the ancient practice of imitative magic—only in this version there's no need for rock, wood, clay, joint compound, or any other goo. It's with our thoughts alone that we'll create the magnetic likeness of what we want: whether radiant health, a new love, or a house with a six-car garage.

Back in my house, I go online and discover that the creator of *The Secret* (the pretty blond woman) is named Rhonda Byrne and she is Australian. It was in 2004 that her life fell apart: "I wept and wept and wept, and I didn't want my daughter to see me sobbing." That's when Rhonda's daughter came to the rescue and gave her the book that changed her life. The book was *The Science of Getting Rich,* published in 1910 by Wallace D. Wattles. According to Rhonda, "Something inside of me had me turn the pages one by one, and I can still remember my tears hitting the pages as I was reading it. It gave me a glimpse of the Secret. It was like a flame inside my heart. And with every day since, it's just become a raging fire of wanting to share all of this with the world."

After that recommendation I feel compelled to rush-order a copy of Wallace D. Wattles's book. When it arrives two days later, I tear open the cardboard envelope and within half an hour I've devoured the slender volume. What was the message that became a raging fire in Rhonda's heart? The very first chapter begins with these words:

> *Whatever may be said in praise of poverty, the fact remains that it is not possible to live a really complete or successful life unless one is rich. No man can rise to his greatest possible height in talent or soul development unless he has plenty of money; for to unfold the soul and to develop talent he must have many things to use, and he cannot have these things unless he has money to buy them.*

Having thus established the necessity of becoming rich, Mr. Wattles goes on to explain that "there is a Science of getting rich, and it is an exact science, like algebra or arithmetic. There are certain laws which govern the process of acquiring riches; once these laws are learned and obeyed by any man, he will get rich with mathematical certainty."

These laws are based on the ancient belief that the essence of reality is thought. As Wattles puts it: "There is a thinking stuff from which all things are made, and which, in its original state, permeates, penetrates, and fills the interspaces of the universe. A thought in this substance produces the thing that is imaged by the thought. Man can form things in his thought, and by impressing his thought upon formless substance can cause the thing he thinks about to be created."

In this formulation, it seems that our thoughts have not only a magnetic but a generative power. And this power not only can but *should* be used to create the material things that we wish for. As Wattles writes: "To become really rich is the noblest aim you can have in life, for it includes everything else. . . . All that is possible in the way of greatness and soul unfoldment, of service and lofty endeavor, comes by way of getting rich; all is made possible by the use of things."

*Things.* He says it so bluntly. So unapologetically. And as I walk further into the raging flames of this brave new world, I am more and more stunned that the same metaphysical belief in the primacy of thought that led the ancient sages of India to renounce worldly things should encourage others to go after them hook, line, and sinker.

At the same yard sale where I bought the tape that exhorted me to float my desires in the air like pink balloons, I also bought a book called *It Works*. It's been sitting unopened in my pile of wish books, but I pounce on it now. Described on its front cover as "The Famous Little Red Book That Makes Your Dreams Come True," it's a miniature volume with a copyright date of 1926. Its author goes by the initials RHJ, and within moments it's clear to me that RHJ is cut from the same cloth as Wallace D. Wattles, and that *It Works* belongs to the same ancestral line as *The Secret*. The famous red book begins with the question "What is the Real Secret of Obtaining Desirable Possessions?" It proceeds, in nineteen tiny pages, to give the answer:

*"If wishes were horses, beggars would ride" is the attitude taken by the average man and woman in regard to posses-*

*sions. They are not aware of a power so near that it is over-
looked; so simple in operation that it is difficult to conceive,
and so sure in results that it is not made use of consciously,
or recognized* as the cause of failure or success.

There follows a list of hapless folk, including Jimmy, who gazes
longingly as a new red roadster goes by, Florence the telephone
operator, who covets a ring in the jeweler's window, and President
Bondum, who "in his private sanctorum, voices a bitter tirade
against the annual attack of hay fever." The error that these people
are making is that they give no thought to what they really want.

And yet, "To get what you want is no more mysterious or uncertain than the radio waves all around you. Tune in correctly
and you get a perfect result, but to do this, it is, of course, necessary to know something of your equipment and have a plan of
operation."

A few sentences later, RHJ reveals that the most important
piece of equipment is a mighty power that lies within us, anxious
and willing to serve us, and capable of providing that which we
earnestly desire. "Other learned writers use different names and
terms, but *all agree that it is omnipotent.* Therefore, I call this
Power 'Emmanuel' (God in us)."

He goes on to explain that occasional or halfhearted wishing
will not form a perfect connection with the omnipotent power
within. In order to connect with that power, he provides "Three
Positive Rules of Accomplishment." They are:

1. Read the list of what you want three times each day:
   morning, noon, and night. *If you want money, write
   down the amount.*
2. Think of what you want as often as possible.
3. Do not talk to any one about your plan except to the
   Great Power within you which will unfold to your
   Objective Mind the method of accomplishment.

In the few pages that follow, RHJ advises one to be quite specific with one's list: "If you want an automobile, *decide what kind, style, price, color,* and all the other details, including when you want it. If you want a home, plan the structure, grounds, and furnishings. Decide on location and cost. If you want money, write down the amount. If you want to break a record in your business, put it down. . . . You must be definite, and when you are, the results will be surprising and almost unbelievable."

RHJ does not explain what he means by your Objective Mind, but presumably he means a mind that is in touch with the mighty power that lies within us, anxious and willing to serve us, whether to provide the red roadster or deliver us from hay fever.

After reading both *The Science of Getting Rich* and *The Famous Little Red Book* I call Rosemary on the phone. It's been a week since we watched *The Secret* together, and now I finally feel ready to confess to her that the focus on *getting things* makes me extremely uncomfortable.

"Oh," she says, after a pause. "Yes, I think many people feel that way. But you see, that's just the way they try to draw people in. They start with where people are, with their very simple, concrete desires. And then those desires can be refined. It's a way of bringing people in the door, creating the widest possible entrance gate. You start with wanting things—more money, a bigger house. And then gradually you realize that it's qualities that you want to cultivate and to draw into your life."

"Qualities?"

"Yes, like peace, love, generosity."

As Rosemary speaks, a bell is ringing in my mind. A loud and surprising bell. For the model she's describing is in essence the same as that described by Plato, some four hundred years before Christ! In one of his most famous dialogues, *The Symposium,* Plato depicts his teacher, Socrates, at a dinner party, where he and his companions are discussing the nature of desire. Socrates is almost the last to speak, and he frames the discussion in a way that is radically different from those who went before him. While most of them made a rather harsh distinction between base and more noble desires, Socrates does not. Rather, he speaks of desire as being on a continuum, all the way from the sexual rutting of animals to the soul's longing to be one with the Heaven of Ideas. And though he definitely believes that the aim of human life is a gradual refinement of desire, he marvels at the same life energy that drives us, animates us at every step of the way.

Now I'm amazed, and even a tad horrified, to recognize that this Platonic idea is present even in *The Famous Little Red Book*! According to RHJ, because the scope of what we can attain is so very great, the first list of desires should

> *consist only of those things with which you are quite familiar, such as an amount of money or accomplishment, or the possession of material things. Such desires as these are more easily and quickly obtained than the discontinuance of fixed habits, the welfare of others, and the healing of mental or bodily ills. Accomplish the lesser things first. Then take the next step, and when that is accomplished, you will seek the higher and really important objectives in life, but long before you reach this stage of your progress, many worthwhile desires will find their place on your list.*

So here, too, in this little red pamphlet I found at a yard sale, is the notion of stages, progressive desires, an infinitely expanding ladder of wishes.

· · ·

Toward the end of September, the summer grows fiercer even as it gives way to fall. One morning, seduced by the intensely golden light, I put on my sneakers and step outside. Making my way down the road, I note more signs of summer's surrender: the violet grapes on a neighbor's arbor, the fallen apples under another's tree, the bulrushes starting to split their seams. Down at the pond I see a tall, willowy woman with long dark hair who is coming in my direction. Though the morning is already hot and the day promises to get much hotter, she's wearing a long-sleeved dress of a dark, gauzy material that goes down to her ankles. And though I've never met her before, I instantly know who she is.

Raquelle.

For years people have been telling me, "You have to meet your neighbor Raquelle."

She's a kind of priestess, I've been told. A sort of witch—but a good witch. She's lived in India, she performs sacred dance, and she channels divine energy.

I introduce myself, and we talk briefly. "People have been telling me about you, too!" she says. "We should get together and talk about our writing." I didn't realize that she was a writer, too. Immediately, I sense her intensity. Her eyes are large and dark, and they look right into mine. She's probably in her early forties, but there's something girlish, almost babylike, about her face. Her voice is soft but resonant, authoritative even. It's impossible to imagine her making chitchat. There's some unusual combination of gravity and gaiety that both her voice and her movements convey, and just standing there among the bulrushes, I feel mesmerized. Then she breaks the spell by telling me she needs to get back to her house. It appears that she's been ill for some time, struggling with some sort of chronic fatigue.

About a week later, I find a letter in my mailbox that reads:

*Dear friends,*

*As many of you know, I have been going through a prolonged ordeal in the form of a mysterious and depleting illness. I have every faith that this deep descent into darkness is preparing me to transmit an ever steadier and more radiant light. But the process of preparation is draining all my resources now, and that is why I am putting forth this appeal. Though it is very difficult for me to do so, I am asking my friends to help me in any way they can. I would be forever grateful for any offerings of food, money, or time. And it would be an enormous help to me if anyone would like to buy my book.*

Reading the letter, I feel a great pang for her. As a woman living alone, my greatest fear would be to fall into a lingering illness. And writer to writer—of course I'll buy her book. I dial the phone number that she provided in the letter, and when she answers, I hear the fatigue in her voice.

"I thought I'd come over and buy one of your books, Raquelle."

"Well, you haven't really seen it," she says, sounding doubtful.

"I'm looking forward! And first I'm going to the grocery store. Can I bring you something to eat?"

"I'd love some ground turkey."

"White or dark?"

"Dark."

Though I've walked past the back of Raquelle's house a thousand times or more on my way to the pond, I've never been to the front door, which is set far back from the road. I knew that the house was old, and I could tell it was big, but I pictured it a sort of ramshackle hunter's lodge in which Raquelle, pale and somewhat waiflike, shivered in underfurnished rooms.

But the moment Raquelle opens the door, my preconceptions fall away. The house is, indeed, an old wooden lodge, with hardwood floors and dark wood-paneled rooms. But it's been renovated, meticulously maintained, and beautifully appointed. It's majestic, with leaded-glass windows and carved wooden doors. Various surfaces—mantels, tabletops, the tops of windowsills—are hung with exquisite bolts of iridescent silk, threaded with gold.

"Would you like to come into the temple?" Raquelle asks. She leads me into what most people would refer to as a living room.

But it is a truly impressive space. The furniture—settee, armchairs, a daybed with a wrought-iron frame and velvet mattress—is on a grand scale, as if made to order for a castle. From the cathedral ceiling, a shaft of light plunges to the floor. There's a magnificent wooden staircase that, just before it arrives at the second story, provides a kind of balcony that looks down on the room below.

"That looks like it would make a wonderful stage!" I say to her. "Have you ever had performances in here?"

"Oh, yes," she says, looking slightly perplexed. "Didn't you ever get the flyer for my "Channeling the Goddess" workshop?"

I do remember having gotten a flyer in my mailbox about a year ago. It showed a photograph of a hand holding a flaming torch, and it announced an evening of prayers and sacred dance, to be performed by Raquelle, with a suggested contribution of twenty-five dollars. Something had irked me about that last point, and I hadn't responded. But now, standing in this space, I can well imagine Raquelle with her long dark hair and a flowing dress, dancing up and down the stairs, standing on that balcony and channeling the goddess. Why shouldn't she have asked for a contribution? So far as I can tell, she doesn't seem to have any sort of regular job. And the rent on this huge house, where she lives alone in her illness, has got to be a pretty penny.

"How did you come to live here?" I ask her.

She tells me that she had been living quite happily in Vermont. But she began to feel a deep intuition that she should move to California. She went online, read about this house, and moved out here, sight unseen!

While the tea water boils, she takes me into a little room that is piled high with copies of the book that I had offered to buy. "Here," she says, laughing, and heaving one of them into my arms.

It's a huge, heavy tome—bigger than the Manhattan phone book. It must weigh twenty pounds. It's called *Opening to the Sacred*, and it's absolutely sumptuous. Its cover is dark, satiny brocade. The glossy, high-rag-content pages are multicolored and separated by sheets of vellum. Facing the text on most of the pages is an elegant envelope. You open the envelope and pull out a card that bears an elaborate collage created by Raquelle. They are really quite striking, and they appear to me like a kind of psychedelic, New Age, Pre-Raphaelite Hieronymus Bosch swirl of imagery, full of figures and symbols.

Glancing at the table of contents, I see that the book represents a mystical journey. It's divided into stages, each introduced with a meditation by Raquelle. Though her own writing is interwoven throughout the book, much of the text is drawn from other poets and seekers. Nietzsche, Rumi, Rilke . . . It's an impressive list.

The cost, I note, is $260.

Not quite what I had anticipated when I walked over with my little packet of ground turkey.

Raquelle laughs; she knows what's going through my mind.

"Now you know why I told you to wait and see it!"

"It's stunning, Raquelle. How did you come to create it?"

"It just came through me," she says. "I really had no choice in the matter!"

As I get to know Raquelle better, I will learn that this is a kind of refrain in her life. As with her moving to this magnificent house—sight unseen, and on the other end of the continent from where she lived—she proceeds through intuition, the reading of signs, the sense of being guided by some power deeper than her own will. And she doesn't seem to allow the cost of things to detract her. The book, for instance. Since my mind is already swirling with numbers, I find myself doing an instant calculation. The book looks as though it must have cost at least $100 a copy to produce, and she had a thousand of them printed up at her own expense. That's $100,000! Some, no doubt, would call it hubris, but I'm amazed by her courage.

I am even more amazed, after we take our cups of tea and sit before the fire in the temple, when we find ourselves talking about the men in—or out—of our lives, and she tells me about her most recent quest for love.

Nearly two years earlier, she began to feel a very strong conviction that the love of her life was waiting for her in Big Sur. Over a period of several weeks she asked for guidance in her meditation, and the conviction grew stronger. It also grew clearer and more specific. She was to drive to Big Sur on a particular Saturday and find her love waiting for her at 2 P.M. in the café at Nepenthe, the Route 1 restaurant perched on a cliff overlooking the Pacific.

The day came. Raquelle drove down the coast. She went into the café at the appointed hour—and whom should she find but a fellow she had known in high school back in Vermont. She sat down beside him, and they talked for two hours straight, pouring out their life stories. She had never been attracted to him, and she wasn't now—but through connections that she made through him that day, she met a man she fell deeply in love with a few weeks later. He was a sculptor who lived high on a forested ridge in a cabin that he had built himself. He and Raquelle felt a powerful attraction to each other in body, mind, heart, and soul. It was the sort of attraction that comes over you in an instant and that seems like a form of recognition, as though you have loved each other for lifetimes. Over the following year they continued to see each other, traveling back and forth between Big Sur and the wine country. They became engaged. And then, two weeks before the wedding day, he broke it off. "I don't want to be married to a goddess," he said. "I don't want to live in a temple."

It was in the wake of that profound heartbreak that Raquelle first experienced the symptoms of the illness from which she's been languishing, and trying to heal herself, ever since.

* * *

By the time I leave, the afternoon has turned to evening and in my hands the little packet of ground turkey has been replaced by Raquelle's giant book, *Opening to the Sacred*. In an act of great generosity, Raquelle decided to give me the book, in exchange for future participation in one of my writing groups. Stumbling along the dark road, I feel in a somewhat altered state, as though I've been sipping nectar with Isis or Demeter and come back lugging her gift of a tabernacle.

When I enter my own house, it feels small and stuffy, with its faint odor of gas from the stove and a clutter of papers everywhere: stacks of my students' writings, bills. . . . How does Raquelle do it, I wonder? I know she doesn't live on air. But there's something so ethereal about her: with her willowy body, her long silky hair and gauzy clothes, her house fit for the Faery Queen. She took me on a tour of all the rooms, and I didn't see a single corner that showed the seamy side of life, the evidence of earthly coping. Every surface gleamed, looking ready to serve as an altar or pedestal for some exquisite talismanic object: a purple geode, a dancing Shiva, a bronze Kwan-yin. How does Raquelle navigate the material reality of life? Is she paying her bills? As I lie in bed that night, I feel an odd contradictory impulse: to rescue her from her unearthliness, and to learn the secret art of her unearthly lavishness.

When I fall asleep, my dreams are imbued with Raquelle's glittering presence, but when I wake up in the middle of the night, I'm back in my own dark thicket of worries. What will happen to George? What should we do about my mother?

When I reach to turn on the light, I discover that I am not alone. Once or twice before, Nicholas has driven up after I've already gone to sleep and then slipped soundlessly under the covers beside me. It's the best possible surprise, the perfect antidote to my night fears. I'd love to wake him up so we could murmur together for a while, but I refrain. I know he has to get up before dawn to make it to his inner-city classroom. Since I did not turn on the light, the moonlight is streaming in through the blinds, throwing a pattern of stripes on the walls that makes the whole room look like the inside of a wicker basket. Pulling the blanket up over my eyes, I curl up next to Nicholas and attune to his quiet breathing, letting it take me deeper, deeper, down into the peaceful darkness, a place where worries will not find me.

But just as I'm about to cross that final border into sleep, I startle awake. Like the princess who feels the pea, I am acutely aware of something beneath my mattress. It's something very small, but it feels enormous. It's the thought-made-thing, the paper wish that brought this beautiful man with his two bruised shoulders to lie beside me.

* * *

In the morning when I wake up, Nicholas has already gone.

In the kitchen I find that he has placed two of my smallest matching bowls side by side, and in each bowl he's placed a tiny sugar spoon. It's a visual joke, a reference to the strange fact that ever since we first met, I've been accosted by stories about women over fifty bearing twins. If I'm standing in line at the grocery store, a giant headline or spread of celebrity pix will leap out at me. Jane Seymour! Joan Lunden! A parade of quinquagenarians holding their very own pair of newborns. Then, at a dinner party—without my having prompted her in any way—a friend told both Nicholas and me about a friend of hers who had recently given birth to twins at fifty-three. The next day, when Nicholas and I chanced to walk into an antiques store, the first thing we noticed was a beautiful green baby carriage, French, circa 1850. It had a landscape of willows and swans painted on its metal sides, and it had not one but two little black leather seats.

"For the twins!" Nicholas said.

He thinks it's funny, and he's taken to starting sentences with "When the twins come . . ." But, I confess, it's making me nervous. I've put that huge *History of Celibacy* back on the shelf, and it's wonderful to have a man in my life again, but twins at fifty is a bounty I would rather not have. So how should I take these repeated references in the field, which are starting to seem relentless? As a warning, a joke, a sign?

Meanwhile, beside the two little bowls on my kitchen table there's a pile of my wish books, and though there are several I haven't read yet, I find myself reaching for Paul Pearsall's *Wishing Well*. And then—could this really be a totally random occurrence?—I turn directly to a passage that I don't remember having read before:

> *The best wishers are worriers. One of the signals you can use to tell you when a wish is called for is worrying. If you don't worry you can't wish well, because worrying is an essential precursor of a well-made wish. . . . Our ability to think about consequences, reflect on them, try to sense them, and even ruminate a little about what "might be" is one of our most important adaptive skills. It's a means of rehearsing "what ifs" and "what will I do if" and running over and over again in our mind the worst-case scenarios without having to actually experience them. The key is to know you're worrying and when to stop worrying and do something or wish for something. Worry can be a tip-off that a wish in the domain of your worrying may be in order.*

Tip-off received. It seems I've got to take the energy of my worrying about my mother and transform it into yet one more wish. I've got to take the contraction of my anxiety and allow it to expand into a potent plan of action. Look at Raquelle: though it's clear from her appeals for donations that she's not working with unlimited resources, she doesn't seem to let practical worries get the best of her. She begins with a thought in the mind, a vision of what she wants, and then lets herself be led *where it listeth*—even if it means leaving everything behind and traveling across the continent to a sight-unseen residence. And look at her now—in her beautiful temple of a house, with its royal furnishings!

I take out a pen and paper and begin to write:

*I wish for my mother to be safe and near her children, in a beautiful and very European sort of place where Luigi will want to visit often.*

What's the most European place I can think of around here?

It's the town of Sonoma, not far from where I live. It's the former Mexican capital of California, and it's built in the Spanish style, around a plaza. I would like for there to be two bedrooms, so that someone can stay with my mother to keep her company. And it would be wonderful if there is a pool, because she loves to swim . . .

I know that Paul Pearsall would urge me to become more serene before setting out, that Carole would tell me to stop and make a shrine, that Wallace J. Wattles would tell me I haven't practiced hard enough to fully impress my thoughts on matter, and that RHJ would tell me I need to be more specific ("If you want a home, plan the structure, grounds, and furnishings. Decide on location and cost . . ."), but I feel that time is short. And in that place where human power meets human powerlessness, I must not scamp my work. Quickly, quickly, I throw on my clothes, jump into my car, and drive to the Plaza in Sonoma to look for the place I've wished for.

# CHAPTER TEN

# October

*Body/Mind: Trusting Connection*

It's October, and on the vines the grapes are heavy, purple, and covered with dust. The grasses look as though they could burst into flame, and I'm remembering how it was when at last I moved back to California after more than two decades of living under that leaden gray shield of the snow belt. We moved at the end of summer, and in October I went to visit a friend who lived near Oakland. Originally from New York, she'd been living in California for nearly as long as I'd been living in her part of the world. She and I went for a late-morning walk around her neighborhood. It had been an unusually cold and foggy summer in the Bay Area, and she was chattering away, exulting in the breezy warmth of the day. "Isn't it balmy?" she said. But I was on edge, uncomfortable in my skin and unable to concentrate on our conversation. "Isn't it balmy?" she said again.

"Something doesn't feel right," I said. Then we looked up in the sky, and there it was: the first coil of black smoke from the Oakland fire that was about to burn more than two thousand homes.

What is the kind of knowing that begins as a physical sensation, a state of the body, well before it translates into words or even a conscious thought? What is the kind of knowing that can be stored in the body through twenty years of exile, latent as a seed under the desert sand, and then burst into bloom as soon as certain precise conditions are met?

It's a knowing with the body, the way animals know—and people, too, when they are attentive. Just think of the stories one hears about people who knew that they were seriously ill, even though they had no symptoms and sometimes even in the face of skeptical doctors. I have more than one friend who's told me that they would not be alive today were it not for a warning that came to them in a dream.

How do we explain the place where such dreams come from? It's the body's mind, the mind's body. And it's the place where, over thousands of years, human beings have most intently focused their wish power, in the passionate—and sometimes desperate—desire to believe that *if only we can think the right thoughts and say the right words, we can transcend the limitations of the body.*

•   •   •

I'm thinking of these things because I'm on my way to visit my friend George in Santa Cruz, while his wife, Vicki, is out of town for a brief and much needed rest. I first met George and Vicki nearly thirty years ago when I was a graduate student in Toronto and babysat for their two young children. They've often told me that my intense homesickness for Santa Cruz was part of what inspired their decision to move. And now, as I drive, I'm trying to prepare myself for what I may find when I arrive there.

George has always been a fountain of energy, leaping through rooms, breaking into dance at the least provocation, wiggling his ears, singing in tongues. Though he's actually Jewish and from Massachusetts, he's always looked to me like a kind of wild Indian holy man or music maker, with his brown skin, big dark eyes, and beaklike nose, his long thin body and unruly black hair. He's a mix of contradictions. Serious, philosophical, and reverent when it comes to the meaning of life, the rearing of children, and the fate of the earth, he's simultaneously spontaneous, goofy, silly to an almost manic point at times, like some trickster spirit, a Jewish Hindu coyote priest, philosopher, and political activist.

For the last twenty years, George has devoted much of his life to the story of a brave little girl and her wish.

When we first met, George had just left behind a promising career as a professor of political science. Then the family moved from Toronto to Santa Cruz, and—without any experience or training—George set out on the risky path of making films for children. The first one was based on the true story of Sadako, the little girl from Hiroshima who developed leukemia in the aftermath of the bomb. A friend who came to visit her in the hospital reminded her of the magic power of cranes. "Cranes live for a thousand years," the friend said. "If a sick person folds a thousand paper cranes, the gods will grant their wish to be healed." With hope in her heart, Sadako began to fold her cranes. Ten, one hundred, two hundred . . . They sat on the sills of her window and hung in long strands from the ceiling of her hospital room. Friends, relatives, classmates began to send her beautiful papers so that she could continue to fold. "Three hundred . . . four hundred . . ." She had folded nearly seven hundred cranes when at last she succumbed to her illness. After her death, her classmates founded the Paper Crane Club in her memory, and word of Sadako spread throughout Japan. Since 1958, thousands of people from all over the world have come before the beautiful statue of Sadako that stands in Peace Park in Hiroshima. It shows Sadako, holding a golden crane with outstretched arms. On the base of the statue, Sadako's young friends had these words engraved: "This is our wish. This is our prayer. Peace in the world."

And so it is that George, a wildly energetic American man in the prime of life, found himself possessed by the powerful spirit of a frail Japanese girl. Over a period of years, the house in Santa Cruz was transformed into a kind of shrine to Sadako, with paper cranes flying from the rafters and nesting on every tabletop and windowsill. He traveled around the country, showing the film at schools and libraries and teaching hundreds of children, their parents, and their teachers to fold paper cranes. When the big Santa ~~Loma~~ ~~Prieta~~ ~~Cruz~~ earthquake hit in 1989, George was in Hiroshima, presenting his film as a tribute to Sadako and to all those who shared her tragic fate.

Now George himself is ill. For weeks he's been lying in bed in the house in Santa Cruz. After his initial diagnosis, it appeared for some time that he was keeping the illness at bay, and so he felt encouraged in his refusal of medical treatment. But then he began to develop disturbing symptoms: pain in the hips, difficulty moving.

Since I heard about his initiation into Christian Science, I've been trying to learn more about it. My grandmother Grace, who lived about the same time as Mary Baker Eddy, was a believer. She never talked to me about it, but because she lived it there was something very palpable that she transmitted. She wasn't a purist, and in dire circumstances she would consent to see a doctor. But for the most part, she stayed away from the medical profession. And above all, she believed in keeping one's thoughts focused on goodness, truth, and light. You would never hear her complaining or uttering a negative judgment about anyone or anything—not even when she succumbed, periodically, to the terrible dark depressions to which she was prone.

I've been reading a book called *God's Perfect Child: Living and Dying in the Christian Science Church.* The author, Caroline Fraser, was raised in an observant Christian Scientist household. On the very first page she writes,

> *In Sunday school, we learned that . . . God was All. Matter was nothing. At the age of four or five, I gazed at the top of the Sunday school table, at my knees going under it, at*

*the plastic chairs, at the scratchy sisal carpet. The table and*
*the chairs and the carpet and the knees* looked *real, but*
*they weren't. They weren't even there. They were matter,*
*and matter was Error, and Error did not exist.*

Gradually I'm coming to understand that Christian Science seems to fuse two contradictory philosophies, both of which are very ancient. On the one hand, it is a form of radical idealism, for which the core principle is All is Mind (or Spirit). Thought alone is real, and what appears to us as the physical world is an illusion; *the knees, the plastic chairs, the scratchy sisal carpet are not real.* Yet at the same time, Christian Science has a great deal in common with certain ancient dualistic religions that posit two separate and conflicting orders of reality: Spirit and Matter. Among these is Manicheaism, which emerged in southern Babylon some two hundred years after Christ and became one of the most widely influential religions of the ancient world. For Manicheans, the central task for human beings is to wholly identify with God, in whose likeness we are made, and thus experience freedom from the darkness of Matter. As an ancient text puts it: "If you do not make yourself equal to God, you cannot apprehend God, for like is apprehended by like. Outleap all body and expand yourself to unmeasured greatness: outstrip all time and become Eternity; so shall you apprehend God."

This is precisely what George has been attempting, as he lies hour after hour, day after day, in his bed in Santa Cruz. In our conversations he has made it clear to me that in becoming a Christian Scientist, he has embraced the belief that if we can train our mind to focus on the eternal, then we can indeed outleap the limitations of our bodily form and our earthly existence.

But for Vicki—and for the children, who are now young adults—George's refusal to acknowledge that he is sick with a potentially fatal illness has been very difficult. Not only has this prevented him from getting medical treatment, but it makes it extremely difficult for them to talk with him about plans for his care, and it also means that they can't share their own anxieties with him. When Vicki broaches the subject of his illness, she feels that George wards her off, believing that her negative thoughts are quite literally harmful to him. And even when I called a few days ago to tell him "I want to come and visit you soon," there was a pause. I could tell that he didn't like the sound of urgency in my voice. And then he said, "You know I always love to see you, Noelle. But don't come to put another nail in my coffin."

Like all the people who care for George, I would like to be able to support him in the way that he wishes to be supported. But the truth is, I have always been profoundly suspicious of people and practices that deal with painful situations by refusing to think about them. Some years ago I lived next door to a woman who, throughout her small mouse-infested house, had stuck yellow Post-it notes that read: "Those squeaks I'm hearing are NOT mice!" Every time I visited her, there seemed to be more mice, and she seemed more and more anxious and on edge. When at last I broke down and brought her some Havahart traps, she was furious with me—as if in acknowledging the mice I was reinforcing their existence. To me, her reaction seemed absurd—and potentially dangerous. What if one day the intruders were not mice but thieves?

As I read more about Mary Baker Eddy, I'm learning just how vigorously the negative thoughts were swept from her door. It seems that, as time went by, she became increasingly obsessed with the "malicious animal magnetism" that she felt was being directed at her by disloyal former students. Caroline Fraser writes, "M.A.M. was not only in the mail, it was widespread throughout the physical world, a colorless, odorless, insidious influence affecting Mrs. Eddy's health, her food and clothing, the air she breathed, and the weather outside her home; it also preyed on her students and aides. It made lost objects impossible to find and ruined the printing of her books. It required constant vigilance." In the last years of her life, her poor staff had to take turns maintaining a con-stant round-the-clock vigil, using the power of their own positive thoughts to repel the relentless waves of vicious incoming M.A.M.

Alas, the more I learn about Mary Baker Eddy, the more disen-chanted I'm becoming. Though she clearly had prodigious gifts for guiding and inspiring her thousands of disciples, she seems a clas-sic example of what can happen to people when, as the Jungians say, we try to "repress the shadow." As Jung himself said, "What remains unconscious will return as fate." In Mary Baker Eddy's case, it seems that her fate was to grow more and more paranoid as she tried harder and harder to shoo those dark thoughts away.

• • •

I arrive in Santa Cruz at dusk, and when I step into George and Vicki's house, it's very quiet. It doesn't feel like a house that is laps-ing into chaos through the force of illness. There are freshly picked flowers on the table in the living room, and it smells as though bread has been baking in the kitchen.

"George?"

George calls my name, and I follow his voice down the hall to the room where he lies in his bed.

When I see him, I have to keep from gasping. He's so thin, his face seems so drawn, and his large eyes look enormous.

I feel almost afraid to put my arms around him, but he reaches out to hug me, and then I sit in the chair beside him. I've brought a bouquet of bright orange tiger lilies, which I put on his night-stand. And in my picnic basket I've brought hot chicken soup and rolls, which, he tells me, is the very thing he's been craving. As I set out these offerings, I'm aware of how much I need them. They are little buffers, signs of my own relative power and well-being, evidence that I still belong to the place that Sylvia Plath described as "a country far away as health." I think of how the spiritual teacher Ram Dass, recovering from a major stroke, described how much harder it is to receive than to offer help.

But within moments, lying there hollowed out in his bed, George puts me at ease. He asks me about myself, my daughter, the drive I've just made down the coast. We slurp our chicken soup together, and gradually it's as though I come to room temperature, adjusting to the zone where George now lives. As though the molecules of panic evaporate from my skin until I can just be there beside him, inhabiting the same atmosphere, breathing the same air, feeling acutely alive together in this nether zone, this dusk-filled room.

Our minds have always wandered freely, leaping from one idea to the next in a very fluent conversation. But it's strange now, because despite the underlying fluency, there are these huge things we can't talk about, like pain, illness, death. I don't want to spend my precious time with him in metaphysical arguments.

So I ask him about Sadako, and what her life reveals about the power—or powerlessness—of the wish.

George tells me, "When I go around the country introducing children to Sadako, they often ask me, 'How come she didn't get her wish?' And I tell them, 'Well, what does it really mean to *get your wish*?' Because there's that other meaning of 'to get,' which is *to understand*.'"

As George continues, what I *get* is this: Sadako's personal wish for herself to stay alive, to be cured of radiation sickness, was not fulfilled. But over the course of her brief life, that personal wish was transformed. It became the medium of her connection to thousands of people around the world, a connection that continues to this day. It became the small opening for a tremendous outpouring of human kindness and generosity. It became the ongoing reminder to wish and to work for a world in which all children are safe from the terrible suffering of war.

Listening to him, I think of something that a young poet friend of mine, Kythe, told me recently, when I asked her about the place of wishing in her life: "I've learned that deep down we're never truly separate from what we wish for. We may not always seem to get the literal thing that we wished for. But then we learn to wish better."

"That's absolutely right," says George.

"Would you say that's what happened to Sadako?"

"Yes."

*And for yourself?* But something keeps me from asking that question. Perhaps it's that I don't want to ask George to evaluate himself, to judge his own progress.

Years ago, when I read the book called *Who Dies?* by the writer and grief counselor Stephen Levine, I encountered his distinction between curing and healing. It's not always possible to be physically cured of a disease, but in the process of dying we may find that profound psychological and spiritual wounds are being healed.

Sitting there in the darkening room, I know that George has wished to be cured. He has believed that his thoughts had the power to vanquish illness. Seeing the state of his increasingly frail body, it seems to the rest of us that the experiment has failed. Yet having spent these hours in his presence, I feel refreshed. I definitely feel less afraid of illness and of dying. And despite my very mixed feelings about his newfound beliefs, I know that they have played a role in what has transpired between us. Because the quality of our visit would simply not have been possible if he had allowed himself to be overwhelmed by pain or dazed by medication or obsessed and anxious over the latest test results or overcome by bitterness at his condition. Despite the weak and emaciated state of George's body, after spending a handful of hours beside him I find that my heart feels lighter.

"It's really all about fear," he says to me when I take his hand to say good night.

"Fear?"

"Yes. It's amazing what can happen when fear is gone." He's too tired to say more.

The next morning when it's time to say good-bye, I don't break down as I expected to—and it's not because I'm holding it in, either. Despite all I felt I couldn't say when I was with him, I don't have any sense of stones unturned, because somehow, with and without words, we have both managed to express the essential: *I am alive with you in this moment, and I treasure you.*

. . .

Driving home along the coast route, I have the sensation of parting two seas. To my left is the vast silver blue of the ocean; to my right is a field of bright orange pumpkins.

Will George ever be able to leave his room and see the world again?

We don't know.

But it's clear that what he's asking of us is to help him face the unknown without fear.

*It's really all about fear,* he said.

If he hadn't been so tired last night, I would have liked to talk with him further. And if only I hadn't felt the need to protect him from my own doubts, I would have liked to tell him about my own most intense encounter with fear.

It happened during my experience of childbirth. The labor was long, and for hours the pain was beyond anything that I'd ever imagined the human body could feel. Yet, through most of it, I was able to stay quite calm and focused. I followed my breath in and out, and it seemed like the most wonderful affirmation of the power of meditation—especially because I've never thought of myself as being very physically strong. At a certain point the doctors and nurses began telling me, "You're exhausted. You're wearing down." They began to urge one intervention after another: we'll give you pain medication, we'll give you an epidural, we'll stop the labor so you can rest, we recommend a caesarean. But I refused. I felt they couldn't see that I'd discovered the most amazing reservoir of energy. I felt exhilarated, almost ecstatic. If I could transcend this level of suffering, then nothing could ever harm me! I felt utterly free. And then something happened. Through a combination of pain and exhaustion, the scales tipped, and I lost the thread of awareness. It was as though my mind shattered, and I became engulfed by fear. I felt as though I was drowning in a tidal wave. One of the nurses seemed to understand what was happening, and she called my name: "Noelle! Noelle!" I swam in the direction of my name, and a few moments later my daughter was born.

Though my own experience with extreme fear ended joyfully, it haunted me for years. Seeing George has brought it back up to the surface. And so it is that driving past the ocean, the fields, that he may never see again, I find myself with yet a new wish: *May George find his way past all fear.*

· · ·

A few days after my return from Santa Cruz, an envelope arrives in the mail, sent by a childhood friend. When I open it up, a shiny coin falls into my hand: a Sacajawea dollar. "Dear Noelle," the accompanying letter reads,

> *Since I know you are interested in wishes, I thought you might like to try this technique. Believe it or not, it was recommended by my physician—but it's very low tech. All it requires is a Sacajawea dollar and a wart that you wish to get rid of. And here's what you do: You go for a walk down a country road, holding the coin in your hand. After you've gone a ways, you stop and rub the wart vigorously with the coin. And then you throw away the coin and leave.*

And so the next morning I set out from my house, ready to perform my own mind/body experiment on the small wart that I've had for some time on my right index finger. As I walk down the path toward the pond, I can't help wondering how it was that Sacajawea, of all people, became the goddess of wart removal.

Sacajawea, who stepped into the canoe and went off into the great unknown with her newborn baby and two white men, Lewis and Clark, who were as foreign to her as the moon.

*Sacajawea, goddess of long absences, vast homesickness, will you forgive us for making use of you for our small disappearances?*

Arriving at the rim of the pond, I rub my wart and toss the coin into the reeds.

Halfway down the road, I see Raquelle walking a short distance ahead of me. She herself looks like a beautiful Indian maiden, with her dignified pace, her willowy stature, her long flowing dark hair. When I catch up to her, she tells me that she's still struggling with her mysterious illness but that she's excited about some new connections for her book. It seems that one of the producers of the movie *What the Bleep Do We Know!?* has taken an interest in it, and there's a rumor that Madonna might like a copy.

"What have you been up to?" she asks.

"Well, at the moment, I'm trying to wish away a wart."

Raquelle laughs. "You've got to talk to my friend Rupert!" she says. We walk down to the edge of the pond where Rupert is dangling his feet over the deck. He's a slender, dark-haired, midlife man, and though he smiles in greeting, his face looks anxious and preoccupied.

"Tell him what you're up to!" Raquelle says. And when I tell him about my wart and Sacajawea, he tells me that he has long had an interest in the power of the mind to affect the body. It turns out that he's a publisher and that one of his bestselling books was on the mind's healing power. He thinks he has an extra copy in his car, and as we walk back up the road to find it, he begins to pour out a very sinister story.

One of the books that he recently published was a very critical study of certainly highly placed American politicians with links to the religious right. Since the book came out, both he and other people involved with the writing and publishing of the book have fallen prey to mysterious illnesses: fevers, fatigues, rashes. It's something that he doesn't feel at liberty to talk about at great length, and I don't press him.

But neither do I dismiss what he says. When I was ordering the long list of wish books, I discovered a book whose title I could not resist.

"Have you read a book called *The Men Who Stare at Goats?*" I ask Rupert.

He looks at me as though I'm getting ready to make a joke at his expense, and so I explain to him that it's a serious and rigorously researched book. According to its author, the journalist and documentary filmmaker Jon Ronson, certain highly placed officials within the United States military and governing agencies have long been exploring the potentially lethal power of mind over matter. Hard as it is to believe, large sums of American tax revenue have gone into experimental attempts to thwart the enemy by becoming invisible, walking through walls, implanting negative thoughts, and cultivating a paralyzing gaze—a gaze that can make hamsters keel over and goats stop dead in their tracks. Ronson traces three decades of such practices, which he maintains continue to this day in Afghanistan and Iraq and within the Department of Homeland Security.

Having read this book, I don't doubt that a U.S. government agency might perform malevolent thought experiments on perceived enemies like Rupert and his comrades. But I can't help wondering: How much does Rupert's belief in the power of mind over body make him vulnerable to being manipulated by others? As Cavendish writes in *The History of Magic,* "Confidence in magic can cause it to work. When a spell is cast to heal someone who is sick, and he believes in it, his belief may help him to recover. When a spell is cast to murder a man, and he believes in it, his belief may kill him."

Once again, I think of George saying, *It's all about fear.*

. . .

Meanwhile, my own mini–mind/body experiment is not going so well.

A week or so after flinging the Sacajawea coin into the reeds, when I go to the doctor for my annual checkup, I show her my wart and ask her what she thinks about warts and wishes.

"It's true," she says. "Warts are very susceptible to thought energy. That may be why warts and witches tend to go together, because there really is something kind of magical about warts, and the way they can be made to appear and disappear. But what you have there is not a wart. It's a keratosis. It's not dangerous in and of itself, but it does indicate that you've had a fair bit of sun exposure. It's not likely to grow, but you'll most likely have it for the rest of your life."

*For the rest of your life.* Though it's a very small bump, the finality of her words make me shudder. And as I look down at my keratosis, I remember the words of the writer Philip K. Dick: "Reality is that which, even when we wish it, does not go away."

But is that really true? Aren't there times when the most intractable reality does indeed seem to bend or to bow? For spontaneous remissions are real, too: the inoperable tumor that mysteriously disappears, the relentlessly progressing disease that mysteriously reverses itself. Are such occurrences miracles? Many people believe that they are. Others believe that once we finally gain an adequate scientific understanding of such occurrences, they will no longer seem mysterious or miraculous.

. . .

While still thrashing about in these questions, one day I come across an essay in *Harper's Magazine* called "Pathologies of Hope." It's by the well-known writer Barbara Ehrenreich, who has herself survived a bout with cancer. In the essay she reveals her resentment and distrust of the new field of "positive psychology," which is devoted to the scientific study of happiness.

> *If health and well-being in general are at stake, the positive psychologists would argue, why not indulge in some positive illusions even at the cost of "realism"? There's no question but that extreme, locked-in negativity in the form of depression is a risk factor for physical illness, but the evidence for the health-enhancing effects of positivity is surprisingly muddled. A frequently cited 1988 article arguing that positive illusions, such as unwarrantedly high self-estimations, promote mental health has been disputed. Nor are positive-thinking people necessarily happier than pessimists or realists, since anyone who self-reports positivity is equally likely to self-report happiness. As for "success": in workplaces that enjoin a positive attitude, one would do well to conform, but the halls of fame are lined with the busts of major depressives, including Max Weber, William James, John Donne, and Samuel Johnson.*

I'm not sure that I follow her on the logic of self-reporting, but given my own philosophical bent, I do understand her decision not to engage in "positive illusions," no matter how beneficial their effects. With regard to her own medical ordeal, Ehrenreich writes that she got through it in a state of constant rage. "The trick, as my teen hero Camus wrote, is to draw strength from the 'refusal to hope, and the unyielding evidence of a life without consolation.'"

*The unyielding evidence of a life without consolation.*

Is it, indeed, so unyielding?

Or is it possible that to omit the second field of flowers—the flowers that were able to pierce through Viktor Frankl's numbness—is every bit as delusional as to omit the first? As Frankl wrote of that second field, the one I failed to remember: "One day, a few days after the liberation, I walked through the country past the flowering meadows, for miles and miles, toward the market town near the camp. Larks rose to the sky and I could hear their joyous song."

What would Barbara say to Viktor: "Close your ears!"?

• • •

To quiet the voices that have been whirling around in my mind, one evening I take pen and paper in hand and go down to the bench by the pond. With the fat autumn bullfrogs bellowing around me, I scribble for a while until I come up with a schema that brings me some ease. For when I put it on paper, the whirl seems to sort rather nicely into three broad categories of people:

1. There are those who refuse to think happy thoughts unless they are first convinced, beyond a shadow of a doubt, that the world is indeed a good place to be in.

2. There are those who prefer to think happy thoughts because it makes them feel better—never mind whether those thoughts accurately reflect the nature of reality.

3. And there are those who insist that if they think happy thoughts, they will actually change the nature of what happens to them and the world around them.

Barbara Ehrenreich obviously belongs in the first category, along with her teen hero Camus. And some of the positive psychologists whom she excoriates endorse the wisdom of the second category. George, despite his skeptical roots, is doing his best to be in category three—along with other Christian Scientists and any number of contemporary New Age thinkers, including disciples of *The Secret*. But then there are some people who are hard to place.

Paul Pearsall, for example, who seems to overlap the categories. In the grip of his near-fatal illness, he became deeply skeptical about what he calls "relentless hopeful optimism." In fact, he even came to appreciate the power of hopelessness. He writes:

> No one gave me a book about the joy of hopelessness, so I had to put my own mind to the issue. The more I thought about hope as being a way—but not the way—to deal with adversity, the more I also began to find value in giving up hope as a way to think differently about my life, particularly during times of my deepest despair.
>
> I began to fear that constant hoping might cause me to sacrifice today for the illusion of a better tomorrow. I wondered whether I was allowing others to see my present as devoid of meaning. . . . Constant hoping led me into reckless regard for how I was evaluating my own present.

Yet it was within the context of abandoning hope that he experienced the power of the wish: "When I was dying and spending what everyone thought would be my last night alive in the intensive care unit, I saw a shooting star."

Though the star was only the nurse's tiny flashlight, it inspired Pearsall to make his wish. He wished that he might feel the presence of those he loved who'd gone before him. And in the morning when he woke, he heard the doctor saying, "This is a miracle. Remove the tube. He's not finished yet."

* * *

What can account for such a miracle?

It seems that when we arrive at the extreme edge between life and death, it can sometimes take something very small to tip the scale: a subtle form of assent, a kind of homeopathic "yes" to life, a mustering of vital energy. And isn't this assent, at least in part, what happens when a placebo works, that the patient's belief in the remedy, the expectation of healing, somehow engages the body's own natural resistance to illness?

*He turned his face to the wall and died.*

This phrase recurs in the writings of concentration camp survivors, describing the moment when a fellow inmate relinquished the will to live. Having survived for months under the harshest conditions, the person seemed to die instantly after letting go of the tiny thread of desire. There was a movement there, a final spurt of energy: "He turned his face to the wall . . ."

But what if the spurt went the other way?

Many years ago, I translated a book called *Life Begins Today* by a Frenchman named Jacques Lusseyran. Though he had been blinded in an accident when he was eight years old, as a teenager during the Nazi occupation of France, he became an important figure in the French resistance. Eventually, Jacques and a number of his closest friends were betrayed and rounded up, and Jacques was sent to Buchenwald. Because he was a gifted translator, the Nazis did not immediately destroy him as they did most people with disabilities, and so not only did he survive his experience in the camp, but he helped others to survive it. Among the extraordinary things he did was to organize poetry readings among the inmates. Drawing upon the memories and the multiple languages of hundreds of exhausted, terrified, and starving men, he revealed the healing power of poetry. Huddled together in the ice-cold washrooms, they would recite aloud to one another. And as they did, they discovered to their amazement that their suffering diminished in the most tangible ways. As Jacques put it, "Quite simply, poetry warmed us."

A further discovery for Jacques was that, in the midst of their misery, his comrades were not particularly drawn to the poets who dwelled on life's suffering. *Au contraire!* They were drawn to the bons vivants, to the ones who expressed their joie de vivre through the chantlike rhythm of their verse and the vivid earthiness of their imagery, whether evoking the pleasure of a cigarette or the beauty of a young girl's waist.

For a group of freezing, starved, utterly uprooted, and humiliated men, the act of remembering and celebrating what was worth staying alive for was a kind of medicine, a spark of vitality, a "spurt of energy" that pushed in the direction of life. As Jacques puts it, "To nourish the desire to live, to make it burn: only that counted. Because that is what the deportation threatened to destroy. You couldn't let yourself forget that it is always the soul that dies first—even if its departure isn't perceived—and that the soul brings the body down with its fall. It was the soul that had to be nourished, first."

At its roots, the word *consolation* means: "with courage." For his comrades who were living an inch away from death, it seems that Jacques's poetry readings provided just enough courage to keep them from making that small—but irrevocable—movement of turning to face the wall.

*   *   *

From such situations of extremity, is there anything that can be gleaned for our more ordinary, everyday life?

One hot, breezeless day toward the end of the month, Nicholas and I decide to head toward the coast. Leaving town, we come to a street corner where a strange man is sitting on a bench, dressed in layers of mismatched clothing. The light turns red and we're stuck there, with our windows wide open, alongside the strange man. He's got a very big head, and his limbs are sort of flailing. He's making strange, unintelligible sounds, and his face is contorting with tics.

Nicholas rolls his window down farther. "How's it going?" he asks the man.

The man's limbs flail even more flagrantly, and his sounds get louder. Nicholas picks up on the man's sounds, which have a kind of rhythm. It's a long red light, and Nicholas starts tapping the rhythm on the steering wheel, the dashboard, turning the man's unintelligible sounds into a kind of jazz riff. The man is now wriggling with such pleasure, he looks as though he might suddenly grow wings and fly off his bench. The light changes, Nick toots the horn, and we go off, with Nicholas still chanting the rhythm.

This is the man I drew to my door. Money runs through his fingers and he lives in a rooming house, but in a single moment he's able to ease the isolation of a profoundly disabled man.

And actually Nicholas is happy now, with his new job. Every day he brings me another story. Yesterday it was a painfully shy child who Nicholas had noticed was very responsive to music. He put on some wild sitar ragas with an irresistible beat and got the child dancing on tabletops. When the boy's mother walked into the classroom and saw her son, she burst into tears of relief. Today it was a profoundly depressed child of low IQ whom Nick invited to draw with crayons on colored paper. When he returned, he found that the child had painstakingly stripped the wrappers from the crayons, broken the crayons into bits, and glued them onto folded-up paper cylinders. Did Nick scold him for breaking the crayons? No. He told him, "You're an architect."

In Nicholas's presence, children flourish.

To flourish is to bloom, to grow, to do the opposite of languish. And lately I've been struck by the link between flourishing and wishing. For isn't this the primal wish of every living being: to flourish? And in order to truly understand another living being— whether a little girl, an old man, a dolphin, or a lemon tree—isn't it necessary to know precisely what makes them *flourish,* as a genus, a species, an individual? Which is to say, isn't it necessary to know *what they wish for*? And what of the earth itself? Is it crazy to imagine the wishes of a languishing planet?

• • •

When at last the morning comes for my expedition to Spirit Rock, I am once again in the old white cow of my Volvo. I take the back roads, and it's a beautiful drive: the golden hills, the dark green windswept trees. As I drive, I'm listening again to the first tape in

Jack Kornfield's Buddhist psychology series, and it's about desire. He's telling a story about readjusting to life in the United States after his years of monastic training in Southeast Asia. Having found himself a girlfriend, he soon became aware of his own unhealthy disconnection from desire. His girlfriend would ask him, "What would you like to do this evening?" And he'd say, "Oh, anything." She'd say, "Would you like to go to a movie or to a restaurant?" and he'd say, "Either or both would be fine." "Well, if we went out to a restaurant, what kind of food would you like?" "Oh, anything is fine with me." "Would you like Thai food, French, Italian?" "Anything." Finally she couldn't take it anymore. She told him, "I want you to get a little notebook and every day notice and write down some things that you desire."

Hearing the story, I find myself identifying with both sides: with Jack's desire to float in a state of open receptivity to anything, with his unwillingness to trade that open receptivity for a plate of Italian food or the latest French movie. And at the same time, with his girlfriend's frustration. From my own experience, I know what it's like to be the one who carries the burden of choice in a relationship: Should we get a sofa? What kind? Would we like to go on a vacation? Where? Should we have friends over for dinner? Who? Though it might seem easy to be with someone who has no preferences, it can be wearying in its own way, and lonely. There's some truth in the old proverb "A man who is too good for this world is no good for his wife."

When I walk in the meditation hall, Ajahn Jumnian has already begun. I feel happy just seeing him. He's in his seventies, but he looks much younger. He wears the saffron monk's robe tied around one shoulder, and it reveals his big, meaty arms. Beside him Jack looks rather pale and thin, as though he were the one following a monastic regime in a forest monastery. Jack K. could eat no fat, the monk could eat no lean. Ajahn Jumnian. Aunt Jemima. It's not just their names that are alike. It's the spirit of rotund, overflowing generosity. Ajahn Jumnian radiates energy, laughs readily, and from time to time—whenever the conversation seems to get too serious—he performs a little trick of making the muscles of his upper arm vibrate in a comical circular twitch.

If you happened to walk in at such a moment, you might mistake him for some roly-poly, happy-go-lucky guy. You might not imagine the immensity of suffering he's witnessed, the immensity of responsibility he's taken on. From the time he was quite young, he was recognized as a healer in his village, and for many years he practiced in what was essentially the ancient shamanic tradition of his people. But then, in his early thirties, he decided to devote himself entirely to the study and practice of Buddhism. During the war in Vietnam, conflict spread to a part of Thailand where Ajahn Jumnian was the abbot of a monastery. Though his monastery became a refuge for people fleeing the violence, he himself did not stay safely within its walls. Every morning he would wake up and—at great risk to himself—traverse the war zone looking for the wounded. Then—at even greater risk to himself—he would carry them back to the monastery and watch over them until they died or were healed.

Now he's telling a story about a woman from his village in Thailand. This woman was married and had a young son. She worked in a beauty salon, and because she was very conscientious, she had many customers who came to her to have their hair shampooed and cut, their nails trimmed and polished. One day a funeral procession happened to pass by on its way to the cemetery up the hill. She heard the chanting and saw the monks go by, bearing the dead body on a pyre, and suddenly, she couldn't help herself. She ran out of the salon, leaving her customers sitting in their chairs, and joined the procession. Thereafter, she found herself irresistibly drawn to the cemetery every day. After work, before going home to her husband and son, she would climb the hill to the cemetery and sit there for an hour or more, among the ashes of the dead. Her husband and the other villagers thought that she had lost her mind. But somehow she encountered Ajahn

Jumnian, and he confirmed that she had awakened to an authentic spiritual quest. The hairdresser shaved her head, and together they found a way for her to develop an intensive meditation practice, without abandoning her husband and child.

During the morning break, I go up and ask Jack to tell Ajahn Jumnian that I have a little statue I'd like to give him. It's the one I bought in San Miguel de Allende last year, on Good Friday, and now I feel like I must have bought it for him. Jack translates, "It's a lady skeleton in her beauty salon, with a row of other skeletons sitting under hair dryers." Ajahn Jumnian laughs. When he does, his whole face lights up and his big meaty arms jiggle.

I ask Jack what he's been up to, and he tells me that he's starting a new book on Buddhist psychology. "I've just been listening to your tapes!" I tell him. "I need to ask you more about your problem with desire—"

"Which problem with desire?" He laughs, as though for him desire were a thousand-headed Gorgon.

"The story you tell about returning from Asia, about how you had to learn to want things, and your girlfriend made you keep a list—"

"Oh, that," he says, and pauses for a moment. "My wife would probably tell you that I still have trouble! But I don't feel that I struggle so much anymore. There are some things that I very clearly prefer. It's not difficult for me anymore to say, 'I'd rather go to a Japanese restaurant than have Korean barbecue.'"

I'm struck by the way he uses the word *prefer*, which seems much more restrained than *want* or *desire* and which is inherently comparative. When I fell in love with the shiny black Jaguar, all comparisons were swept aside. I didn't "prefer" it to the white cow of my Volvo. I was overcome by it. It filled my universe.

"And why was it hard for you to *prefer* one thing over another?"

"I think because the monastic training reinforced a kind of detachment that I already had. You know, you go out in the village to beg, and you just accept whatever gets put into your bowl."

"Do you have a sense of where that original detachment came from?"

"Well, I think it was in part a defense mechanism for me. My father was a very angry and sometimes violent man, and my way of coping as a child was to detach, to try to make myself peaceful. So that's the pathological side of it. But I do believe that there is also a dharma side to detachment, the appreciation of life as it is, without all our preferences—"

Before I have a chance to press him about that word *preference,* the bell sounds, and we all return to our cushions. Ajahn Jumnian asks if anyone has any questions relating to their meditation practice, and—to my amazement—I hear my own voice saying: "I have a daughter who's a teenager now, and my question comes out of my experience of her birth."

I tell him the story, about staying calm for hours and hours of intense pain and then something snapping, the mind shattering.

"You had an experience of total fear," he says.

"Yes."

"Many people die in this state."

"Yes, I know. That's why I'm telling you this. Because I don't want to die in that state."

"Listen carefully. *If you truly do not wish to, then you will not.*"

In the large meditation hall, tears stream from many eyes.

I feel a relief on George's behalf. And relief for myself. Because inside the cage of my ribs, a tap is turning back into a knock, and something is finally opening. Inside a space that has been tightly constricted, something is giving way. And though it hurts, it's a good hurt. It's as if someone or something is making room for a bird to return, a bird and its hunger.

• • •

After the midday break, Ajahn Jumnian presents us with an exercise. If we do it faithfully every day, he tells us, it will restore a sense of balance to our lives. Here's how it's done: From an upright start-ing position, we bend over until our foreheads touch the ground. Then, as if lifting the immense weight of the earth itself, we raise an imaginary orb and hold it over our heads. We hold the orb sus-pended for one long moment, then return it to the ground at our feet. Three times over, we take on the weight of the world, then re-lease and let it go.

At the end of the afternoon session, Ajahn Jumnian announces that he has something to show us. Unfolding the outer layer of his monk's robe, he shows us what he's been keeping close to his chest. Pinned to the saffron fabric are hundreds of medals, amulets, and pouches of coins that have been given to him as gifts.

Sitting at his feet, the meditators gasp.

He beams.

"Together these weigh one hundred sixteen pounds," Jack translates for him.

We gasp again.

Rather than simply renounce the accumulation of earthly goods, he managed to turn it into an ascetic practice. It seems like a won-derful joke—but the best is yet to come.

"And now before you leave here," Jack is saying, "Ajahn Jumnian would like you to join in a chant with him and, one by one, to come up and receive his blessing."

Ajahn Jumnian begins the chant, slowly, with each syllable dis-tinct. It sounds a bit like the most sacred of Tibetan chants, *om mani padme hum,* which means "the jewel in the heart of the lotus," but it's not a chant I've ever heard before.

*O-mane-kam*

*O-mane-kam*

Repeating the chant very slowly, we begin to form a line. One by one each person who goes up to Ajahn Jumnian receives a lit-tle pat on the head, a sprinkling of water, and a goody bag.

"He's asking that we chant faster!" Jack says.

And when we do, *O-mane-kam* turns into *O money come,* and everyone is laughing.

. . .

On the way home, dapples of late-afternoon light hang like coins in the leaves, like the coins on the inside of Ajahn Jumnian's robe. Last year in the same Mexican church where I briefly joined in the stations of the cross, I had another vivid encounter. In one of the side chapels, I came across a diminutive Jesus, about the size of the Patty Playpal I had as a child. He was dark-skinned and had the narrow, somewhat pointed face of the local indigenous people. His black hair appeared to be real, and he had lifelike porcelain eyes, which gave him a startlingly alert expression. His leather face was twisted in agony under its crown of thorns, and little rivulets of blood ran down his cheeks, his chest, his limbs. Yet he was covered with money! Paper peso notes were rolled up and pinned to the bloody little cape that draped around his shoulders. There were photographs: smiling faces of children, a bride in her gown, an elderly couple. And here and there were simple handwritten notes: "For a happy wedding!" or "Please make our son well!" or simply, "Gracias." The dark-skinned Jesus seemed to bear it all equally: the thorns, the blood, the pesos, the requests for favors, and the gratitude for favors shown.

In *The History of Magic,* Cavendish draws the distinction between low and high magic. Where low magic operates on the material plane, high magic involves the transformation of oneself.

*High magic is an attempt to gain so consummate an understanding and mastery of oneself and the environment as to transcend all human limitations and become superhuman or divine. . . . Low magic is comparatively minor and mechanical, undertaken for immediate worldly advantage, to make money or take revenge on an enemy or make a conquest*

*in love. It tails off into the peddling of spells and lucky*
*charms. The distinction between the two types is blurred in*
*practice and many magicians have engaged in both.*

*Blurred in practice* . . . A large part of being a wish snob, I realize, is *refusing to blur,* maintaining a rigid distinction—not only
between sacred and profane desires but between low magic and
high. Yet who are the wisest, bravest, and most compassionate
people I can think of, whether living or dead? There is one who
multiplies loaves and fishes, one who recommends calling on
Gwan Shi Yinn if you want "an uncommonly pretty daughter with
well-formed features," and another who chants O-*mane-kam.*
Blessed are those who blur.

• • •

A few days after I return from Spirit Rock, I get a call from Jack.
Would I like to edit his new book about Buddhist psychology? His
working title is *The Secret Beauty.* Before I can exclaim over the
synchronicities in my life, the references to beauty—both inner and
outer, temporary and eternal—we're on to the nitty-gritty. We don't
discuss numbers, but he indicates that if we should choose to work
together, he would give me part of my editing fee in the form of an
advance.

When I hang up the phone, I feel so elated that I dash out my
door for a run in the open air. Circling the pond, I find myself
thinking of that wonderful line from the ancient Roman poet
Ovid, "Let your hook always be cast. In the pool where you least
expect it, will be fish." It's true. I would never have expected that,
in the place where I went to recover the bird of my soul, I might
discover the fish of my down payment. At least a portion thereof.
But do I dare to call it *grace?*

# CHAPTER ELEVEN

# November

## *Abundance: Realizing the Dream*

It's November, and the rains have come, falling in silver sheets from the sky and soaking into the parched earth. Once, long ago, a man from Pakistan told me that in his country the metaphors are reversed: dark clouds portend happiness, and rainwater brings a shower of blessings. In Zen, too, clouds have a positive connotation: they represent the sacred mystery of life; they dissolve the sharp edges of separateness; they gather the many into the one and reunite the opposites; they represent the soft, receptive yin of not-knowing, without which there can be no bright yang of awakening.

One rainy afternoon I'm in the copy shop, making copies of reams of French documents. Though my mother has always been very meticulous about her finances, it seems that for some time now the bills on her French apartment have gone unpaid. Because I speak French, it falls to me to disentangle the chaos. Worrier that I am, I've been feeling overwhelmed by the task. In my living room, where the wish books were strewn across the floor, now there is a sea of threatening papers. And the French don't mince words. If the taxes aren't paid within a matter of days, the apartment and its contents will be seized and become the property of the state. Then there are menacing letters from the gas and electric and phone companies. To make matters more complicated, my mother insists that she paid the French taxes, and a trail of Italian documents shows that she did indeed make a valiant attempt. But where did the thousands of lira that she withdrew from her Italian account end up? It's clear they never made it to the French *trésorerie*. Though I need to make copies of everything, there's something that feels counterintuitive about the process: there are already far too many of these threatening and confusing documents, and they seem to be multiplying at a terrifying rate.

Leaving the copy shop, I see a small sign on the door of the adjoining building: BRINGING SPIRITUALITY INTO YOUR FINANCIAL LIFE. It's a talk being sponsored by the Shambhala Center, our local outpost for Tibetan Buddhism. I jot the date down in my book.

* * *

Meanwhile, I still haven't found a place for my mother to live, and the sense of urgency is growing. The plan is for Luigi and my mother to go together in December to her new place of residence. He'll stay through Christmas and then return to Italy. His presence, we hope, will help smooth the painful transition for my mother, and help her to feel that there's a link between her life in Italy and her life in California. But none of this is possible if I can't find the right place to rent, and that's turning out to be more difficult than I imagined.

And so, stashing the reams of threatening French papers in my car, I decide to grab my umbrella and go out hunting. I trudge through the Plaza, which—except for a few mud-splattered ducks—seems empty of living beings. Walking past the Mission with its whitewashed adobe walls, its tile roof, and ancient flowering cactus, I stop to peer over the heavy wooden gate into the inner courtyard. There's something calming about its view of an old stone well and spreading olive trees. Two blocks farther, I find a curving street of red-tile-roofed townhouses I've never seen before. It's a cul-de-sac, lined with sycamore trees, and halfway down the block is a communal swimming pool—exactly what I'd envisioned for my mother. As I come to the end of the street, I feel my heart beating loudly. I cross and walk down the other side of the street, and there it is: a white stucco townhouse with its red tile roof and a wrought-iron gate. On the gate a discreet sign announces, FOR RENT. I jot down the number, then walk to the nearby bookstore, where I buy myself a guide to the Big Island of Hawaii.

• • •

"Noelle, you've got to come and see my coffins!" That's the message I find on my answering machine when I return from Sonoma. It's Carole, inviting me for a spur-of-the-moment dinner. Coffins and dinner: how can I refuse? I throw on some dry clothes and drive through the pounding rain, wondering what on earth Carole is up to now. At the word *coffins* I'm picturing some Day of the Dead–type miniatures sculpted from joint compound, but when I peer through the door of the studio what I see is a row of full-sized cardboard coffins, leaning up against the walls. Carole is standing with her back to me and a brush in her hand, painting big flying bears on one of the coffins. When I rap on the door, she turns and gives me a giant grin that makes her look like a combination of magical rabbit and some kind of wild Mexican fiesta skeleton lady.

As always, when I step over the threshold into Carole's world, I have that feeling of stepping into a world of unpredictable happenings and shape-shifting dimensions. But should I be worried that Carole is suddenly consumed with a passion for coffins?

She explains to me that she and Don turn sixty this year, and though they're both healthy and happy, it seems a good time to acknowledge that they're not immortal. On their recent trip to Mexico, they got swept up in the wave of a giant Day of the Dead procession that carried them to the cemetery and deposited them on an unclaimed tombstone. There—surrounded by hundreds of townspeople holding candles, pushing wheelbarrows full of marigolds, and bearing platters of food, pitchers of drink, blankets, pillows, musical instruments, radios, and even small color TVs— they munched on sugar skulls and, like so many visitors before them, found themselves both astonished and moved by the Mexican people and their intimate relation to death.

"So when we got back from San Miguel last week, I went online and discovered that you can buy these cardboard coffins, and I bought a batch. They're just thirty-five dollars each, if you'd like to buy one and paint it for yourself."

Worlds within worlds. Is it any wonder my head is spinning? One moment I'm with George, who appears to be dying and in whose presence one cannot speak of death. The next moment I'm with Carole, who appears to be in the bloom of health and who is adorning her cardboard coffin with flying bears.

"Carole! Supper's ready!" An unfamiliar voice calls from the balcony above.

"Who's that?"

"That's my rent-a-grandma. Didn't I tell you? I'd been feeling sad that I don't have any grandmothers anymore, and one day it occurred to me that I should just post a note at the senior center. And that's what I did. "Grandmother wanted to do grandmotherly things: bake cookies, mend clothes, knit, crochet, et cetera." You wouldn't believe how many calls I got! So I picked Marjory, and she's great. I pay her ten dollars an hour, and she comes about five hours a week. She bakes cookies. She knits. She just sewed a batch of fish hats I designed, all satiny and full of sequins. It's great for both of us!"

We go upstairs where Don and Marjory, a round and archetypally grandmotherly-looking woman with a long silver braid, have combined their talents to produce a meal of braised tofu with bok choy, brown rice, and triple-fudge brownies. As we sit down at the table, I'm struck that all three of us—the husband, the grand-mother, the French-speaking friend—came to Carole in much the same way. Whatever skeptics might think about the magic of Putting It Out There, we are certainly proof of the power of sign-age in Carole's life, whether a printed card, a posted note, or a classified ad.

After dinner, Don goes off to practice his taiko drumming, Marjory goes home to darn Carole's socks and watch television, and Carole and I curl up on the sofa in her living room.

Within moments, I've spilled out all my anxieties about my mother's situation, about the complications in France, the piles of bills, the unpaid taxes, the threatening letters, the uncertain fu-ture. Somewhere in the midst of my riff, I realize that—apart from our discussions about real estate and "shifting the paradigm"— I've never really asked Carole about her relation to money, and how as an artist and single mother she came to be so good at mak-ing it, keeping it, growing it.

She tells me that growing up in middle-class San Diego, she had been shielded from any experience of real material need. Then, after completing art school in San Francisco, she relinquished a graduate fellowship and opted to go "off the grid" with the young man—also an artist—whom she'd fallen in love with. They married and moved to Mendocino, where the plan was to live on a wildlife preserve with a group of like-minded people, having as little as possible to do with the world of money. "The idea was that we would be one another's living insurance policies. If you needed something, you'd either grow it or make it or exchange something to get it." When Carole became pregnant, she began to feel more acutely the precariousness of their existence. Her hus-band, she says, was a dreamer. "His feet didn't really touch the earth. And it didn't help that he was stoned much of the time, either!" One day, when they were getting very low on food and supplies, Carole went to a crafts fair to try to sell some of her weaving. When she arrived, she had sixty-five cents in her pocket, with which she bought two oatmeal cookies. There was a good crowd of people at the fair, and she was hopeful that she would make a lot of sales, but Saturday went by, then most of Sunday, and no one had bought anything. The hunger pangs were growing sharp, she was feeling faint, and she was frightened for her unborn baby. A strong wind blew through the leaves above her head, and when she looked up, she realized that all the while, she'd been standing right under a big walnut tree, heavy with walnuts. She threw some rocks up in the tree, and the nuts came down. She feasted. And then, just as the fair was about to close, a woman came and bought five hundred dollars' worth of her weavings.

It was a momentous experience for Carole, one that taught her something about risk and trust that she's been living by ever since. Eventually she left both Mendocino and her husband and moved with her little son to San Francisco. There she had the good fortune to meet Michael Phillips, whom she describes as a financial genius, wizard, and visionary. President of a major bank at the age of twenty-eight, he helped to birth the very idea of the credit card, and along with a friend he wrote the book *The Seven Laws of Money*. With his help, and that of certain other people whom Carole regards as guides and guardian angels, she made her way as an artist "in the real world." First she founded a collective of women weavers, then an art gallery. At each step, she tried to live what she'd learned on that day under the walnut tree, about the edges of life, and the help we find there.

"Whenever I have an idea about something I really want to do, I try to explore every angle until I can find something solid. I think of it as being a trapeze artist. There's the moment between when you let go of the bar and when you grab on to the next one. And a creative life is lived in that space. You have to trust that the miracles—the walnuts, the woman who comes at closing time and buys five hundred dollars' worth of your weaving—will be there when you need them. As a single mother trying to raise a small child in the city, it wasn't easy. There were always so many bills. Toward the end of the month, I would start to panic. I would think, 'I can't do this.' But again and again, at the very last minute, some miracle money would show up. Until finally I learned I didn't have to panic. And that's what I tell people: 'If you're willing to trust in this process—and work your ass off—then you can live the creative life of your dreams.'"

Speaking of which: Carole tells me that she and Don are going to France for Christmas. They're getting ready to sell the first house they renovated in the village near Toulouse. "You've never seen my dream house there," she says. "And now we're getting ready to sell it. Why don't you come visit us before we do?"

I tell her I'd love to but I can't, because in December I'll need to be around for my mother and Luigi. And before that I'm going to Hawaii.

"Hawaii," Carole murmurs, and in her eyes I see a look I've come to recognize that's like haze with a glint of steel. "That's another place where I've always wanted to have a house and a gallery."

Back in my own house that night, I have the first Carole dream I've had in quite some time. It's similar to one I've had before in which Carole and I are riding through tall grasses on bejeweled elephants, only in this dream she and I are zooming through the clouds on painted coffins.

The next morning, when I pull up to the curb in my old white cow, the landlord of the red-tile-roofed townhouse gives me a wink. "Had that awhile?" he asks. He seems to be a friendly, middle-aged man, and he tells me that he owns an auto shop that specializes in Volvos. As he leads me through the wrought-iron gate, I'm chattering away about forty-eight-year-old NPR listeners, but then he opens the front door to the house and I fall silent. It's as though, in an instant, a dark cloud has lifted—a cloud whose weight I hadn't really gauged until it lifted. If I really knew anything about feng shui, I'd say that the house has simultaneously powerful, calming, and unobstructed chi. Spacious and full of light, it reminds me of my family's long-ago house in Santa Monica Canyon. It was the house my mother loved best of any house we ever lived in.

When the landlord tells me what the rent and utilities come to, I wince: it's much more expensive than we had planned to budget. But I can't shake the sense that it's right for us, at this juncture of my family's life. Somewhere in the back of my mind, I remember the words that a wise friend once told me: "When you take something good away from someone, you have to give them something good in return." This feels like a house where my grieving and uprooted mother could flourish, and where Luigi might be enticed to visit.

I fill out the application, take a card for the landlord's Volvo shop, and then drive home to wish and to worry.

•   •   •

For two days and nights it rains without stopping, and on the third day the sun comes out and the landlord calls to say that the house can be ours. Without even bothering to put on my shoes, I rush outside and run down to the pond, letting the mud ooze between my bare toes.

But that very night when I wake at the hour of the wolf, I am once again vibrating with anxiety. The house doesn't have a stick of furniture! Was that why the chi was zooming through the rooms with such power? I'll be away at the workshop in Hawaii for nearly a week toward the end of the month—how will I ever furnish the house in time for my mother and Luigi's arrival?

Suddenly I've turned into the fisherman's wife, unable to bask in the magic flounder's generosity, immediately aware of the next lack on her list. Why is it that, rather than feeling more confident in the wake of a wish fulfilled, I return so quickly to the sense of scarcity?

*You're using up all the sand!*

That's what a little girl said to me once, when I was a little girl myself and building an elaborate drip castle, with a moat and a drawbridge and bits-of-shell-encrusted towers, on the beach in Santa Monica. I'd invited the girl to join me, but she declined. Remembering her now, I can't help wondering if my own perpetually recurring sense of scarcity is as deluded as hers. With each wish that comes true I seem simultaneously to become aware of a new wish and to assume that all my wishes are used up.

And so, though I don't have the energy to get out of bed and fix my gaze on a living thing, I do my best to follow Paul Pearsall's protocol. Putting my hand on my heart, I take a deep breath and launch yet another eight-syllable wish: *Please may I find fur-ni-ture soon.*

* * *

One rainy day follows another, and on the evening of the third day, I'm in my kitchen washing dishes when from somewhere outside I hear a cat meowing loudly. Grabbing my umbrella and going out into the street, I discover that my neighbors, Stephen and Christina, have also responded to the cat's plaintive cries. As we hunt about in the wet bushes and stare up into the dripping trees, they ask me, "How are things with your mother?"

I tell them about the new house.

"You don't need furniture by any chance, do you?" they ask.

"You're kidding!"

It seems they have a basement full of furniture that they've been wanting to clear out for ages: a bed, two tables, a desk, lamps, and chairs.

"Come and see!" they tell me.

We linger a few moments more, straining our ears through the sound of the rain and peering into the foliage. But the invisible cat who drew us all outside has stopped meowing, and so I follow them inside and gaze, with wondering eyes, at my mother's new furniture.

. . .

*And then I found, quite simply, that my dream had become my address.*

That's what Proust said when he first went to Venice, and I never imagined that it could seem so wonderfully apropos in my own life. But this morning I got the keys for the townhouse in Sonoma. Then I drove to the airport and boarded the plane that will take me to my dream address: *Hawaii.*

Outside my window, the clouds themselves look like small white islands floating in a sea of sky. Inside the plane, the seats are upholstered with a pattern of giant tropical flowers, and the stewardesses have orchids in their hair.

I wish that Nicholas could be with me.

And I wish we hadn't had an argument last night.

Before being separated by ten days and thousands of miles, I suggested that we go out for a special dinner. And before Nicholas could opt for burritos, I made a reservation at the little bistro in my town. It's a place that might be described as "modestly chic," and it's certainly not extravagant. But from the moment we walked in the door, Nicholas seemed ill at ease. He read the menu with a frown on his face, grilled the young waitress about her culinary terms, and by the time she brought our artful little salads, he had worked himself into a thoroughly prickly state.

"It's eight dollars for this little bunch of stems?" he said. "That's a rip-off!"

"Nicholas," I said, "it's arugula. With crumbled chèvre."

"Well, I'd rather have a big plate of iceberg with ranch dressing. I've been working hard all day, and I'm hungry."

"Would you like me to see if we could make you a big spinach salad?" the young waitress asked. "We might have some bacon bits."

"No, that's all right," said Nicholas, stabbing with his fork at a tiny piece of nasturtium. "What's this?" The waitress gave me a soulful look and left, and Nicholas devoured his salad in two bites, then pushed the plate aside. I could feel my ire rising. I tried, for one valiant moment, to channel Aunt Jemima. But I couldn't. I felt her siding with Nicholas, laughing at the tiny salad of spiky greens and shaking her head at the hefty price.

"You know, Nicholas," I said, "if I go to a diner, then I don't expect to have a salad of arugula with crumbled chèvre, and if I come to a place like this, I don't expect a salad of iceberg lettuce with ranch dressing. It seems to me that it's all about appropriate expectations."

"I hate the word *appropriate*," he said. "In fact, I think it's probably the word I hate most in the English language. It's so incredibly bourgeois." We ate the rest of our meal in silence, then drove home gloomily.

"So this is our first argument," I thought.

A woman I know is a marriage-and-family counselor, and over several years I helped her write a book in which she distilled her method of working with troubled couples. The book is called *The First Argument: Unlocking the Code of Intimate Conflict.* Her theory, in a nutshell, is that the first argument that a couple has lays the template for all future arguments between them. Over the years, the particular issue may vary, but the underlying dynamic will not. So if you can see what the underlying dynamic was in your very first argument and get to the root of it, you can spare yourself years of misery.

Nicholas and I made up later that evening, but it was a kind of smoothing over. And as I let myself slip into sleep beside him, I had a slightly sinking feeling. I knew it was not the last time that we'd experience some version of this argument, this push-and-pull between two poles.

*Arugula versus iceberg.*

After all, wasn't this the argument that I'd been having with myself for years?

• • •

When I get off the plane in Kona, I see a young woman with long wavy blondish hair standing with a hand-painted sign that says "Noelle!" The sign gives me a rush of happiness, a moment's illusion of belonging to this beautiful place.

Even when I bought my ticket, even when I sat on the plane looking down on the miles and miles of ocean, I didn't fully believe that I would actually set foot in this land with the magic name: Hawaii. But as we drive away from the airport, everywhere I look there are beautiful names full of vowels.

The young woman's name is Julie, and as I've arrived at rush hour and the traffic on the one road leading away from the airport is terrible, we have a long time to talk. She tells me that she's engaged to be married to a man named Kalani. His name means "chief," and from the time he was a little boy, his grandfather raised him to be a healing kahuna.

We make one stop along the way: at an outdoor market to buy some Crocs for several of the women in our group. Julie says the clunky-looking plastic clogs that come in a brilliant array of colors are perfect for walking on lava beds, and the idea is so thrilling to me that I buy myself a pair in fluorescent purple.

Back in the car, we finally leave the heavy traffic behind, and the steep hills on either side reveal themselves, through layers of dense vegetation. At last we turn off the main road and follow a long and winding dirt road down, down, until it flattens out and Julie pulls up beside a grove of trees and stops. Though it's growing dark, from the moment I step out of the car there's no doubt that we've arrived at a tropical paradise. Nearby, the waves are crashing. Up above, giant palms are bearing their clusters of co-

conuts. Around us, there's a profusion of flowers so big and so bright that they can't hide their colors in the dusk.

Julie leads me up the wooden ramp that leads to the main house, and there is Irene, smiling at me as she did in the warm turquoise water on that day when I couldn't stop crying. She's wearing a long, flowered dress, and she drapes a lei of magenta orchids around my neck. Putting a finger to her lips, she leads me to the temple room: a giant white circular tent billowing up above a gleaming wooden floor, set high on stilts and surrounded by a wooden balcony that leans out toward the ocean. In this room, sitting on pillows or reclining on rugs, the other women in the workshop are gathered, and they are rapt with attention. In their midst is Julie's fiancé, Kalani. He's a robust man, with a very open, mirthful face and long wavy black hair flowing down his back. He's wearing a brown sarong that reveals the top of his broad chest and his muscular arms, and he's playing a ukulele. With a smile, he motions me to sit down, and I take my place on the rug not far from him. Within a few moments, I understand that he's giving a vocabulary lesson that is also a lesson in Hawaiian spirituality. He'll say a word, sing a little chantlike song about it, and then explain its meaning. The word I've happened to walk in on is *haole,* Caucasians. Kalani explains that the word means "without the breath of soul." The next word is *okole,* which according to Kalani means "sphincter" or "asshole." That strikes me as somewhat hilarious, and Kalani's eyes are sparkling with humor. I can't help but wonder if he's just pulling the wool over our *haole* eyes, but as he goes on speaking I find myself ready to believe that the *okole* has a serious place in the ancient Hawaiian understanding of how to conduct oneself on this precious earth.

We take in, we take out. The *okole* helps us to attain the proper balance between the world inside us and the world outside. It helps us to cleanse ourselves by letting go of what we no longer need.

With a lei of magenta orchids around my neck and a new appreciation of my asshole, I'm struck that Hawaii has already both matched and subverted my expectations.

. . .

That night after supper, I make my way to my little nook, which is way at the back of the property. Most of the other women are sleeping in beautiful hand-carved Balinese huts, large enough to contain not only a bed but a chair, a dresser, and a desk. My space is so narrow that there's just room enough for the single bed, which is pushed right against the thatched wall. Though there's a beautiful, multicolored quilt on the bed, it's covered with a dark sheet to protect it from gecko shit. I crawl into the bed and lie there, looking through the screen at the moon. It is brilliant and nearly full, and it looks the same as it did to me the night before in California. But it's shining on leaves that are huge and tropical. In the near distance, I hear the waves crash. Over my skin, a breeze blows that is just as I've always heard it described: *as soft as silk.*

. . .

In the morning when I wake, there's an instant of shock that turns immediately into enchantment. The shapes that greeted me in the dark have taken on vivid color. Those big black leaves outside the screens have turned a variegated mass of brilliant greens, entwined with yellow, orange, and violet flowers. And the air is throbbing with the song of birds I've never heard before, along with a constant low-grade rumble—something between a croak and a purr—that I later learn is the music of geckos.

I make my way to the main house, along winding paths that I now see are black and white: crushed black lava and crushed white coral. Everywhere there are statues of Buddhist and Hindu figures: sitting Buddhas, laughing Buddhas, goddesses with many arms, and many versions of Ganesh, the round-bellied elephant god. Each one of them, set in its bower of trees and flowers, seems to be on the brink of becoming animate, of turning to flesh and saying *Welcome!*

So this is what it means to be *dazzled.* Years ago when I looked that word up, I discovered that its root denotes a mild form of shock. In the face of something dazzling, one feels slightly paralyzed, overwhelmed, blinded by an intensity of light. I'm glad I arrived at this place in the dark. Glad I had a night's sleep in my thatched nook before going out to greet paradise in living color.

In the kitchen Julie has made a breakfast of eggs and muffins and mangos and melons. When the other women go into the main house for the morning's watercolor workshop, I decide to go out and see the ocean whose waves I've been listening to all night.

In front of our little Balinese village, there's a dirt road. Beyond it lies a jagged, convoluted bed of hard black lava against which the waves are crashing. I take the dirt road until it peters out, then I clamber over the lava bed until I arrive at the sheltered curve of a beautiful beach. Pink cliffs, laced with masses of leaves, fronds, and flowers, climb toward the clouds behind me. In front of me, the ocean is warm and turquoise. Sinking into the warm white sand, I rest my head on my towel and close my eyes.

From outside I'm sure I look like a lucky lazy tourist, with time to snooze on a tropical beach. But inside me, there's a struggle going on. For weeks now I've been worrying about my mother, about George, and now I don't know where to put the worries. And though, once again, I remind myself that my worries accomplish nothing, if I try to let them simply drop from consciousness, then I feel somehow as if I'm being callous and disloyal, abandoning those I love to their suffering.

*I can be rich and I can be poor.*

Suddenly those words from Saint Paul spring into my mind, and I wish that I'd remembered them the night when Nicholas and I got tangled up over arugula and iceberg.

Why is it so hard to hold simultaneous contradictory realities?

And really, isn't it the case that we are always living within simultaneous contradictory realities? If it's daylight or summer or peacetime where we are, then it is night or winter or a war zone somewhere else.

*The poor you have always with you,* said Jesus, letting the precious oil run over his face.

Is this the true meaning of "abundance consciousness"—not to deny the reality of scarcity, deprivation, and all manner of suffering but to celebrate that which is good and beautiful in the very midst of it?

Two nights before I left for Hawaii, I went to the Shambhala Center to hear the talk on "bringing your spirituality into your financial life." One of the two presenters began by saying that in Tibet, to be very wealthy does not mean that one is any less spiritual. Indeed, wealth is considered a sign of great merit, the result of good deeds and accumulated blessings from the past. It is also the opportunity for exceptional generosity, and thus the ongoing accumulation of good merit. What is considered very unfortunate, however, is for someone to die wealthy. For to do so indicates that they squandered the lucky opportunity for generosity.

Something rough, wet, and sandy is brushing against my face, something round and warm is burrowing under the small of my back, while something else is bouncing on my stomach. I open my eyes and discover that I'm being attacked by a litter of furry puppies. A few yards off, three young Hawaiian children in bathing suits—two black-haired, skinny-limbed boys and a round little girl—are laughing.

"Are these your puppies?" I call to them.

"Yes. Do you want one?" they call back. They run toward me and fall in the sand beside me so that I am surrounded by children and puppies. "Do you want one?" they ask again.

"I wish I could have one," I say.

But it's not really true. In this moment, in this tumult of fur and sand and skinny-limbed children, both my wishes and my worries have evaporated, like drops of glistening oil in the sun.

· · ·

In the afternoon I give a writing workshop. We start with an exercise that I call "Write where you are." You think of whatever feels like the last "chunk" of your life (whether the last week, month, year, or years), and then you start by describing it as if it were a landscape. What sort of landscape was it? A clearing in the woods, a steep mountain grade, a desert, a maze, a tangled thicket of thorns? It's a way for people to get some perspective on their own recent history, while simultaneously helping the rest of the group to understand "where they're coming from." I let the women write for about twenty minutes or so, until most of the hands have stopped their scribbling, and then we go around the room and read aloud.

*A sunken island, a dry riverbed, a burning lava flow.* As always, I'm moved by the range of images that people arrive at, and by the level of difficulty in their lives. Three women in the group are dealing with the illness of an aging parent; one recently lost her husband of thirty years; another is recently divorced. But of all the women, there is one who pours her story out like a vial of acid, stinging our eyes, burning our throats with its fumes.

Maryann. She appears to be in her sixties, with a rather birdlike face, pale skin, short cropped hair.

"I can't think of a landscape to describe my last year," she begins, sounding indignant. "Well, yes I can. It's been hell."

She goes on to describe a year of physical torment: something strange happening to her digestive system, so that the muscles of her esophagus and her intestine are out of synch with each other, making it nearly impossible for her to eat and causing excruciating pain. After months of tests and no diagnosis, it was finally discovered to be a rare kind of cancer, so that now she's had rounds of chemotherapy. She's still in a very fragile and precarious state, and several times during the last few days it looked as though she would have to cancel the trip at the last minute. In fact, it's probably pretty crazy of her to have come so far, to such a remote place—but she needed to get away, and she wanted to paint. Besides, apart from her doctors, she doesn't seem to have much to stay home for. She's divorced, and though her grown daughter lives in the same town, she's apparently too busy to look after her mother. Though Maryann seems full of fear and grief, what she expresses is an intensely bitter anger, and a profound suspicion of any easy form of consolation.

Fortunately, in the format of my writing workshop, there's very little talking about what people have written. We write, and we read, and we listen, and sometimes we respond with an "Ohhhh" or an "Ahhhh" or a "Wow." Maryann's words are met by an intense silence, in which it seems to me that you can actually feel the rest of us trying to absorb the waves of pain. And then we go on to the next exercise.

· · ·

Late that night after supper, when most of the other women have retired to their huts, I'm on the balcony of the main house, leaning out into the night air, seeing the moonlight reflected on the water, and thinking how different the darkness feels on this, my second night, now that I know the brilliant colors of the leaves and flowers that lie between me and the ocean.

Suddenly there is Irene at my side, beautiful in a long flowing dress and holding a candle. "How are you?" she asks. "And how did you feel the workshop went?"

Within a matter of moments, I am exuding waves of anxiety about Maryann. "What will we do if she gets really sick?" I ask. "What can we do for her? I feel like we should do something special for her. Should we have some sort of healing ceremony?" Irene lets me go on for a while, and then she says very firmly,

"Stop!" I look at her somewhat stunned, and she says again, "Just stop." And then she goes on a riff.

"Don't grab on to her suffering," she says. "Just let her be. Don't focus on her illness. Don't remind her of it. She doesn't need to be singled out. She doesn't need to have some special healing ceremony. Just let her be here with the rest of us in this beautiful place. That's what she needs."

Then she tells me that as a fairly young woman, her mother was diagnosed with breast cancer. She lived with it for years as Irene was growing up, but she rarely spoke about it. She never wanted it to become the family's focal point. When she was feeling well enough, she always got herself up and beautifully dressed and entertained her friends and tried to live with every ounce of zest and grace that she could manage. Of course, I find myself thinking of George again and of what for me is that profoundly mysterious question: When is it wise to bring our attention to bear on suffering, and when is it wise to close our eyes to suffering and focus elsewhere?

For now, I feel that Irene has arrived beside me in the dark like a kind of priestess, an avatar, an oracle.

*Don't attach to suffering.*

How many times, in how many guises, must I hear this message before it truly penetrates?

In the flickering light of her candle, in the silvery light of the moon, Irene and I say good night and retire to our separate rooms.

. . .

The next morning after breakfast, just as I'm heading back to my hut to gather my books and papers and find a place to write, we hear a cry from the beach: "Dolphins!" We've been told that the beach at Hale Aloalo was a haven for dolphins, a cove where they come to feed and rest, but so far no one in our group has spotted any. Now, from the storeroom under the main house, in a chaos of hands and feet the women grab fins and snorkels and head for the beach. I've never worn a snorkel or fins before, so I just pull on my sneakers and do my best to fly over the black lava bed and down to the water's edge.

At the farthest edge of a very long reef, almost at the horizon line, I can see the silver arcs of the dolphins' bodies rising and falling back into the turquoise water. I swim and swim, farther out than I've ever swum before. Though we ran down to the beach in a pack, I seem to be following my own course through the water, and suddenly I feel very small and alone and it's hard not to think of sharks. I swim and swim and it starts to feel a bit like a mirage: I think I'm getting close to the shimmering goal and then it recedes, and another expanse of turquoise opens up before me. *Don't think, just swim,* I tell myself, and I swim until at last the movement of dolphin bodies is in a circle around me. I feel as though I can't quite see them, because their movement is so rapid and so liquid, but I can feel the waves their bodies make rippling out and underneath me.

I'm just treading water in a kind of a daze when all of a sudden a voice says, "Put this on!" From somewhere a young woman has swum up beside me and is putting her snorkel mask over my head.

"But I've never worn a snorkel!" I say.

"Just try," she says.

I snort and gasp, breathe water in and gasp some more.

"It's hard at first," she says, in a voice with a light accent that I can't quite place. "I know. It was hard for me. But just try it. You'll be happy you did."

I sputter and gasp and yank the mask this way and that until finally I seem to be able to breathe.

"Put your head down and open your eyes," she says.

And when I do, I see, just below my navel, a vertical line of dolphins extending down, mothers and babies just floating: big, here, alive, now, real, glinting silver in the turquoise water. I feel that I have entered another dimension of time and space. I am an interloper, and in this moment, through the rapidly fogging glass of my mask, I am allowed this glimpse into the life of another species.

But awe is an emotion that both fills and empties. I feel filled with amazement and depleted, a small pale human mammal, out of my element. My body is beginning to feel cold, and it's a long way back. Taking off the mask, I return it to the young woman who showed up by my side. "Thank you," I say—but the words seem utterly unequal to what she's given me. "What is your name?" I ask.

"Myrna."

After what seems a dangerously long time for my almost bare and shivering body, I make it back to the beach. Then I return to my hut, climb into the bed with its dark cover now spattered with bright orange gecko shit, and sleep for two hours until my body has thrown off the cold and absorbed at least a portion of the awe.

. . .

Later that day I join the other women in the painting workshop. It's now been thirteen years since my desire to paint again fueled my first attempt at Putting It Out There and brought me to Carole. But apart from those first few weeks of trading French for studio space, I've done precious little painting. It wasn't long after meeting Carole that my life fell apart, and by the time it was put together again, I'd taken on so many new responsibilities that the longing to paint got pressed down again, turned back into that ongoing, low-grade ache in my arms.

But now, what excuse could I possibly invent? It's hard to imagine a more perfect time or place. The women around me are intensely focused on their paintings, most of which are some silver, gray, and turquoise version of the dolphins. The white curtains of the room are billowing out into the fronds of the palm trees that surround us. The sounds are: breezes, waves, the clank of bamboo chimes, the clink of paintbrushes being rinsed in glass jars.

Just every now and again, someone calls out "Whale!" from

our midst and we all leap up, knocking over stools and jars of brushes, so we can rush to the rail and look out to see a great black body, giving off its intermittent gush of spray, traveling by so close that we can see an eye, a bird on its back, an unusual marking, a barnacle clump.

Whales in the front yard! Whose life is this, and is it possible that such a life could ever just be someone's ordinary life, their regular routine, their daily dose of whales?

In my back pocket, I feel a buzz. I'd set my cell phone to vibrate. I've never had a cell phone before, but with my mother not well, I felt I should have one with me. I haven't used it since I've been here, and I have no idea if it will even work over thousands of miles of ocean. I lift the phone out and say "Hello?" but what I hear is chaotic: a lot of static, children's voices in the background, a child screaming in the foreground, and a man's voice saying, "Lakeesha, Lakeesha, that's Jared's. You have to give it back to him. Jared, calm down. Lakeesha . . ."

It's Nicholas! A butt call from Nicholas! With his cell phone in his back pocket, he must have brushed up against a desk or chair and somehow activated my phone number. It's happened two or three times before, and each time it's amused me to get an inadvertent slice of his life in the middle of my own. Each time I've felt what a different weekday world he inhabits from mine. But never before, in the sudden juxtaposition of our lives, have I felt the difference so radically. There he is, in an underfunded inner-city classroom that is narrow, shabby, crowded, and windowless. And here I am, with my paints on the wooden deck beside me, and the sound of the bamboo chimes.

*Nicholas, Nicholas!* I want to say into the phone. *Here, have some of it!* Maybe one day it will be possible to hold your phone and send not just the sound and the image but the feel of the breeze, the smell of the ocean in the air, the awesome immensity of a whale. But the static, crackle, and wailing go on, with poor

Nicholas sounding more and more exasperated. I shut the phone off and stick it back into my pocket.

Again I'm struck that, if only we had eyes and ears to see and hear it, this simultaneity of worlds is always going on. While some are lounging on beautiful beaches, others are languishing in prison cells or crowded slums. As a teenager, I had a book of photographs I loved. It showed graffiti from the student uprising in Paris in the spring of 1968. My favorite one of all was *Sous les pavés, c'est la plage!* "Underneath the cobblestones lies the beach."

Now, on this balcony in Hawaii, I understand this phrase as intimately connected to wishing. It's not that the cobblestones aren't real; after all, the students in Paris heaved them up from the streets and used them to make barricades to protect themselves from the police, and some of them hurled them at the police and inflicted real damage. Rather, the truth of this phrase is that there are simultaneously other layers of reality that are accessible to us, if only we can open to them. This, I am coming to see, is the true meaning of abundance. Whatever hard surface layer of reality may present itself, it is only a single facet of the whole. And when we are able to look around or below or beyond it, possibilities shimmer, and worlds within worlds reveal themselves. Dolphins extend below our navels and above our heads, starlight reaches us from thousands of years ago.

I once read a story about an American woman who had dedicated her life to ending world hunger. She told of coming to a place deep in the Saharan desert, where the tribal people were on the verge of dying from thirst. Having met first with the community's leaders—who were all men—she did a radical thing. Sensing that the women had something very important to impart that they would not reveal before the men, she gathered them together. One by one, they told her that the wisest woman among them had dreamed that there was a lake hidden deep beneath the sands, and they believed her. Something made the American woman believe in them. She returned with equipment for drilling. They dug and dug, and there it was: a beautiful shining lake beneath the sands! And just recently I learned that scientists have discovered, through satellite photos, a vast lake basin below the desolation of Darfur.

Now, before settling back down to paint, I look at the women around me. As if playing a game of freeze tag, each one is held in a focused pose, whether standing, squatting, or kneeling with brush in hand. Just over my shoulder, there is Maryann. Bending over her easel, she is rapt. She's painting the reflections of clouds on wet sand, and she's managing in a single medium to capture the radically different textures of water, clouds, sand. Where is her illness in this moment? It's out of the limelight: that's what Irene was trying to tell me. And when it's out of the limelight, then something else can come forth. Maryann has dropped below the cobblestones, and found a beach.

• • •

The next morning I wake up early before breakfast. Sitting on my porch, I listen to the wild and utterly un-mainland songs of the birds, and I look out at the guardians of the night: the sitting Buddhas, the leaning bodhisattvas, the laughing Hoteis, with their round bellies and raised arms. And Ganesh. Ganesh the elephant god, reclining in his folds of fat, wreathed in jewels, his giant wrinkled ears the epitome of his ridiculous majesty, his sumptuous goofiness.

A few feet away, there's a standing Buddha in a hibiscus bower. His face is drawn, his eyes look out from nearly hollow sockets, every rib stands out on his chest. This is the Buddha in his "ascetic pose," representing the first phase in his quest for enlightenment, when he took up extreme ascetic practices.

I try to take in the two of them without blinking, but the effort is dizzying. It almost seems as though I should close one eye and then the other, because there's something so startling about holding the two of them together in my gaze.

And then, as though I had the ancient gift of theurgists to make the statues talk, I feel as though I hear a voice—a strange voice, somewhere between a neigh, a bray, and a snort. "You didn't realize we were such friends, did you?" Ganesh asks.

* * *

"The queen's bathtub! We're going to the queen's bathtub!"

Bolting up from the porch, I yank on my sneakers, grab my towel, and race to catch up with the other women who, wrapped in towels over their bathing suits, are making their way down the winding path in their fluorescent Crocs. I've heard them talking about the queen's bathtub before, but I don't really know what they meant, and I haven't been able to find it for myself.

We go through the gate onto the dirt road, past a little row of shacks and beach houses, as we head toward the lava bed. The air is a little hazy this morning, and the ocean is a darker shade of blue than it's been before.

"See, that's what's left of the queen's beach house," one of the women says to me, pointing to a single weathered wooden wall. I'd looked at that wall before and admired its faded colors: green with a layer of pink showing through. I'd wondered why the wall was there, freestanding and with the glass of its single window still intact.

"Do you really mean the queen?" I ask.

"Yes," the women say. "I think you missed the story Kalani told on our first night. Queen Liliuokalani used to come here. This was her beach. And where we're going really was her special place.

Queen Liliuokalani, the last monarch of Hawaii. As a child I loved to look at her picture in my encyclopedia. She was a magnificent woman, with her statuesque body in ruffled Victorian satin, with jewels and flowers in her coiled-up black hair. She loved to sing and wrote the music for "Aloha Oe." And she tried so valiantly to resist in the face of overwhelming American power.

Before being deposed, she lived in a beautiful palace, but it seems that she loved to come to her little beach house and to bathe in her tidal pool.

We make our way over the lava bed, getting closer and closer to the sea.

"Here it is!"

It's a giant tide pool, with steep sides carved by the waves in such a way that it does indeed resemble a bathtub.

"Kalani told us that the water in these pools is very healing," one of the women says. "And especially in this one."

We lower ourselves in and sit down. The stone seats are covered with velvet seaweeds, the plushest seats you could imagine. Tiny shells, opalescent bits of mother-of-pearl, float over us. Mollie sits across from me. Her husband is actually a descendant of Queen Liliuokalani. Due to some family dispute, he lost out on all the money. The two of them are in the process of selling their house on the Big Island and will soon be moving to Nevada. Nevada: Could there be a place more unlike this iridescent green watery land? I know that for her this retreat has been a kind of ceremonial leave-taking, preparation for a wrenching departure. Yet in this moment, you'd never know. With each surge of the wave, our bodies sway, our limbs fly up, and huge purply brown, shell-encrusted bouquets of seaweed come floating to the surface. We shriek with laughter, like children on an amusement park ride, and no one laughs louder than Mollie. Then the wave recedes and we are dignified as queens again.

There are four of us in the tub. There is also the felt presence of Queen Liliuokalani, Hawaii's dark Madonna. And for me there are two other palpable if invisible presences: in this sumptuous tub, which is hard as rock and draped with silky layers of seaweed, fat Ganesh is spouting seawater from his trunk on the bony ribs of the fasting Buddha.

·  ·  ·

When we get back to the main house, breakfast is in full swing.

Across from me Maryann is eating from a big bowl of hot cereal with fruit.

"You're going to eat that?" I ask.

"You bet," she says. "Painting makes me hungry."

She hasn't been able to join in our treks to the beach, to scramble over the lava beds, float in the tide pools, or swim with the dolphins, but she's been having her own adventures with paper and paints.

"Painting, eating, sleeping: I could live like this forever," she says. This is the woman who, a few short days ago, had described her life as a living hell.

* * *

On our last night, we put on our fanciest dresses and our Crocs and make our way over the lava bed just as the sun is setting. The waves are crashing fairly high against the rock, and the salty spray is hitting against our faces. But we stand there until each one of us has had a chance to perform the evening ritual that Kalani taught the women on their first night, before I got there. First, he told them, you find a piece of rock to stand for whatever it is you need to let go of. Then you throw a petal into the sea to stand for what you wish for. The other women came prepared with pebbles from the beach, but I am empty-handed. I'd assumed that hard pieces of black rock would be a dime a dozen on the lava bed. But actually, it's not that easy to find something small enough to pick up. The top layer of the lava presents a myriad of knobs and bumps, but when you pull at them you find that they're immobile, stuck. The lava bed resists me, a hard black mass, a perfect image of attachment to suffering.

A few feet away from me, there's Maryann. She's standing there in the pink orange light, having thrown her rock and cast her flower.

Since I don't have an actual rock to throw, I will throw in the rock of my fear for her, of my compulsion to keep her illness in the limelight. In doing so, I remember the exercise that Ajahn Jumnian gave us, when he said: *You imagine that the world, with its sorrows, is heavy as a boulder and you are lifting it up, up toward the sky. Then you set it down again, as though it were as light as a feather.*

Though I don't have a rock, I do have a flower in my pocket: a single white plumeria. It's so light that it clings like a moth to my fingers, but I load it with a very big wish: *May I always remember the second field of flowers.* To send the plumeria on its journey, I have to lean rather perilously over the dark edge of the lava bed and then blow with all my might until it flies into the great whooshing lungs of the sea.

. . .

When the plane lands the next evening in San Francisco, I can see from the runway that there is a driving rain. Nicholas is waiting for me, beyond the baggage claim, and in his sopped clothes he looks pale and exhausted. After a long day in his inner-city classroom, he's come through sheets of rain and rush-hour traffic to meet me. I throw a garland of magenta orchids around his neck, and we drive to my house through a storm of hail in his battered red car.

By the next morning, the storm has passed. After breakfast, Nicholas and I take a walk down to the pond, to see how much the water has risen. On the way, we pass Raquelle and Rupert, who are heaving a heavy gold bodhisattva into the trunk of his car.

Nicholas leaps forward to help them, and I follow.

"Rupert bought this statue from me," she says. "And you're invited to my moving sale tomorrow!"

"You're moving?"

I'm stunned. How could anyone but Raquelle live in that beautiful house with its vaulted ceilings, its stained-glass windows and indoor balcony?

"Yes!"

Unlike the statues at Hale Aloalo, this bodhisattva seems heavy and thinglike—perhaps because she's resisting her fate?—and we struggle to get her into the car.

Before Nicholas and I continue our walk, I manage to whisper in Rupert's ear, "Is she all right?"

"I hope so," he says, looking pale and full of dread, as though he's still being hounded by the sort of men who stare at goats. "She's been advised to go bankrupt."

. . .

Down at the pond, the rain has brought the water to the very rim.

Standing on the muddy trail, Nicholas and I look across to the island. In precisely our spot, the spot where we lay in the summer's sun to read and doze, two white herons are standing in their one-legged way. Do herons bring good luck the way cranes do in the folktales of so many lands? Do they mate for life like geese? We don't know, but we can't help but feel that they represent some alternate version of ourselves, an auspicious omen of a paired future.

At my feet among the reeds at the water's edge, I see something glinting. Stooping to pick it up, I rub its mud off on my pants: it's Sacajawea.

Hurling her into the water, I make a wish for Raquelle, ignoring the eight-syllable rule. *May she have an abundance of health and money and readers wealthy enough to buy her magnificent book.*

"She'll be all right," says Nicholas.

"What makes you say that?"

"It's the way she lives her life. The way she frames things. If life gives her a lemon, she won't just make lemonade, she'll make—"

And before Nicholas can finish his sentence, I know how to fill in the blank. Raquelle would make the most exquisitely fluffy lemon mousse, with a dozen organic egg whites whipped light as air, and she'd serve it in a silver chalice.

Making our way to the little dock, we sit on its wooden bench and mull our plans for Thanksgiving. Nicholas has grave misgivings about a holiday that is so linked to the tragic encounter between an indigenous people and their white conquerors. And for me, the trip to Hawaii—site of another tragically conquered people—has intensified the mixed feelings I already had about an occasion in which the mystery of scarcity, abundance, greed, suffering, and celebration are so interwoven. "Well, don't be too complicated," says a voice in my mind. It's a familiar voice, both robust and honeyed. "There can't ever be harm in giving thanks."

It's none other than Aunt Jemima. I haven't encountered her in a while—perhaps she thought I didn't need her in Hawaii—but now with her blessings, we swallow our doubts and plan our feast. At her insistence, there will be a maple glaze on just about everything: the turkey, the yams, the pies. And between ourselves, Nicholas and I come to an easy and even mellifluous agreement that in the large wooden bowl, carved with dolphins, that was my gift to him from Hawaii, there will be an all-you-can-eat salad of arugula and iceberg lettuce.

# CHAPTER TWELVE

# December

## *After Wishing: In Praise of What's Here*

Hawaii would have been the perfect place to conclude my experiment in desire: having bathed in Queen Liliuokalani's tub, I stand at the edge of the black lava bed and, with the red-orange sunset doing its slow fade behind me, I throw the white flower of my wish into the frothing sea: *The End*. But as the queen herself knew, sometimes life has other plans: volcanoes erupt, storms slam through houses made of palms, white men arrive in boats, and a radically different chapter unfolds.

Not long after I returned from Hawaii it became clear that, while my sister went to bring my mother and Luigi back from Italy, I would have to go to France, to face the dreadful tax officials who'd been hounding my mother and to try to sell her apartment. It would have been a great comfort if Nicholas had been able to come with me, but he'd already made plans to go to Oaxaca for his Christmas break, and his tickets were nonrefundable.

Two days before leaving for France, I asked Nicholas to join me in a little ceremony to celebrate "closing day" on my house. After several hours of signing papers and writing checks in the mortgage office, I returned home to find him waiting for me in the driveway in his battered red car. After a hard day in the class-room, he was asleep at the wheel, and when I peered through the window I saw that the interior of his car had begun to look more and more like his principal residence. Since I met him in June, he'd moved out of the rooming house and into his parents' spare bedroom, and from the look of things, he was keeping himself ready for the next transition. The piles of books were still there, of course, with my own book—the one that had drawn him to me—prominently displayed, and now somewhat faded, in the back window. There were the piles of paper, the clipboards and CDs that had always been there, but now there were also towels and items of clothing, a thermal coffee mug or two, tubes of toothpaste and shaving cream, a collection of stuffed animals for his classroom, a jar of salsa for his burritos.

At the slightest tap to his windshield, he opened his eyes. I don't know why it continues to move me that he's such a light sleeper—could it be the combination of chaos and attentiveness in his life? He may be distracted and disorganized when it comes to time, money, and things, but he's intensely present to living beings. Emerging from the car in his rumpled state, he threw his arms around me and said, "Congratulations, bitch goddess householder pig!" Which, considering his feelings about the history of private property, the displacement of native peoples, the enclosure riots of 1607, the disappearance of the small family farm, the Enclo-sure Act of 1832, and the forced urbanization of British peasants, was actually quite sweet.

He told me that I was beaming, and I could feel that I was. To my surprise, it wasn't anticlimactic to buy the house I'd lived in for so long, and I was actually feeling rather triumphant. Nicholas took my arm and we walked around the house together, in a sort of circumambulation. At the base of the chimney, my eye fell on something I'd never seen before: a tiny door. When I opened it, a cloud of soot blew out, and through the cloud I discovered that there was an immense reservoir of powdery gray ash behind the little door. "I think ashes are good for roses," Nicholas said. And for some odd reason, it was on hearing these words that my heart fully swelled with pride of ownership, and I thought to myself, "When I come back from France, I'll plant rows of roses and I'll cover their roots with layers of ash from my secret cache. And then I'll throw myself into an orgy of renovation, replacing the bullet-riddled window, tearing up the dreadful brown linoleum in the kitchen and covering it with terra-cotta tile . . ."

Nicholas had brought a bottle of champagne, and we went inside and made a toast: to my new house, to our imminent travels in vastly different directions, to us. Then he added, "To the twins!"

· · ·

And now I'm in the plane, on my way to France by way of Frankfurt, where I will have a four-hour layover before boarding my plane to Marseille and then making my way to Aix-en-Provence. I wasn't happy about the complicated itinerary with its hours on German soil, but there weren't many flights to choose from so close to the Christmas season. So here I am, staring at a computer screen that keeps flashing the word *Fluggeschwindigkeit* and sitting next to a big, broad-shouldered woman with blue eyes, ruddy cheeks, and grayish-blond hair. Somehow I know that she will be able to tell me the meaning of this outrageous word.

"It means the speed of flying," she says with only the slightest German accent. Then she tells me that though she was born in northern Germany and is returning to visit her mother's grave, she's lived in the States for some forty years now. Her name is Frida.

"You must have been a child during the war?" I ask.

"Yes."

She goes on to tell me that she had a great deal of fear as a child, but it wasn't so much the war that caused fear—it was Gyp-sies. From their farm, she and her siblings had a long walk to school, nearly two hours in each direction. She was the littlest one of the batch, and—though they'd been fiercely admonished not to—the older children would run off way ahead, leaving her alone to trudge along the winding path through the dark forest. She'd al-ways been warned never to do so, because at any moment the Gypsies might come and kidnap a little blue-eyed, blond-haired child. "To this day," she tells me, "I have nightmares about that path in the forest."

Then she tells me that one evening a Gypsy man showed up at her father's farm, surrounded by his scraggly gang of dark-haired, dark-eyed children. He was a cobbler, and he offered to make shoes for Frida's family. As their shoes were on the brink of falling apart and winter was fast coming, Frida's father settled on a price with the man, and he and his brood went off.

The next morning when Frida's family went into the barn to milk the cows and collect the morning's eggs, they found that all the chickens had been stolen. They followed muddy footprints deep into the woods until they came to a trampled-down place. There, around the still-glowing ashes of a fire, they found tiny bones and a huge mound of feathers.

"That's something I'll never forget," she says. "That huge mound of feathers in the middle of the dark forest."

The flight is long. We sleep, we eat, we fall asleep again. At one point when I wake up, Frida is asking me in a panicky voice, "Have you seen my pin?"

"Your pin?"

"You didn't see the pin I was wearing?"

When I tell her no, she looks very unhappy, as though my fail-ure to notice the pin has further compounded its absence.

"It's gold. Real gold. It belonged to my mother. I must have lost it when I went back to the restroom. I lost it and somebody took it."

"You don't know that somebody took it."

"Somebody did. I'm sure of it. It's very valuable. Somebody stole it. That's what people do. I can't believe that on my way to visit the place where my mother is buried, I've lost the pin that she gave me." And she buries her head in her hands.

I ring the bell for the steward.

"My neighbor here has lost a piece of jewelry," I tell him.

He goes to the back of the cabin, and within moments we hear his voice through the PA:

"Attention, passengers. Someone has lost a piece of jewelry that has a lot of sentimental value. Please check around your seats and on the floor beneath you to see if you can find it."

From the seat behind us, a hand emerges. In the hand is a shiny gold pin. "Is this it?" a young dark-skinned man is asking. "It was on the floor beside my feet."

Frida thanks him profusely, then gives me a look in which relief, embarrassment, and disbelief seem equally mixed. *See how our thoughts make our world?* I feel like saying—but I resist. I didn't grow up in wartime Germany, with a terrifying walk through the woods every day and desperately hungry people butchering my family's chickens. She fastens the gold pin back on her lapel, and this time I notice that it is an intricately carved feather.

• • •

In France, too, a cold wind is blowing, bringing fine black sand from North Africa and depositing it on the windowsills and the balcony of my mother's apartment building in Aix-en-Provence. I arrived yesterday midafternoon, after the all-night flight, a bus, and a taxi. When at last I entered the foyer, carrying my suitcases, I winced: the American woman who has not yet bought the apartment has already substituted her name for my mother's on the mailbox.

Nearly twenty years ago, my mother had a wish: to move to southern France, buy an apartment, and paint. Through her own magical/unmagical combination of resolve, hard work, and a few well-timed strokes of good fortune, she made her wish come true. The apartment is filled with her paintings. Whether large or small, figurative or abstract, they are odes to her life in Europe, to the ochre and russet of old stones and tiles, the grays and greens of cobbled streets and cedar trees, the blues of fountains and windy skies, and neon splashes of graffiti.

Now it's time to let it all go. For the law of impermanence is fixed and unwavering: everything changes. Without the reality of change, wishes couldn't come true and thus bring about a new reality. Yet the very same law also decrees that, one day or another, the new reality will grow old and give way to a newer one. One perhaps not wished for.

If it's difficult for many of us to permit ourselves to wish in the first place, it's even more difficult for most of us to let go of a wish that's come true. One of the things I've noticed about people who seem especially adept at the art of wishing is that they're also good at surrendering the fruits of a wish and moving on to the next one. They seem to embrace the principle of change, of constant movement, ebb and flow, as though it were the very medium they worked in.

Carole, for instance, can appear quite ruthless: shifting gears, disbanding projects, selling one house to buy another long before many friends and associates see it coming. Just recently, for example, she decided to close down the communal studio that she'd created in California. The other artists were distraught. "But we love it here!" "You've worked so hard to make it perfect!" "We're just really settling in!" Carole, however, remained adamant: she wanted her share of the money out, and she wanted to consolidate. Within a few months she had created a new communal studio in the garage of her own house—and now, she told me, the artists are happy as clams. It seems that her commitment is never so much to the new reality she's created but to the process of creating it. And when I think of Raquelle and the grace with which she let go of her beautiful house and so many of her talismanic possessions, I see that the same is true for her. Just recently I received a group e-mail from her in which she sounded positively ecstatic. She announced that the first run of her book had been selling like hotcakes. There were only a few left at the bargain rate of $260 before the price jumps to $500 on the second run. And she'd been invited to channel the goddess through sacred dance at no less a venue than the Cathedral of Notre-Dame de Chartres.

But here I am, in Aix-en-Provence, wearing the raggedy work clothes I brought with me from California and feeling well out of range of my inner goddess. There's an immense labor involved in letting go of the life that grew from my mother's wish. As she isn't well, and as I speak better French than my siblings, it falls to me. By day I get a crash course in the tangled web of French real estate. At night I pull staples from the scores of her paintings that, stretched on wooden frames, are stacked under sofas and in various closets. Once I've pulled the staples out, I leave the canvases—some quite huge—draped over chairs and pile the wooden stretcher bars out on the balcony. I sort through mounds of clothing, boxes of photographs, letters, and documents. I go up and down the stairs to the basement, putting out trash, hauling up more canvases and boxes. It's an exhausting labor, both emotionally and physically.

One night, well after midnight, as I'm hauling another large box of belongings, I suddenly feel pain radiating out from my heart. It's a mild pain, but it's one I've never felt before, and it's frightening. I feel so alone here. What would I do if I really thought I was having a heart attack? I don't even know what number to dial in case of an emergency.

Suddenly I hear the sound of sirens, those French sirens that always sound to me like an animal's mournful wail. The sound gets closer and closer until finally it stops just below my mother's apartment and bright pulsing lights come in through the windows and race through the rooms.

*Ask not for whom the bell tolls . . .*

I go out on the balcony. A crew of emergency workers has fanned out on the yard below, and they're coming my way. One of them looks up at me and asks if I know where Madame Tourneau lives. But I've never even heard of her.

"*Non, hélas,*" I say.

They enter the building through the front door and climb the stairs, past my mother's apartment. For well over an hour, I can hear some sort of commotion from one of the apartments above me. Finally I fall asleep, curled up tightly on the living room sofa, still wearing my dirty work clothes. In the few hours of night that remain, I have frightening, emergency dreams. When I wake up in the morning, the winter sun is shining brightly and all is quiet—ominously so.

After breakfast, I cross paths in the foyer with Rose, an older woman who lives in the apartment just above my mother, and who has always been very kind to her. "Did you hear what happened last night?" she asks.

"I heard the sirens. I saw the ambulances," I say.

"It was Monsieur Tourneau. From the sixth floor. In the middle of the night he complained to his wife that he wasn't feeling well. She called the ambulance, but by the time they got here he had already died." Tears are streaming down her face, and before I can say anything, she continues. "And last week we buried my thirty-seven-year-old daughter-in-law. My little granddaughter is only six, and now she has no mother. Can you imagine?"

Yes, I can. No, I can't. I only know that last night there were strange pains that fanned out from my heart, at the hour of my unseen, unknown neighbor's death. And that here, in one apartment building in southern France, there is a convergence of sorrow.

When, ten days after my arrival, I've removed the staples from nearly all of the paintings, decided the fate of most of the other belongings, and survived a series of encounters with notaries and tax collectors, I set off to visit friends in various parts of France. Having completed this round of my heavy labor, I'm longing to float for a bit in lightness of being, in forgetfulness of sorrow.

But everywhere I go, I seem to hear a bell tolling. . . .

When I arrive in Lyon, my friend Sonya opens the door. Tall with big dark eyes and a razor wit, she's one of the few people I know who can make me laugh just by directing her gaze at me. Yet her life has been full of sadness. Her brother, Michel, was my first love. He's the one I met when my ski went over the mountain slope. The one who died on Mount Everest. That was long ago, and since then there have been other tragedies and a great many difficulties in her family's life. In the house in the Alps where I spent a summer with them long ago, Sonya's mother, Lilly, died in a fire. Her father, Maurice, was shattered. And now, for some time, Sonya's daughter, a young woman in her twenties, has been prone to a host of disturbing symptoms. In the last letter I received from Sonya, she told me that for the past year her daughter had experienced such terrible pain in her jaw that she found it impossible to speak. "Not a word," Sonya tells me when we find a moment alone on my first night there. "Can you imagine?"

No, I can't. I can't imagine what it's like for a mother to have her beautiful daughter fall silent for a year. It seems like something out of a fairy tale, something that would call for a handsome prince to ride up on his stallion and plant a single, healing kiss on her sad, sealed lips.

But Sonya and her husband, Hervé, have instead engaged a team of specialists—a psychologist, an orthopedic doctor, a physical therapist, and a masseuse—to help her. Gradually she's been getting better. Though her jaw is still painfully tight, she's begun talking again. Their lives are returning to something that looks somewhat like normal.

Does wishing have a place in their lives? I wonder. In the morning, over our *petit déjeuner* of coffee, milk, bread, and jam, I ask them. The question seems to make Sonya uncomfortable, as though reminding her of everything in her life that has been the absolute opposite of anything she would ever wish for. As though she doesn't dare enunciate what I know is her deepest wish: *May my daughter be well.* She murmurs something vague like "We are really so privileged."

But Hervé surprises me. Though he's generally rather quiet in conversation and not given to oracular pronouncements, he seems to have strong feelings about this subject. Leaning over the table, he tells me, "I don't have wishes for myself anymore."

"Why?"

"Because I have arrived at a certain wisdom. Just the other day I was talking with a man I know who's about my age, in his early sixties. This man kept saying, 'I should have done this,' and 'If only I had done that,' and I felt sorry for him. At this stage of life, what's the point of thinking like that? We adults have made our lives, and now it's time to appreciate what we've made. There's so much to experience! That's what I mean when I say I don't have wishes for myself anymore, because wishes are for the future. Now, when I wish, it's for others—and especially for the children. Not just our own children. In making the lives we have now, we adults have transmitted a future to our children. They have to carry forward with what we've left them. And so it's for them, and their future, that I make wishes."

When I leave Lyon, I take the train that heads northeast, toward the city of Nancy in the forested region of the Lorraine. It's a long way, and as the train moves deeper through the darkening day of the darkening year, my thoughts keep coming back to Hervé. Though it seems to me that a healthy man in his early sixties—and beyond—might well have wishes for his own future, I'm struck by his emphatic sense of life's seasons. He seemed to speak, as a farmer might speak, with the same clarity about when to sow and when to reap. Often, when I've heard people discuss wishing as a function of time and the stages of life, there's been an element of resignation, even bitterness in their tone—as in, "Now, it's too late to wish." But I didn't hear that tone in Hervé's words. Rather, I heard hope and generosity. I heard his resolve to enjoy the ripe fruit of his own life and to save his wishes, like seeds, for the fields of the young.

Now the train is flying past frozen fields and pine forests laced with snow. When we arrive in Nancy, another old friend is waiting for me: Jacques. He and my father met in Paris shortly after World War II, and I've known him since I was a small child. He's in his eighties now. His hair is white, and he looks stooped. But I recognize him instantly with his broad chest, his ruddy, big-eared face, and his bright blue eyes.

We drive back to the village, Deneuvre, where Jacques was born and raised. Its small, shuttered houses line the narrow cobbled streets, which lead, at the crest of a hill, to an onion-domed church. Dark pines and heavy gray clouds form the horizon: we are far from Provence here, close to Germany.

When we enter his house, I realize I'm looking for Colette, Jacques's wife, who died twelve years ago. Everything looks just as she left it, the dark browns of the carpet and somewhat sagging sofa and armchairs, the long wooden dining room table, her worn brass pots in the kitchen. On the windowsill, I even see a glass bottle filled with cherries floating in *eau-de-vie*. That's what Colette and I did together, the last time that I saw her. It was early summer, and we picked cherries from the tree in their garden. Then we rinsed them, removed their stems and pits, and placed them in a glass bottle of *eau-de-vie*.

Now Jacques is preparing supper for me. In all the years I've known him, I've never seen him cook. "Well," he says to me, "Colette has been gone a long time now. I had to learn." With his big hands he's peeling tiny speckled quail eggs for our salad. He serves it with a roasted chicken that he bought at the charcuterie. For dessert we have ice cream, with cherries in *eau-de-vie*.

. . .

The next morning, when I come downstairs for breakfast, Jacques is already drinking his *café au lait* in a bowl and shuffling cards at the long wooden table. He and Colette used to begin the day by playing cards together, and now Jacques plays solitaire. "Shall we go and see Hercules today?" he asks me.

Since I was last in Deneuvre, an ancient Roman sanctuary was discovered in a field, one dedicated to Hercules. Known as Herakles to the Greeks, for centuries he was worshipped throughout the Mediterranean world. This far north in France, it's rare to find a shrine in his honor. This one seems to have flourished for at least a hundred years, not long after the birth of Christ. Then marauding Christians attacked the site, toppling its pagan statues, smashing its columns, and uprooting its stone paths. Now, in a museum in the center of the village, the site has been carefully reconstructed.

"You know, I don't remember much about Hercules," I say to Jacques as we walk down the winding street from his house.

"*Alors,*" Jacques says, sounding as casual as though he were telling me about one of his neighbors, "Hercules was the child of Zeus, and his mother was a mortal woman named Alcmene. As you can imagine, Hera was jealous of Alcmene and resentful of her child. When Hercules grew to manhood, Hera resolved to push him to the very limit of his capacities. She gave him twelve labors, one after the other. Because of his great courage and physical strength, he triumphed and Hera rewarded him with the gift of immortality."

The main room of the museum is quiet and dimly lit. When we enter, I feel a wave of something like dizziness, a mild case of whatever it is that divers experience when they suddenly drop deep below the sunlit surface of the sea and enter another dimension of space and time. I was expecting one large statue and a bit of broken crockery. But before me, in a very large space that reproduces the size and proportions of the original site, a pool of water bubbles up in a stone basin, as if from a deep spring. Beyond it rise the columns of a temple. And around the pool stand a line of carved stone statues of Hercules. Some of them are only a few feet high, but many are bigger than a real man. Most of the statues show Hercules in one of two poses: poised for battle or at rest. In all of them, he has a noble, bearded face and a shaggy head of hair. His naked body is muscular, and he holds a club in one hand and his lion's pelt in the other.

From the various plaques on the walls, I gather that this sanctuary was all about wishing. People would come to the basin of water, to drink from it and make ablutions. Then they would pray to Hercules to grant their wish. To encourage him to do so, they would make an offering. One of the plaques explains that there are two kinds of offerings. There is the *offrande propitiare*, an object presented to a divine being in the hope of obtaining some favor. And there is the *offrande gratulatoire,* which is the object given in thanks after a wish has been granted.

"The *offrande gratulatoire* is an ex-voto," Jacques says. "That's what most of these statues are. You know, a *voto* is a vow, a wish. When you made your wish, you would promise a tangible offering to Hercules if your wish came true. And when it did, you had to make good on your promise with a plaque, a statue—whatever you could possibly afford. The larger statues would have cost the annual income of a wealthy person."

Many of the statues bear the Latin phrase *Votum solvit libens merito.* "He has freely and willingly fulfilled his vow." Looking into the stone eyes of each Hercules, I want to know: What vow did you accomplish? What wish did you grant? Beside me, Jacques reads from the museum brochure: "A healing god, Hercules helps his devotees in their terrestrial life. Having triumphed over death, he also guides them to immortality." There it is again: the reminder not to be a wish snob. The same god who opens the door to eternal life can also confer an earthly blessing: a fertile field, a healthy child, a battle won.

With his shaggy head, his naked, muscled body, his club and lion pelt, Hercules seems a world away from Tinker Bell and all her ilk, with their gossamer wings and fairy dust. Yet for all his power, he's ready to lend an ear to the full range of human desire, granting wishes both large and small. Before I leave, I nail a piece of paper to the trunk of Colette's cherry tree: "Hercules, please help me to resolve my mother's financial affairs in France."

. . .

From here I go to visit Carole in her village of Sorèze, near Toulouse. She's come to arrange the sale of the first house she worked so hard to restore—the one that came with waist-high medieval dust and bats flying through the holes in the walls. Though she's loved it, she feels it's time to move on. There's a house on the Mediterranean that she's made an offer on. Another in San Miguel de Allende that she's fallen in love with. And then there's the lure of Hawaii. She's bought a book, *1,000 Places to See Before You Die,* and she and Don are planning to make their way around the globe.

Carole told me to wait for her in a little café in the central square, and though it's all arranged, I can't help but do a double take when she appears. After all, when I last saw her, she was painting a cardboard coffin in California, but now here she is, bounding up to me in a village in southwest France, wearing a red beret and red high-top sneakers. Carole, the queen of Putting It Out There, whom I met when I answered the little ad that said "Free use of studio in exchange for speaking French." Though we're far from home, it seems somehow as though we've come full circle. Greeting me the French way with three kisses to my cheeks, she takes my arm and we set out to her house, just a few blocks away. Winding our way through the narrow streets, it's clear that everyone knows Carole *la californienne.* As we pass by the charcuterie, the *boulangerie,* the *tabac,* people smile and call out *"Bonjour!"* in a way that strikes me as not at all characteristically French.

It turns out that this town was the site of a famous boarding school that was founded in the fifteenth century and educated the sons of illustrious families—not only from France but from Europe and the Americas—until very recently. This school was the heart of the village, and its boys and their visiting families supported the village shops, restaurants, and hotels. Ever since it closed, the town has been languishing. With the arrival of Carole *la californienne* and her brigades of visiting artists, people began to feel hopeful again, as if new life was stirring. Carole even had talks with the mayor about turning the massive school building into an artists' collective, with studios, galleries, workshops, and festivals.

We've arrived at the door of her house. From the outside, except for its bright blue shutters, it blends in indistinguishably with the row of ancient crooked townhouses. But when we step inside, I feel as though I've walked into a jewel box, with refracted color bouncing off all the walls and echoed in mirrors. I gasp.

"I wanted it to feel like you were living inside a Bonnard painting," Carole says.

Prominent on the living room wall is a large painting of a dark-haired woman, seen from behind, standing by the steepled church that I've just seen in the center of Sorèze and surrounded by a giant rippling field of sunflowers, with a blazing blue sky above. Painted across the bottom of the painting are the words "She thought the light would make her well."

"I love that title. Is there a story behind it?"

Carole gives me a startled look. "Didn't you know I had Lyme disease? For five years, I was basically immobilized, bedridden."

"You never told me."

"I didn't?"

"No."

"Are you sure you didn't forget?"

"How could I forget something like that?"

"You have no idea how happy you've just made me!"

"Why?"

Carole tells me that for years she felt subsumed by the illness. Even when her energy finally began to come back, it was still her reference point. Everything she did or thought was influenced by her fear that the symptoms would return, her relief that they hadn't yet. Then she strained her back after a day of lugging art supplies, and she went to the chiropractor. He asked her, "Do you have any conditions that I should know about?" She started to dredge up the whole Lyme disease story, then stopped herself. "It was as though a loud voice from deep inside was telling me, 'Stop. You don't need to define yourself that way anymore. It's time to go forward, to open up to everything new that wants to come into your life.'"

"Like a little village in France."

"Yes."

She takes my hand and leads me upstairs to her studio, where the walls are still covered with her paintings and they seem to be vibrating with an energy so intense that I almost feel as though I've entered an aviary or aquarium of giant tropical birds or fish that might just leap from their frames and fly or swim, and from somewhere I find myself remembering a line from the poet Rilke: *Out of the darkness a blaze of colors appears . . .*

Below the paintings, lining the perimeter of the room, is a jumble of boxes, some still empty and some full to the brim with paints and rags and palette knives. As well as I've come to know Carole, I still can't really fathom that, after so much grueling work, she could leave behind this place that she has made so beautiful, this place that came to mean so much to her and that did so much for her. Does she suffer from a chronic restlessness, an inability to be content? Shouldn't she keep it as a kind of permanent shrine to her healing, to the place where the light made her well?

"Most people in my life are a lot more resistant to change than

I am," she tells me. "To me it's all a kind of dance: you move toward a goal, you create it, attain it—and then you let it go."

"But what about all the other people you've drawn into this place: the artists who come to paint with you, the villagers and all the hope that you've inspired?"

"They'll carry on without me! That's how I do it. I like to wish a world into being. I dream up the most miraculous thing I'd like to have happen in my life that I don't really know how to do. I feel this enormous excitement when the kernel of the dream starts to twinkle. I work hard to make it happen. And I work hard to share it with other people, and perhaps even find a way to make their livelihood within it. But then I let it go. It's like I create these planets, but then I hand them over to others and move on to the unknown."

"But doesn't it get really scary sometimes?"

"Yes, but it's exciting. And the way I see it is, now I have all the information I've learned from the last adventure. So the next one in my life is going to be even better!"

As Carole talks, she's returned to the labor of packing, stuffing more things into the partially empty boxes and shaking them gently to make their contents settle. Wanting to help her, I pick up a box to do the same and then let out a shriek. A box turtle, about the size of a dessert plate, was stationed behind the box and is now lumbering my way.

"That's Garibaldi!" Carole says. "The turtle I got when I went to visit your mother. Didn't she ever tell you about him?"

"Garibaldi? You mean the turtle you stole from the people of Venice? What were you thinking?"

"Well, you know, when I saw him hiding under some bushes in that park, I just knew I had to have him. And I felt like he knew it, too." And Carole tells me how it was, during the years with Lyme disease, when everything became agonizingly slow. It would have been hard for anyone, but for her it was a radical shift in identity. She had always been a person of exceptionally high energy, flying through life like an acrobat, while keeping twelve spinning plates in the air. She had to discover a whole new way of functioning, of being in the world. Then one day while staring at a blank canvas, she saw the image of a turtle and she realized: *That's it! My totem animal!* She knew that the turtle was sacred to many indigenous peoples, a steadfast and dignified creature for whom there is no shame, no catastrophe in going slowly. And so the turtle, multiple turtles, began appearing in her dreams, her drawings and paintings. That's why, when a real turtle crossed her path in Venice, she scooped him up, put him in her purse, and took him back with her to France as though by divine decree.

• • •

From Sorèze I travel to Paris, where I've arranged to stay four nights alone, to give myself a breather before heading back for the final whirl of packing and coping with French Realtors, notaries, and bankers in Aix.

My hotel, l'Apollinaire, is close to the Luxembourg Gardens. It's a place I've loved since childhood, and what strikes me now is that within its fenced boundaries, it's a world that seems to exist to grant our every wish. For children there's the carousel, the puppet theater, the central basin with its miniature boats, the booths selling candy and bubbles and balls and pinwheels. There are private nooks and shaded alleys for lovers, young and old, as well as those craving solitude. There are the lanes where old men play *boules*. There are cafés for crêpes and sandwiches and warm sugared waffles and wine and coffee and tea. There are fountains, a reflecting pool, an art museum.

It's winter now, and many of the garden's riches lies in wait, pruned back, under wraps, behind closed doors. But when I enter it on my first day, the riches seem latent, ready to unfurl with the spring's green leaves. Meanwhile, winter reveals the underlying plan of the garden, its foundation of generosity. Through grand open spaces and narrow passages, I roam, greeting certain trees, statues, and fountains like old friends. Under the long alleys of bare trees, I smell the chestnuts roasting.

Then, on the far side of the garden, I enter another world. I'm walking down a river of blue gravel, and high above me, hanging from ropes and printed on giant squares of diaphanous fabric, are faces. They are faces of people from around the world: a turbaned man; a dirty little girl with a jewel between her eyes; a dark-skinned, maybe Tamil boy with wide, dark eyes. There are around a dozen of these huge diaphanous photographs, and as different as the faces are from one another, there is something in their expression that unites them. Each of them looks out, into the sky, with the same expression of utterly crushed hope and inextinguishable longing. Down below them, on the blue gravel, the dots of light from the hanging bits of mirrored glass dart and swirl. I look to see if there's a sign posted anywhere, giving some information about the work, but I can't find one. A woman in a fur coat passes, and when I ask her, "Do you know anything about these photographs?" she says, "I don't know. Someone told me they're slaves from around the world."

Crossing the garden again, I decide to go into its small art museum. There's an exhibit of contemporary art, and what I'm most struck by is a collection of garments, made of seaweed. VÊTEMENTS MOUES, FAITS D'ALGUES DE MER the sign reads. "Clothing _____, made of seaweed." I can't remember what *moues* means. I decide to ask the gallery attendant, a woman about my age with large blue eyes and bright red hair. She tells me that *moues* means "transformed"—as in "mutation." We begin to talk, and her co-worker, a tall, dark-haired woman who's about our age, joins in. The red-haired woman is named Gabit, which she tells me is a Hebrew name. The dark-haired woman is Sabine. When I ask them what they do, Gabit tells me that she's done all kinds of things, but that her passion is the theater. Sabine tells me that she's a philosopher and an art critic. When they find out that I'm a writer and

that I'm writing a book about wishing, they both become animated. Sabine tells me, "I believe in the power of wishing, but I
believe it's mysterious. And I believe it should stay that way. It's
something I refuse to investigate."

Gabit tells me, "I definitely believe in the power of wishing!
You know, I haven't taken my break yet. Would you like to come
with me and we can talk about it?"

She leads me outside the museum to a greenhouse, where the
air is warm and dense with moisture. We walk under a canopy of
flowering vines, past all kinds of lush leafy plants whose names I
don't know, until we come to an alcove full of flowers I recognize:
hibiscus, plumeria, bromeliad.

"Hawaii!" I say to her. "I was there just last month."

"You're so lucky!" she says. "I've always dreamed of going
there. That's why I come here, every day, on my break."

We sit down on two green metal chairs, and Gabit pulls a pack
of cigarettes from her pocket. "Do you mind if I smoke?"

"I don't mind. Do they let you smoke in here?"

"*Boeufffffff*. There's never anyone here." She leans back in her
chair. "So I wanted to tell you a story that I don't tell many people. Because, you know, especially in France people tend to be so
skeptical."

"Well, maybe like what your friend Sabine just said. That she
believes in the power of wishing, but she thinks it's something
that you shouldn't try to understand with the rational mind—like
love."

"I agree that it's mysterious, like love. But I don't think that
means one needs to talk about it in whispers. When I find someone who understands, as you seem to, then I like to acknowledge
what a powerful force it's been in my life. So let me tell you just
one story.

"It was fifteen years ago, and I was in a desperate state financially. I didn't know where to turn. And suddenly I conceived an
immense desire to go to the church of Saint-Sulpice, and see the

Delacroix. I'm Jewish, you know, and I'd actually never been to the Saint-Sulpice. So I go in there, and I'm looking for the Delacroix, and what do I see but a painting of the Passion of Christ. I don't even remember who painted it, but it's a big dark painting, and it's Christ in agony on the cross. And you know, for a Jewish girl, that's something you have an aversion to. You recoil. But suddenly I hear a voice inside me saying, 'Jesus, please, you've got to help me!'

"And later that day, having been to the Saint-Sulpice, as I was walking down a street that I've walked down a thousand times before, I noticed for the first time a building called l'Institut Catholique. As I say, I'd never even noticed the building before, let alone gone inside it. But now I went inside, and what should I see posted on one of the doors but a sign saying 'Library School.' I'd never thought of being a librarian! But I opened the door, and found the course was beginning the next day, and I signed myself up. And I was a librarian for the next fifteen years!"

"And now?" I ask her.

"I'm at another crossroads," she says. "Do you think I should go back to the Saint-Sulpice? I've been invited to go to Turkey, to work as a translator/guide. I'm not quite sure yet. But what I do know is this: our wishes do come true, *mais il faut s'élancer dans la vie*. You have to throw yourself into life."

She has a few moments left of her break, and we sit there, watching the smoke from her Gitane waft through the flowers of Hawaii on a winter day in Paris.

.   .   .

On my way back to l'Apollinaire, I stop at an Internet café to check my e-mail. There's a long message from Nicholas in Oaxaca. He's living with a Mexican family and attending Spanish lessons in the mornings. I would have loved to go with him to experience the famous Christmas celebration there and the swirl of activity that precedes it: the lit-up streets, the carved radishes, the crèches, the costumes, the candles, the candlelit processions. I'd begged him to tell me about the celebration in detail, but his e-mail is all about the signs of mounting political tensions: the printing presses smashed at the office of one newspaper, demonstrations in the streets, worried looks on people's faces, and armed police everywhere. It seemed he joined a demonstration, gave away all his food and pesos to the protestors, got drunk with some of them afterward, then smashed the beautiful black pot that he bought from an old Indian woman.

There's also an e-mail from Liz, the graduate student whose life has been so full of tragedy. It seems that more misfortune has befallen her. "You're not going to believe this, Noelle. I've had a serious health setback. I think I'm going to be okay, and I'll explain more when I see you. But the amazing thing is, I've been seeing a lot more of my daughter. She's been really good to me. I got my wish, Noelle!"

On my last day before going back to Aix, I have a rendezvous with Maurice, another man in his eighties whom I have known for most of my life. He's the father of Sonya and her brother, Michel, and though he's a very modest man, over the years I've come to think of him as one of the most remarkable people I know. As a young man, he risked his life to join the French resistance. After the war he went on to have a long and distinguished career as a lawyer in the Court of Paris, dressed in a long black gown and powdered wig. Yet despite his heavy responsibilities and even despite his family's tragic losses, he's retained an almost childlike ability to celebrate life's simple pleasures: to hike in the mountains, listen to music, enjoy a fine wine. In the smallest, middle-of-nowhere village, he can lead you to a café that serves the most exquisite food, and there he'll keep you laughing for hours with his stories or hold you entranced as he recites poems. I've always thought that he and my hero Jacques Lusseyran, who spread hope in the freezing barracks of Buchenwald, would have been best friends if they'd chanced to meet. And once when someone explained to me that the English word *savor* derives from the Latin *sapere,* which means "wisdom," I thought immediately of Maurice.

On this December day we meet in the spacious living room of his apartment in Neuilly, an elegant suburb of Paris. Except that his full head of hair has turned completely white, he doesn't look any older to me. I last saw him nearly ten years ago, not long after his wife, Lilly, had perished in the fire. Now, after several long and very lonely years, Maurice has found a new companion. Amazingly, she is Austrian, as Lilly was, and she, too, bears the name of a flower: Daisy. She is away in Austria at the moment, so I won't get to meet her. But I've already heard a lot about her from Sonya and Hervé, and they warned me that Maurice has not only emerged from his grief but is nearly out of his mind with happiness.

And indeed, almost as soon as he's settled me in a chair with a glass of the aperitif, made from gentian petals, that he taught me to drink in the Alps, Maurice begins to talk about Daisy and the miracle of their connection.

"What I've learned in this period of my life is that *la vie est une bonne mère.* Life is a good mother. A good mother on condition that we remain in contact with her. If we seal ourselves off, then she can't help us. But if we remain ready, receptive, then she stretches out her hand to help. She gives her children what they need, in their particular circumstances, in their own unique difficulties."

"Do you believe that life helps us in all aspects of our lives?" I ask, thinking about how I began this year, slinking away from a New Year's ceremony in northern California, where people were wishing for world peace, romantic love, slim thighs, and new client referrals.

Maurice shakes his head. *"C'est dans l'essentiel que la vie est une bonne mère,"* he tells me. ("It's in the essential that life is a good mother"). "There are many things that we have to do for ourselves. Life leaves me alone for lots of things. But in the essential, life intervenes to help us."

Later, over lunch in the neighborhood bistro, I tell Maurice about the sanctuary in Deneuvre and the ex-voto Hercules.

*"Je suis un ex-voto!"* Maurice tells me ("I am an ex-voto!"). And he explains that, during World War II, he tried to cross from southern France into Spain to join a branch of the French resistance. But he was caught and sent to a detention camp in Bordeaux, where his fate was uncertain. His mother went to the neighborhood church and offered a novena to Mother Mary. A novena involves a recitation of prayers for a special purpose during nine consecutive days. On the ninth day of the novena, there was an intercession. An acquaintance of Maurice's parents told them that he knew a well-placed lawyer in Bordeaux. The lawyer was able to get through to someone higher up who arranged for Maurice to be released.

"And the amazing thing," says Maurice, "is that through Daisy I've discovered where I would have been sent. She was asked to translate from German into French for a ceremony in the Austrian town of Melk. The ceremony was to honor those members of the French resistance who were sent to a camp in Melk, where many of them died. I met some of the survivors there, and they told me that they had been captured as they were trying to cross the border into Spain, and that first they were sent to Bordeaux."

*"C'est extraordinaire."*

*"Oui, c'est extraordinaire."* Maurice points to the steeple of a stone church a block away. "You can go and see it there, the ex-voto of which I am the living testimony. It's a marble plaque and reads: "Sainte Marie, merci de m'avoir rendu mon fils." ("Blessed Mary, thank you for having given me back my son.")

Returning from my visit to Maurice, in the late afternoon I reenter the Luxembourg Gardens. Once again, I move down the blue River of Sorrow, under the faces of the turbaned man, the dirty bejeweled girl, the Tamil boy with his wide, dark eyes. I walk under the leafless rows of the chestnut trees, past the shut-up candy booths, down the stone stairs to where the gray water of the great round basin reflects the movement of the gray but still somewhat luminous sky. Crossing over to the far side of the garden, I pass men playing *boules*—even in winter. I am fast on the beekeeper's house, close to the exit, when I see a handsome young man, his jaw clenched, striding resolutely out of the park. A few yards behind him, a young woman follows. Fashionably dressed in sleek jeans and a short fur coat, her hair in a sort of punkish pouf, she is shrieking in a loud American voice, "I didn't come for this! I didn't come for this!"

In her rage and despair she appears beyond inhibition, unable to stop herself from driving her lover farther and farther away.

"I didn't come for this! I didn't come for this!"

What *did* she come for, I wonder? Some sort of Parisian honeymoon, no doubt, a December *lune de miel*.

I have an impulse to run after her, to take her arm and tell her, *Come with me!* Then, leading her into the warm, moist air of the greenhouse, I'd lead her into the room full of tropical flowers, the orchids, hibiscus, and bromeliads. Finding two metal chairs alongside each other, I'd tell her, *Have a seat.* Then—if she didn't bolt out the door, resuming her cry of profound disappointment—I'd tell her: *Don't despair.*

It seems you had a wish that didn't come true. And this unmet wish seems to confirm for you that wishes don't come true. That wishes aren't horses and beggars don't ride. That if you wish in one hand and shit in the other, it's the hand with shit that will fill.

But it's not so black and white, so either-or. At least, that's what I've learned this year, during the course of a remarkable journey, to a place I'd never been before. It is a place in which I permitted myself to act *as if* I believe that we live in a world where wishes come true. Thus, you might say, I held my wishes in one hand and with the other I held off my doubt, kept it at bay. And thus, it seems, I made a kind of clearing, a meadow in which—if I were a beggar and wished for a horse—a horse might be much more likely to appear than if I'd never made that clearing.

And thus, despite my skeptical bent and my tilt toward a certain pessimistic melancholy, I've learned that there is indeed a power in wishing.

For at the very least, a wish is a form of focused attention. When we take the time to consciously articulate a wish, then we begin to notice things we haven't noticed before. If what we desire is something as tangible as a house, then we start to notice houses in a way we haven't before, we glean information from all kinds of places that, in the past, didn't even show up on our radar.

When we consciously articulate a wish, then we also give ourselves a kind of permission to receive the thing we desire. We thus remove some of the false obstacles that may stand between us and the thing we desire, the inner voices that tell us, "I couldn't possibly deserve such a thing" or "If I let myself want this, something dreadful will happen."

When we permit ourselves to believe that our wishes have a certain power, then we maintain a more receptive and optimistic attitude. That receptivity and optimism provide us with a kind of fuel, a form of renewable energy. They make us more resilient in the face of setbacks and disappointments. And they also make it more likely that others will be drawn to us, that they will wish to help us in our quest. Indeed, many people have observed a kind of critical mass that is achieved when people dare to pursue a wish. Once, for example, I met six mountaineers who wished to be the first group of women to scale a certain Himalayan mountain. In the final days before departure, they were inundated with supplies from every corner of the globe, gifted with tents, backpacks, camp stoves, and every kind of exotic dehydrated food. When someone dares to hold the shining prospect of a wish aloft, it often seems to draw others irresistibly toward it, with a powerful magnetic pull.

Thus far, each of these aspects of wish power can be explained psychologically. But is there a transcendent dimension to our wishing? Is there, indeed, some form of divine help out there? Perhaps that's something each of us must find out for ourself. For myself, I think of being led from the tarnished gold of my sad dreams to the blazing silence of a golden temple and to the radiant presence of a forest monk who told me that if I truly wished to be free from my own deepest fear, then my wish would be granted. I think of finding my way from the narrow straits of my worry mind to the dolphins shimmering below my navel. I think of painting on a balcony as whales swam by, a phone rang, and I heard the tired voice of the loving man who came to my door, in just the way I wished for. And when I think of these things, I say YES.

When I think of my house, I'm still inclined to say I got it through a combination of focused attention, built-in privilege, thrift, work, familial generosity, and luck. And when it comes to matters as small as wishing for a parking space or a set of lost keys, I am still reluctant to invoke the divine—but I don't feel nearly so shocked that others do. I think of Ajahn Jumnian, with his saffron robe jingling with key rings, amulets, and coins. Of the dark Christ in the Mexican church whose robe was covered with peso notes. And I feel far more willing than when I began to let it all mix up: the sacred and profane, the obelisk and the Patti Playpal, the happy death and the pair of warm puppies, the desire for love, money, real estate, and a single luminous moment of grace.

I've learned that there can be something quite revealing when a wish seems to fail, or to fall short of what we thought we wanted, or when we ourselves seem to fall short of what we wished for. For the gap between what we wished for and what we thought we wanted is a kind of window, an opening where what is unconscious can flow through, taking us to a deeper level of self-knowledge.

Through my friend George and his little Japanese muse, Sadako with her thousand cranes, I've learned that when we feel profoundly disappointed in the fulfillment of a wish, we can either close down in bitterness and fear or allow ourselves to be carried, by a gradually swelling wave, into the flow of something greater than ourselves. And even in less drastic circumstances, we can let our wishes push us beyond our preconceptions, beyond what we imagined it would be like when our wishes came true. The last time I saw Sylvie, she told me: "When you wish, if it's a wish that's really integral to who you are, it presents new challenges. It doesn't just end there, with a state of fulfillment. It takes you to a new edge." Sylvie felt "ready for sweetness" in her life, and when it arrived, she discovered that she had to let go of her own hard shell and face an often frightening sense of vulnerability in her connection to Edward. As the psychologist Marion Woodman says, "Most of us are dragged toward wholeness." And for many of us, the being dragged toward wholeness happens precisely through the mysterious process of wishing: through the gaps it exposes, the new edges it drives us toward, the deeper layers of longing it reveals.

Perhaps more than anything, I feel lucky to have stumbled upon what seems to me now to be one of the great secrets to the art of wishing. It's the secret that I learned, unexpectedly, in the little village in northern France where I visited the shrine of Hercules. It's the distinction between the two phases of wishing: *petitionary* and *gratulatory*. And it's the recognition that, at all times, we can choose to move from one to the other: from the *not yet* of unfulfilled desire to the *already* of what is present. We can do so in two ways: by savoring the particular circumstances in which we find ourselves, and by opening ourselves to the vast reservoir of possibility that is always there for us, lying in wait, ready to be tapped—if only we don't close down in fear, resignation, despair.

If the young woman was still sitting beside me, if she hadn't yet bolted out the door, beginning to shout again, "I didn't come for this! I didn't come for this!" here's what I'd wish for her. I'd wish that she might take a deep breath and notice that, even here in the dead of winter in a northern country, there are these tropical flowers: hibiscus, bromeliad, plumeria. Each is here, now, offering its earthly color and scent, and each is also an emblem of paradise, of the beach below the cobblestones, the lake below the desert sands, the place toward which the arrows of our wishes fly.

• • •

On my first morning back in California, despite jet lag so intense it feels like drunkenness, I force myself awake. Having wrapped myself in layers of sweaters, I make a mug of strong coffee, grab my empty birdcage shrine and a box of art supplies, and drag myself outside to the picnic table. There, in the weak December sunlight, I set about the art of imitative magic. With a bit of chicken wire and joint compound—which Carole decreed to be the secret to the universe—I form a nest with two birds to go inside the empty birdcage. Then, taking a chunk of modeling clay, I fashion an abundance of little clay eggs and set them around the birds. It's my ex-voto, a nest overflowing with even more than three wishes fulfilled.

# Acknowledgments

I am deeply grateful to:

- My friends and family who allowed me to disappear for long hours behind closed doors, especially my daughter, Ariel.

- Barbara Baer, Robin Beeman, Katy Butler, Barbara Feinberg, Jane Kingston, Terry Lowe, Joan Silber, Penny Wolfson, and Deborah Young, who were among the book's first readers. •

- Alexis Hurley and Kim Witherspoon, *agents extraordinaires* at InkWell Management.

- Caroline Sutton, my editor at Random House, who knows how to wield the sword of compassion.

- All those who helped in the production of this book.

- All those who shared their insights with me, including Ania and Gilbert Combes, Jacques Hallez, Kythe Heller, Jack Kornfield, Gillian Lerner, Maurice Parmentier, Vicki Lundgren, and Paul Zehrer.

- Those whose lives, intertwining with mine, found their way into this book: Eliot Fintushel, of course. Carole Watanabe, the book's catalyst, trickster spirit, and guiding light. Marie Gewirtz, Stephen Kessler, Kathrin Parsons, Christine Renaudin, Marcia Reppy, Colette van Praag: each of you has been an inspiration.

• And last, but certainly not least: the man-who-came-to-my-door and made me believe in magic.

# About the Author

NOELLE OXENHANDLER is the author of two previous nonfiction books, *A Grief Out of Season* and *The Eros of Parenthood*. Her essays have appeared in many national and literary magazines, including *The New Yorker, The New York Times Magazine, San Francisco Chronicle Magazine, Vogue, Tricycle, Parabola, Utne Reader,* and *O: The Oprah Magazine.* She has taught in the graduate writing program at Sarah Lawrence College and is a member of the creative writing faculty at Sonoma State University in California. A practicing Buddhist for more than thirty years, Oxenhandler is the mother of a grown daughter and lives in Northern California.

# About the Type

This book was set in Sabon, a typeface designed by the well-known German typographer Jan Tschichold (1902–74). Sabon's design is based upon the original letter forms of Claude Garamond and was created specifically to be used for three sources: foundry type for hand composition, Linotype, and Monotype. Tschichold named his typeface for the famous Frankfurt typefounder Jacques Sabon, who died in 1580.